TAROT
MADE EASY

TAROT
MADE EASY

NANCY GAREN

PIATKUS

Copyright © 1989 by Nancy Garen

This edition first published in
Great Britain in 1990 by
Judy Piatkus (Publishers) Ltd of
5 Windmill Street, London W1P 1HF
www.piatkus.co.uk

Reprinted 1993, 1994, 1996 (twice), 1997, 1998 (twice), 2000

First published in the United States
of America by Simon and Schuster, Inc.

Designed by Barbara Marks Graphic Design
Cover design by Jackie Seow-Pracher
Cover photograph by Simon Metz

British Library Cataloguing in Publication Data

Garen, Nancy
  Tarot made easy.
  1. Tarot cards
  I. Title
  133.32424

  ISBN 0–7499–1009–7

Illustrations from the Rider-Waite Tarot
deck reproduced by permission of U.S. Games
Systems, Inc., Stamford, CT 06902 USA.
Copyright © 1971 by U.S. Games Systems, Inc.
Further reproduction prohibited.

Printed and bound in Great Britain by
Butler & Tanner Ltd, Frome and London

With

love

and

devotion

to my

sister

Patti

CONTENTS

PART 1

TAROT BASICS

◆ WHAT ARE TAROT CARDS? ◆

Simply put, Tarot cards are a means of predicting events or receiving guidance in both our inner (spiritual) and outer (manifest) world.

Every Tarot deck consists of seventy-eight cards. Not all decks are alike but all decks have three basic principles in common, even though the cards, symbols, and interpretations may vary.

1. Each deck is illustrated with symbols that depict experiences we've all had or could have at one time or another.

2. Each deck has two main sections: the Major Arcana and the Minor Arcana (or Lesser Arcana, as some books refer to it). The Minor Arcana is further divided into numbered cards and what is commonly referred to as the Court Arcana.

3. Each deck contains four suits: Wands (or Batons), Cups, Swords, and Pentacles (or Coins).

Traditionally, the Major Arcana depicts the greater events in our lives while the Minor and Court Arcana depict the more mundane, everyday aspects. I've given a more detailed description of the Major, Minor, and Court Arcana as well as the suits in the section on Tarot Symbology for those of you who want to know more.

No one is exactly sure how Tarot cards originated, but it's widely believed that the ancient Egyptian Masons developed them as a means of charting their important metaphysical and transformational discoveries.

Think of them as stories conveyed in pictures. I have used the Rider-Waite deck to illustrate this book, but there are many other decks to choose from and they are all equally valid. The cards are not "magical," "occult," or "evil." They have no inherent powers of their own. Since Tarot decks and books are chosen because you identify with them or they strike a chord within you, *you* empower them with your beliefs, attitudes, and personality and by your level of growth or understanding at the time you choose them.

◆ HOW DO TAROT CARDS WORK? ◆

I can't tell you *how* they work nor can I tell you *how* I walk, think, or digest food. I also can't explain why I know who's on the phone before I pick it up or what causes ESP experiences. I know, however, that it happens and that Tarot cards do *work*.

I believe that there is a higher wisdom or universal truth that we can *all* tap in to and that there are many methods of accessing this information. One of the easiest ways (but by no means the only way) is through the Tarot. Since our minds think in symbols, it's only logical that cards that tell stories through symbols could enhance our intuition.

My esoteric opinion comes from the understanding that *everything* in the universe (you, me, and the things we touch or see) is composed of pure energy, and I believe that this vast ocean of energy substance is God and that everything within it is God too. It doesn't matter if you call it God, the Universe, the Source, or even "the Force"—it's all the same. And, since you and I are also energy, we are the Ocean too, even if we're functioning as drops. This means that to the degree we expand our consciousness and encompass this awareness, we have the ability to draw from it. So, we can think of ourselves as limited drops separate from the Source or we can see ourselves as part of the Ocean, open our inner channels, and receive guidance.

◆ HOW TO USE THIS BOOK ◆

Y ou don't have to know *anything* about the Tarot in order to use this book. Nor do you have to memorize the meaning of the cards or understand their "esoteric" significance. All you need is a deck of Tarot cards and a question. The rest is easy.

Other books give a brief and often vague or symbolic description of the meaning of the cards in the "upright" and "reversed" positions. You then have to wade through a lot of symbolism and try to figure out how it applies to your question. In this book I present a different, easy-to-understand approach to interpreting the cards. So that you can get answers that apply more directly to your questions, I've created thirty-two specific categories of everyday life experience, such as Work, Success, Romance, Finances, and Emotional State, and explained what each card indicates for each of these categories.

Each card begins with a Focus (or general atmosphere) and ends with an Outcome. There are no reversed interpretations because they are not necessary.

Even the most advanced Tarot enthusiast knows how frustrating it is when you want to know something and you get a card that has nothing to do with the question you asked—like asking about love and reading: "Strength of will bringing ideas to pass. Firm rulership resulting in peace and justice," and so on. With this book, *every* card has a Romance category, so if you want to know about love, you will get an answer about love. All you have to do is ask a question, draw a card, then look up the card you drew in Part Four, Interpretation of the Cards, and read the category you're interested in. It's that simple, that specific! You can read as many or as few categories as you like—the choice is up to you.

EXPLANATION OF THE THIRTY-TWO CATEGORIES

1. FOCUS:
The focus category is a capsulized or nutshell version of the events or conditions coming up in your future. It's the crux of the matter, or the foundation on which the rest of the reading is based. The other categories emphasize specific areas of interest under the focus influence.

2. DESIRE:
This category reveals that which you now want, or that which you *will* want in time to come or as your future begins to unfold.

3. ROMANCE:
This category reveals actual events as well as movements of mind in the area of love and romance.

4. THE UNEXPECTED:
This category covers *anything* that comes as a surprise (be it good or bad).

5. OTHERS:
This covers the EFFECT of other people on you, or how another person will INFLUENCE your life.

6. THE HOME:
The home category relates to your home environment or place of residence, and the events or conditions within it. However, if you spend more time at work than home, it could represent that area.

7. TRAVEL:
This category is about short trips, long trips, comings and goings, and/or influences surrounding travel or travel plans.

8. PAPERS:
This category covers *anything* that involves papers, be it forms, books, documents, legal matters, artwork, presentations, ledgers. Anything where something is transferred from thought to paper can be included in the papers category.

9. WORK/CAREER:

This category covers your place of business, career, or area in which you find yourself operating most frequently, be it at home or in the field. This could also include housework, hobbies, school, or projects. If you're looking for work or have a question concerning your work status, this category will show the influences, conditions, or atmosphere surrounding your query.

10. UNIONS:

The unions category reveals "what will be so" about your unions with others, be it personal, business, or otherwise. If your question concerns personal unions, then it will answer in kind. If on the other hand it is about business partnerships or mergers, it will apply to that.

11. EMOTIONAL STATE:

This reveals how you *feel* as a result of the events that are transpiring in your life or affairs. It's a very important category in that it shows the emotional climate and, as a result, gives great insight into whether or not you're experiencing the events on the whole as being "good" or "bad."

12. PLEASURE:

The pleasure category defines the areas or avenues in which you will find the most enjoyment, fulfillment, or satisfaction. If, however, a negative disclosure should fall in this category, it's probably a good indication that you are not having very much fun during the period in question.

13. NEWS:

This category covers all forms of news, messages, or communications that will affect you, your future, or your state of mind.

14. FAMIILY:

This is an all-inclusive category. It relates to sisters, brothers, mothers, fathers, wives, or husbands as well as distant relatives, aunts, uncles, and/or even friends that are so close either in heart or by proximity that they're considered family.

15. THE PHYSICAL BODY:

The physical body category reveals your health, and your mental, emotional, and/or spiritual well-being as well. It's important to note that other people may be experiencing a situation that is so strong that it affects you, or shows up in your reading as happening to you.

16. FINANCES:
This category covers *anything* that relates to money or finances.

17. TIME:
This category won't tell you when an event will happen (like "in November you will . . ."), but it's significant because it deals with the *passage* of time and *how* it will affect your wish or your affairs. It shows *how* or *in what way* the events of your life or things that concern you are shaping up.

18. FRIENDS:
This concerns the effect of your friends on you, or what will transpire as a result of a friend, and can include a relative or a lover.

19. VISITORS/CALLERS:
This category is about situations regarding people that come to visit or call you on the phone, and/or the status of any query in that area.

20. MAIL:
This covers anything that arrives by or is sent through the mail, from letters, cards, or packages to messages in motion, such as United Parcel Service, Federal Express, etc.

21. ANXIETY:
In everyone's life there are problem areas, things that upset, trouble, or create anxiety. This category will define what those areas are or where your difficulties may lie.

22. DISAPPOINTMENT:
This category describes what could let you down, hurt you, or upset you. It's about the things in life that go wrong, fall through, or discourage you. Most of the time it's a progression of the anxiety category, though not always.

23. ENDINGS:
The endings category covers situations or conditions that are being resolved or coming to an end.

24. NEW BEGINNINGS:

This category covers any new undertaking that will spring up and/or change the course of your experience. It can also include life-altering decisions and/or a new turn of mind.

25. INHERITANCE:

Anything that comes to you as a result of another person, place, or thing (be it material or spiritual) will fall in this category. It's not limited to a legacy or contingent upon the death of another, unless it is specified as such.

26. REWARDS/GIFTS:

This category covers anything that is given or that you yourself give. It's not limited just to material goods, as it also covers spiritual or inner gifts (like those gifts of the heart or spirit).

27. SUCCESS:

The success category is not limited to worldly or material success. It reveals what you consider to be your best achievement or greatest accomplishment at the time in question. It may also indicate *where* or *from what direction* your success will come.

28. FORTUNE:

This will disclose what you will be fortunate in or what will occur by chance, luck, or fate.

29. BLESSINGS:

This can be a very revealing category because it foretells that which you'll be grateful or thankful for in times to come.

30. SPECIAL GUIDANCE:

In this section you'll find whatever it is you need to know or understand about your question, as it tells you the underlying, unforeseen, or unknown elements that will make the way easier. It's divided into two parts, the Mundane and the Esoteric. The mundane deals with the practical, down-to-earth aspect and the esoteric deals with the spiritual heart of the matter.

31. BEST COURSE OF ACTION:

This is a very important category because it tells you the best way to proceed or action to take in order to realize your desire, deal with the elements involved, or overcome the difficulties connected with it. It usually works hand-in-hand with the Special Guidance category.

32. OUTCOME:
This is the probable outcome, end result, or summation of the reading.

If you want to know more about Tarot symbology, read on. If you're anxious to start right out doing a reading, turn to Part Three.

PART 2

TAROT SYMBOLOGY

◆ THE MAJOR ARCANA ◆

The most powerful group in the Tarot deck are the 22 Major Arcana cards beginning with the Magician (#1) and ending with the Fool (#22).

(Note: Traditionally, as well as on the card in this book, the Fool has been assigned the number "0". However, I prefer to put it at the end of the book and call it a "0" or "22" because of what the card represents, which is explained in Part Four.)

The reason Major Arcana cards are so powerful is because they predict major issues in life rather than everyday ups and downs, and as a result, they outweigh *all* the other cards in both impact and effect.

Major Arcana cards also indicate the most important positions in a card spread such as in the Keltic Cross, Category, or Zodiac Month by Month spreads.

The numbers on the Major Arcana represent numerological influences which will be discussed in the section on Tarot Numerology and in the card interpretations in Part Four.

◆ THE MINOR ARCANA ◆

The rest of the cards in the Tarot deck make up the Minor Arcana. These cards are divided into four suits: Wands, Cups, Swords, and Pentacles. Each of the suits contains cards numbered from Ace to 10, followed by four Court cards. The Court cards of all four suits together are known as the Court Arcana.

The cards of the Minor Arcana and Court Arcana refer to the lesser events of everyday life. Each of the forty numbered cards and sixteen court cards is illustrated and interpreted in Part Four.

The significance of the Court cards is discussed in detail in the section on The Court Arcana. The significance of the numbered cards is based on the ancient principles of numerology.

The Aces, which are equal to the number 1, represent the beginning of a new cycle and signify conception and innovation. The presence of an Ace in the beginning of a reading marks the impact of a new beginning and fresh start. At the end of a reading, it can represent another new beginning, or sum up the results of all the cards preceding it.

Aces also represent seasons and in a reading can predict *when* an event is most likely to occur.

Ace of Wands: Autumn
Ace of Cups: Summer
Ace of Swords: Winter
Ace of Pentacles: Spring

The numbers 2 to 10 in each suit represent numerological influences which will be discussed in the section on Tarot Numerology.

THE SUITS

The Suits—Wands, Cups, Swords, and Pentacles—are the esoteric formula or key to manifestation on the earth plane.

THE SUIT OF WANDS:

When you think of Wands, think of *ideas,* because Wands are the conception or "seeds" through which the tree springs forth. They are the original thought, intention, or primary element of growth.

Their key words are: *ideas, growth, ambition, expansion.* When there are many Wands in a reading, it indicates that conditions are primarily in the realm of thought, or at the very first stages of development.

THE SUIT OF CUPS:

When you think of Cups, think of *emotion,* because Cups are the feeling or bridge between the original idea and the next stage, which is action. They are the glue or cohesive factor in the development of manifestation and esoterically signify the marriage of thought and feeling.

Their key words are: *emotion, desire, inner experience, spirit.* When there are many Cups in a reading, it indicates that conditions are felt primarily in the realm of emotion, but not necessarily as an outward manifestation.

THE SUIT OF SWORDS:

When you think of Swords, think of *action,* because Swords are the *act.* Esoterically they are like the third part or Holy Ghost in the Christian trinity of The Father, Son, and Holy Ghost. On the mundane level, the Swords oftentimes indicate struggle, because of the difficulties man has to move through in order to turn a thought into a reality on the denser or physical earth plane.

Their key words are: *action, movement, struggle, keenness.* When there are many Swords in a reading, it shows tremendous activity, agitation, or acceleration, because Swords are the last stages of effort before the final result.

THE SUIT OF PENTACLES:

When you think of Pentacles, think of *manifestation,* because Pentacles are the fruits of one's labor, the culmination of the first three ingredients, the end *result* or fruition.

Their key words are: *manifestation, realization, proof, prosperity.* When there are many Pentacles in a reading, it indicates that conditions are taking form, or are in the process of being demonstrated.

THE COURT ARCANA

There are sixteen cards that represent the Court Arcana: the King, Queen, Knight, and Page of each of the four suits; i.e., WANDS, CUPS, SWORDS, PENTACLES.

The Knights have a significant purpose in a reading because they are the instigators of change, marking the beginning or end of a sequence of events. When a Knight appears, a long-term condition will suddenly change.

The remaining Court Arcana (King, Queen, and Page) serve several different functions in a reading. Each of the twelve cards is represented by an astrological sign, and in their first and perhaps most important function they represent people, the types of people defined by their sign.

Second, because they are represented by an astrological sign, the King, Queen, and Page each have months of the year that their sign is related to, the same as in astrology, for example,

> King of Wands: Aries (March 21–April 19)
> Queen of Cups: Scorpio (October 23–November 21)
> Page of Swords: Taurus (April 20–May 20)
> and so on.

Thirdly, they can also depict events and/or the kind of vocation that's associated with the type of person their astrological sign represents.

So, in essence, each King, Queen, and Page has a personality, time frame, and vocational aptitude. Thus, in a reading, a King, Queen, or Page can tell you *when* you will start a job, *what* kind of work you will do, and even the *type* of person you might be working with.

In the following list I've broken down the signs into the types of people and vocations they represent. The vocations I've listed are by no means the only jobs possible, but are an attempt to give additional insight.

THE KING OF WANDS:
Aries (March 21–April 19)

TYPE OF PERSON: Ambitious, optimistic, energetic, direct, daring, headstrong, impulsive, idealistic, confident, capable; but sometimes self-centered, hot-tempered, and impatient.

TYPE OF VOCATION: Planning, constructing, developing, building, real estate, or any area where leadership qualities are desired, because he/she can work alone.

THE QUEEN OF WANDS:
Leo (July 23–August 22)

TYPE OF PERSON: Affectionate, generous, loyal, adventurous, fun-loving, dramatic, determined, impulsive, daring, passionate, proud, honest, aloof, haughty, egotistical.

TYPE OF VOCATION: Actor, entertainer, creator, artist, musician, fashion figure, confidant, professional sports, and any type of vocation where he/she can be number one.

THE PAGE OF WANDS:
Sagittarius (November 22–December 21)

TYPE OF PERSON: Outspoken, direct, charismatic, high-strung, blunt, instinctive, easily bored, sexual, progressive, future-oriented, sportive, subject to wandering, and sometimes edgy or lackadaisical.

TYPE OF VOCATION: Athletics, politics, pilot, teacher, instructor, philosopher, professional student, gadget inventor, band member.

THE KING OF CUPS:
Cancer (June 21–July 22)

TYPE OF PERSON: Emotional, moody, changeable, testing, home-loving, kind, considerate, focusing, worrying, cranky, and sometimes crabby.

TYPE OF VOCATION: Doctor, minister, priest, metaphysician, cook, restaurant owner, astronaut, homemaker. There's more emphasis on home life than business life, but can become well connected with big business and will get help or support if needed or requested.

THE QUEEN OF CUPS:
Scorpio (October 23–November 21)

TYPE OF PERSON: Spiritual, psychic, clairvoyant, magnetic, intense, secretive, sexual, deep, complex, removed, in control, and at times overpowering or aloof.

TYPE OF VOCATION: Occult work, undercover work, physician, stock broker, acupuncturist, dentist, counselor, dramatic actor.

THE PAGE OF CUPS:
Pisces (February 19–March 20)

TYPE OF PERSON: Impressionable, reflective, sensitive, emotional, vulnerable, warm, loving, romantic, talkative, imaginative, intuitive, psychic, youthful, and sometimes flaky.

TYPE OF VOCATION: Working in institutions, self-help organizations, occultist, poet, dancer, set decorator, make-up artist, wardrobe head, or anything that deals with illusion. Works best behind the scenes, or finishes what others start.

THE KING OF SWORDS:
Libra (September 23–October 22)

TYPE OF PERSON: Fair, just, balanced, perceptive, humanistic, poised, sensitive, compassionate, selfless. Can appear wishy-washy because weighs all sides before making decisions.

TYPE OF VOCATION: Lawyer, law enforcer, armed forces, internal affairs, public relations, psychologist, relationship counselor, interior decorator.

THE QUEEN OF SWORDS:
Virgo (August 23–September 22)

TYPE OF PERSON: Mental, analytical, scientifically minded, objective, factual, "Vulcan" in nature, ingenious, perfectionist, discriminating, independent, cold.

TYPE OF VOCATION: Scientist, secretary, analyst, researcher, editor, computer operator, astrologer, numerologist.

THE PAGE OF SWORDS:
Taurus (April 20–May 20)

TYPE OF PERSON: Practical, thoughtful, persevering, possessive, realistic, down to earth, security-minded, patient, sensual, and sometimes reserved. Needs concrete results and knows how to get them.

TYPE OF VOCATION: Serving, singing, sales, finances, negotiations, consulting, leasing, working with buildings or homes.

THE KING OF PENTACLES:
Gemini (May 21–June 20)

TYPE OF PERSON: Mental, versatile, adaptable, diversified, capable, alert, confident, studious, curious, enterprising, skillful, energetic, communicative, changeable.

TYPE OF VOCATION: Writing, directing, lecturing, fashion, arts, motion pictures, radio, dealing with the public at large. Capable of doing two or more jobs at one time.

THE QUEEN OF PENTACLES:
Aquarius (January 20–February 19)

TYPE OF PERSON: Idealistic, public-minded, charitable, magnanimous, determined, opinionated, pragmatic, hopeful, influential, dedicated, aspiring, compassionate, friendly but sometimes impersonal. Is strongly affected by outside events which are usually unexpected or out of his/her hands.

TYPE OF VOCATION: Serving the planet, New Age teacher, minister, healer, psychologist, painter, writer, inventor.

THE PAGE OF PENTACLES:
Capricorn (December 22–January 19)

TYPE OF PERSON: Studious, persevering, productive, professionally inclined, ambitious, patient, responsible, practical, conservative, and sometimes moody, morbid, or subject to depression but never gives up.

TYPE OF VOCATION: Producer, regional manager, chief executive, boss, head waiter, photographer, student, laborer.

◆   TAROT NUMEROLOGY   ◆

Every card in the Tarot deck except for the Court Arcana is associated with a number. These numbers are based on the principles of numerology and represent a material and spiritual evolutionary process that begins with the number 1 and ends with the number 9.

The Major Arcana numbers 1 to 22 follow the same numerological cycle as the numbers 1 through 9 in numerology, but continue in The Wheel of Fortune (#10) on a higher turn of the spiral as a compound number 1 (1 + 0 = 1).

Justice (#11) and The Fool (#22) are master numbers in numerology, but for the purpose of this book and the readings you will be doing, *all* numbers over the number 9 will be reduced and read as single digit numbers.

In the Minor Arcana, the Aces are read the same as a number 1 because they indicate a fresh start or new beginning. There are no 10s in numerology (except as a compound number), so the number 10 in the Tarot is read as a number 1 (1 + 0 = 1) and represents a cyclical rebeginning that signals a major change from one thing or place to another. The number 10 in the Minor Arcana also points to a time when one must come to terms with something that may have been avoided in the past.

In order to help you become more acquainted with how the numbers work, I've divided each one into three facets, which will provide insight into their meaning and special message in a reading. The first facet is the *esoteric,* the hidden or underlying message; the second is the *mundane* (which includes both the positive and negative characteristics of each number), and the third is what it means in a reading when there are multiples (three or more) of the same number present (it suggests that a specific element indicated by that number will be running concurrently with the rest of the events, indicated by your card's categories and some or all of the facets of that number will be involved). For example, many 2s indicate a waiting period where there will be partial success but more to be revealed later.

THE NUMBER 1

ESOTERIC: The message of this number is inspiration or aspiration. It deals with that which is about to form, take shape, or manifest. It is the "I" of God.

MUNDANE: *Positive qualities:* Creation, ideas, beginnings, will, invention, originality, drive, incentive, determination, independence.
Negative aspects: Willfulness, selfishness, undue force.

IN A READING: Many 1s would indicate that a situation is about to begin, or is in the beginning stages, and some or all of the positive or negative elements mentioned above will be involved.

THE NUMBER 2

ESOTERIC: The message of the number 2 is to assimilate and envision. It is the intellect directed, and its function is to imagine. It is the cooperator whose success is not gained by force, but by patience

MUNDANE: *Positive qualities:* Waiting, sharing, balance, receptivity, diplomacy, gentle persuasion, application, agreement, insight.
Negative aspects: Duality, intolerance, impatience, imbalance.

MULTIPLES IN A READING: Many 2s indicate a waiting period where there will be partial success but more to be revealed later. They can also indicate a reconciliation, a reunion, and/or an element of surprise.

THE NUMBER 3

ESOTERIC: The message of the number 3 is expression. It is the cementing factor of the numbers 1 and 2, and its power is through its word, which goes forth in order to bring into being that which is desired and envisioned.

MUNDANE: *Positive qualities:* Communicating, feeling, enjoying, sharing, self-expressing, having fun, playing, love, friendship, popularity.
Negative aspects: Withholding communication, scattered energies, overreacting, overindulging, criticism.

MULTIPLES IN A READING: Many 3s indicate group activities or situations involving more than one person. They can also indicate delay, but with the promise of future success.

THE NUMBER 4

ESOTERIC: The message of the number 4 is manifestation. It is the result of a well-built foundation and proper application. It is that which comes forth as a result of desire, imagination, and emoting.

MUNDANE: *Positive qualities:* Practical application, formation, foundation, concentration, organization, working, building, planning.

Negative aspects: Plodding, exacting or dull work, too much attention on the material, limitation, blocks, and opposition.

MULTIPLES IN A READING: Many 4s indicate fruition or the manifestation of an idea, along with the foundation or "space" where things can grow.

THE NUMBER 5

ESOTERIC: The message of the number 5 is change, expansion, and re-creation. It also represents the desire to know, which demands that one must look to both the material and the spiritual realm in order to extract the truth.

MUNDANE: *Positive qualities:* Curiosity, spirituality, new thinking, new opportunities, magnetism, attraction, good fortune, travel or adventure.

Negative aspects: Defeatism, dogmatism, fear of change, misfortune, failure.

MULTIPLES IN A READING: Many 5s indicate change, challenge, and fluctuations (lucky or unlucky). They also indicate material prosperity but spiritual poverty, if not properly balanced or understood.

THE NUMBER 6

ESOTERIC: The message of the number 6 is adjustment. It is the balancing factor that unlocks the mystery of the number 5, as it provides the ability to discern both the higher and the lower, and brings them into harmony.

MUNDANE: *Positive qualities:* Harmony, balance, compassion, service, responsibility, social consciousness, domesticity, love, care, comfort, concern.

Negative aspects: Disharmony, discord, lack of concern or responsibility toward others, too fixed in opinion or beliefs, anxiety, interference.

MULTIPLES IN A READING: Many 6s indicate adjustments in thoughts, attitudes, or conditions. They also represent the ability to transcend difficulties.

THE NUMBER 7

ESOTERIC: The message of the number 7 is faith—faith in the things that can't be seen, but nevertheless exist. The number 7 must know the ultimate truths, and it is only through experience that its intellectual and spiritual understanding develops, and faith in the unseen is attained.

MUNDANE: *Positive qualities:* Faith, observation, investigation, discrimination, meditation, discovery, knowledge, wisdom, perfection.

Negative aspects: Fear, faithlessness, pessimism, skepticism, doubt, ignorance, escapism.

MULTIPLES IN A READING: Many 7s indicate a period of introspection or solitude. They also indicate unlooked-for advantages or gains through things that come unexpectedly.

THE NUMBER 8

ESOTERIC: The message of the number 8 is power—power that springs from within and enables one to accomplish that which one sets out to do.

MUNDANE: *Positive qualities:* Capability, (spiritual) fortitude, success, recognition, accomplishment, attainment, enlargement.

Negative aspects: Abuse of power, overemotionalism, strain, oppression, and lack.

MULTIPLES IN A READING: Many 8s indicate a positive change of mind or status because the beneficial qualities of the number 8 are rarely diluted, even when some or all of the negative aspects mentioned above are involved.

THE NUMBER 9

ESOTERIC: The message of the number 9 is completion. It must complete whatever it has begun because it is the final stage or culmination of all of the preceding cycles and numbers. But contained within its depth also lie the seeds of a new beginning about to take root.

MUNDANE: *Positive qualities:* Fulfillment, selflessness, impersonal love, magnetism, idealism (in its highest form), light bearer or giver of wisdom or inspiration.

Negative aspects: Personal loss, emotional extremes, having to let go of that which is cherished.

MULTIPLES IN A READING: Many 9s in a reading mean that situations or events are nearing completion, or have just been completed, and another plateau awaits.

PART 3

HOW TO DO A READING

◆   TIPS ON DOING READINGS   ◆

There are as many different ways to lay out the cards for a reading as there are reasons for doing readings. In the traditional Tarot, the Keltic (or Celtic) Cross method, in which ten cards are laid out in the form of a Keltic cross, was the most favored. I've found that the one that's quickest and easiest for you is usually the best.

The layout of the cards is called a spread. To help you get started, I suggest you look over the section on spreads to get an idea of the types of layouts you can do and how they work. There are other spreads used, but I prefer the ones in this book, and have given an example of how to create your own if you so choose. For a quick answer to a question, the easiest method is the One Card Only. Another simple layout is the Three Card Spread. For questions such as "What type of work am I best suited for" or "What type of person is best suited for me," use the Court Arcana method.

For those of you who've never worked with the Tarot before, it would be best to start out with the One Card Only method. It's really quite simple. All you have to do is shuffle the cards while thinking of your question, pull a card from the deck, and look up your answer in Part Four of this book. A lot of books will lead you to believe that reading the Tarot is very complicated and "mystical," but it's not. You can pull cards off the top of the deck, cut them in the middle, or pick them at random. Any way you feel comfortable is the right way to do it. I've been at it for so long I don't even shuffle anymore. I just let my finger go to one card in the box and when I take it out, it's the right answer.

PHRASING A QUESTION

Because the Tarot is a sensitive tool, it sometimes goes deeper than surface appearance and answers your unconscious question. So, try to compose your thoughts as clearly as you can, because if there's a deeper underlying question, you might not understand the message you receive. More often than not, a misunderstood answer is a direct result of an ambiguous question.

One of the best ways I've found to ask a question is to say, "What's so about . . ." or "What will be so about . . ." The reason this is helpful is that it doesn't limit the response or close off areas that you might not have considered at the time of your question.

In asking a question, I've also found it best to put a time limit on it such as: "What's going to come up between now and January?" or "Will I succeed in getting my project launched between now and this time next year?" because it puts a frame around the situation and gives the cards a structure to work within rather than leaving it open-ended as happens with a preface such as "Will I ever."

Another reason it isn't a good idea to form a question around the word *ever* (e.g., "Will I ever be happy" or "Will I ever find Mr. Right") is that the cards simply won't respond. They seem to *know* you'll ask again and so will focus on your current situation, tell you something you won't understand, or give you an answer you don't like. Remember, you *can* always ask again later!

YOUR ANSWER

Once you have a question in mind, think of the category that can best answer it *before* you begin (if you're not sure, refer to the explanation of the Thirty-two Categories of Interpretation). Remember, you're not limited to only one category; you can read as many as you think apply.

Example
A. If your question concerns love, you might read: Romance, Unions, Others, Emotional State, and Outcome.
B. If it's about business, you might read: Work/Career, Finances, Success, Best Course of Action, etc.

In this book, all category entries are written in the present and future tense, so if you ask questions or read card positions that relate to the past as in the Keltic Cross and Three Card Spread, interpret them as if they were in the past tense; i.e., instead of saying "You will," you would say "You were," or "You felt," etc.

Sometimes the answers you receive don't apply to you but to someone close to you, but because you care about that person and he or she affects your life, it will come up in your reading as if it's happening to you.

If you read something you don't like, remember that *you* are the captain of your ship and *you* can change your destiny. Nothing is ever carved in granite.

TELLING TIME

It's difficult for even the most advanced student of the Tarot to judge when an event is going to happen, but I've found that certain guidelines seem to work.
1. The Major Arcana cards usually indicate that the event will happen quite soon.
2. The Aces signify the season.
3. The Court cards predict the months.
4. The Minor Arcana cards denote days or weeks.

So, in doing a reading if you ask when something will happen and you get an Ace, it will probably happen within the season that that card represents (e.g., Ace of Wands: September–October–November). If you draw a Court card, it will most likely be within the months that that card is associated with (e.g., the Page of Pentacles would indicate the months between December and January). If you get a Minor Arcana like the Two of Cups, the event could happen within two days or weeks.

READING FOR OTHERS

If you want to do a reading for someone else or about someone who is not present, simply visualize that person clearly in your mind as you shuffle the cards and then ask the question as if it's from their point of view.

If you want to know what someone else wants or is going to do, you might want to read these categories:
1. Desire: because it will show what they want or hope for.
2. Others: because it gives insight into how you affect them.
3. Best Course of Action: because it indicates what they are most likely to do.
4. New Beginnings: because it shows what they most probably will do.

If you think someone's having problems and want to find out what, read the Anxiety and/or Disappointment categories.

CLARIFICATION CARDS

If you're unclear about the answer you receive in any category or card position, a clarification card can be used. In order to get a clarification card, all you have to do is take another card off the top of the deck (you don't have to reshuffle unless you want to) and place it on top of the card you want to clarify. Then read the SAME category on the new card that you read in the one under it.

You can also follow up on any line of questioning with clarification cards.

EXAMPLE: Let's say that you use the ONE CARD ONLY method and ask a question about your work such as "What do I need to know or understand about this situation?" and you got the Ace of Wands. In reading the Special Guidance/Esoteric category, the message you receive is: "What is unconscious or unmanifested will soon take form. New elements are being conceived, whether they are perceived at this time or not." If that answer leads to another question like "What kind of form?" you can pull another card and clarify the message by asking "What form will this take?"

When you pull another card off the top of the deck, think about the category that best suits the question (in this instance it would probably be New Beginnings) and read that category. If you draw the Eight of Wands, in reading New Beginnings you find "New ideas or opportunities concerning your business will put a new slant on your life or open new doors." If you still want to know more, you can draw yet another card.

Remember, you can clarify any card or position on a spread using clarification cards.

HELPFUL HINTS

Sometimes when you're doing a reading, one card will seem to stand out, come to your attention, or nag at you. This is *not* a coincidence. The reason it tugs at you is that it's trying to tell you something and your intuition is getting the message.

Another interesting thing I've noticed is that if a card falls out of the deck as you're shuffling, it's your answer, and many times you needn't go any further.

ONE FINAL NOTE

Most readings can be done as often as you like, but asking the same question repeatedly will get you nowhere. The Tarot, like the I Ching, knows when a question is being asked over and over again and responds in much the same way as the I Ching: "The teacher does not seek the Tyro, but when sought and questioned, answers fully. If the student importunes, no further information is given."

◆ THE SPREADS ◆

THE ONE CARD ONLY

This is the easiest means of divining an answer, because there is only one card to look at. All you have to do is shuffle the cards while thinking of your question, intuitively pick one out of the deck or turn the top card up, then read the categories that answer your question. You can read them all or only one, the choice is up to you.

1. If your question concerns health, you need only read the Physical Body category.
2. If your question concerns business, read the Work/Career category.
3. If your question concerns love and you want to know how someone feels about you or the effect you have on him or her, read Romance, Emotional State, and Others.

If you want more information, note the Focus and/or Desire categories, as they give you the general atmosphere surrounding the question or a better idea of what you or another really want.

A variation to this type of reading, (which is very good for an "either/or" question) is to divide the deck into two packs, one for each possibility or outcome, and read the top card off each pile.

Example:
During the 1984 presidential election campaign, I was curious as to which candidate was going to win the election. I decided to use the "either/or" method, to see what the cards had to say. I thought about each candidate, shuffled the cards, and put them into two piles—one for Mr. Mondale, and one for Mr. Reagan. The card for Mr. Mondale was the Eight of Pentacles and the card for Mr. Reagan was The High Priestess. Now, since

Mr. Reagan got The High Priestess card, I knew at a glance that he would probably win (since Major Arcana cards always overpower Minor Arcana cards). And, I think the two things that really clinched it for me were reading the Others and the Outcome categories on Mr. Mondale's card, which read: "You will be greatly affected or impacted by an encounter with another" and "You will have small successes but not big ones." After reading that, there was no doubt in my mind that Reagan was going to win the election.

Another way to read the card is to read *all* the categories and let your intuition or gut reaction tell you what you need to know.

Example:
The other day the air conditioner in my car went out, and considering the cost to repair it could be well in the hundreds, I was very upset—especially since I live in Palm Springs and it's nothing for the temperature to soar to 120° on an average summer day. Well, after wrestling with the problem for a while and going round and round in my head, I decided to pull out the Tarot Cards and ask what would happen. I drew the Nine of Swords and intuitively went to the Fortune category. It read: "You will have luck in returning, repairing or replacing something damaged or useless, etc." As it turned out, the only thing that was wrong was the relay switch, a twelve-dollar part!

REMEMBER: If you don't know what category to choose, you can always refer to the category definitions in Part One.

THE THREE CARD SPREAD

This is another easy layout; only three cards are needed. The best way to proceed is to think of your question while you shuffle and then divide the deck into three face-down piles: one for the Past or Basis of the matter, one for the Near Future, and one for the Outcome. It doesn't matter what order you arrange the piles in as long as it feels right to you.

Turn up the top card on each pile. For each card, read first the Focus category and then the categories that answer your question. You can read as many categories as seem appropriate.

Example:

The first pile (the past or basis of the matter) describes the events, circumstance or conditions that have led up to where you are now (this is especially useful when you want to read for, or about, someone else).

The second pile (near future) reveals a new direction or condition that will come into being.

The third pile (outcome) shows the end result, outcome or resolve as a result of the card in the second position.

Now, let's assume that you have a question about money and the three cards that came up were the World, the Ace of Wands, and the Three of Pentacles. Since the category you would choose would probably be Finances, we'll read both the Focus and the Finances categories.

1. Past or Basis of the Matter: The World—Focus/Finances
The focus was on world events or world-shaking events, encounters and gatherings, travel, change, sports, organization, risks, and new opportunities, but also restrictions, walls, or blocks. You acquired money from more than one source, and a tax refund or interest gained on an account may have also come in.

2. Near Future: The Ace of Wands—Focus/Finances
The focus is on potential: that which could be or is about to be, increased business and social activities, and new avenues of fulfillment or promise that come in from out of the blue.

Money will soon be received for artistic, creative, or inspired ventures.

3. Outcome: The Three of Pentacles—Focus/Finances
The focus will be on activities pertaining to work or career goals, papers, mail, literature, words, meetings, plans, construction, and practical application.

You will soon begin a new enterprise that will bring in extra money or supplement your income.

NOTE: both a Major Arcana and an Ace appeared in this reading, so not only did the past have impact, but the future will as well, and since Aces depict seasons, you'll have a good idea when these events are likely to occur (Autumn).

REMEMBER: If you don't know what category to choose, you can always refer to the category definitions in Part One.

If you want to clarify a category you can always use a clarification card (see Tips on Doing Readings).

THE KELTIC CROSS SPREAD

With this spread, you can do a quick reading by using only one category, or you can do an extended version and read several categories of interest. For instance, if you only want to know about your love life, all you need to read is the Romance Category in all ten positions. If, on the other hand, you want to know what's coming up in a variety of areas, you can pick a category for each.

REMEMBER: Since the categories in this book are written in the present and future tense, it will be necessary to read positions that refer to the past in the past tense.

LAYOUT AND PROCEDURE:
1. Shuffle the cards while thinking of your question.
2. Lay out ten cards face up in the positions shown in the diagram.
3. Each position has a particular significance which is explained below. Read the same category on each of the ten cards.

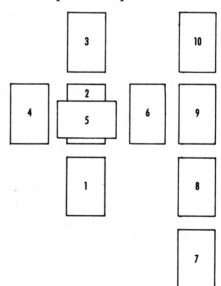

SIGNIFICANCE OF THE CARD POSITIONS:

1. BASIS OF THE MATTER, OR THAT WHICH BROUGHT YOU TO NOW:

The card in this position represents the foundation that molded your past or created the basis of where you are now.

2. WHERE YOU ARE NOW:

This position indicates the circumstances that are present in your life which motivate your question or cause concern.

3. HOPES OR FEARS:

This is an important aspect of your reading because it reveals the inner workings of your mind as a result of your past and present and is ofttimes the determining factor and possible outcome of your reading, depending on the forces working for or against you and the card in the tenth position.

4. PRESENT AND PASSING:

This covers not only your recent past, but long-term blocks or influences as well, and though its effect may still be felt in your present and perhaps very near future, its influence is passing away and moving out of importance.

5. FORCES FOR OR AGAINST YOU:

The card in this position plays a major role in determining the outcome of your reading, because its influence is the crux of all preceding events. If the card that falls in this position is positive, then the conditions surrounding your query will be working in your favor. If, on the other hand, the card has a negative connotation, then those influences will be opposing.

6. THE NEAR FUTURE:

This card will indicate how you've emerged from your recent past, as well as any new factors that come into being.

7. HOW THE NEAR FUTURE WILL EVOLVE:

This position reveals the way in which you've responded to the near future and how or in what way the future is evolving.

8. NEW TURN OF EVENTS AND/OR THE EFFECTS OF OTHERS ON YOU:

This card indicates new developments or perhaps unexpected changes that will alter your course or shed new light on existing situations; it includes the effects of others, if another plays an important role in the outcome of your question. You may want to observe the Others Category here as well as the one(s) you choose.

9. YOU IN THE ENVIRONMENT OF THE FUTURE:

The card in this position is very revealing because it represents *you* in the environment of the future, how your surroundings will affect you, and how you will think in times to come. It gives tremendous clarity as to the effect the future will have on you, and what tomorrow may hold.

10. OUTCOME OR SUMMATION:

This is the summation or outworkings of all of the previous cards. Read the categories you have chosen *and* the Outcome Category.

REMEMBER: If you don't know what category to choose you can always refer to the category definitions in Part One.

You can clarify any category or position with a clarification card (see Tips on Doing Readings).

A SIMPLIFIED VERSION OF THE KELTIC CROSS

You can simplify a Keltic Cross by using only six cards and laying them out as shown.

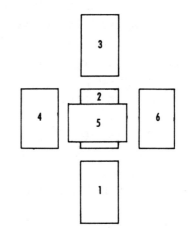

LAYOUT AND SIGNIFICANCE:
1. YOUR EXPERIENCE TO DATE
2. WHERE YOU ARE NOW
3. THE NEAR FUTURE
4. YOU IN THE ENVIRONMENT OF THE FUTURE
5. BEST YOU CAN HOPE FOR
6. OUTCOME

Example:
QUESTION: "Will I have a significant love relationship this year?"

1. YOUR EXPERIENCE TO DATE: TEN OF SWORDS—ROMANCE

Though the worst is over, your anguish continues because you haven't been able to bury the past or start anew. You vacillate between "Do I want it or don't I" and the moment you try to pin anything down or make a firm decision, the situation changes.

2. WHERE YOU ARE NOW: FIVE OF SWORDS—ROMANCE

Though you're longing for love, you won't settle for someone who sells you short or doesn't return your affection in kind.

3. THE NEAR FUTURE: KNIGHT OF SWORDS—ROMANCE

Though you don't see it coming, you will soon be swept up in a powerful love affair that is going to change your life dramatically.

4. YOU IN THE ENVIRONMENT OF THE FUTURE: TWO OF WANDS— ROMANCE

A lonely or unhappy soul is going to enter your life who may offer to take care of you or propose some type of living arrangement. This could be (but is not necessarily) someone who is already married.

5. BEST YOU CAN HOPE FOR: ACE OF SWORDS—ROMANCE

You will get an unexpected message, call, or response from someone who has a crush on you or loves you; or, this could indicate a new love that will take you by storm.

6. OUTCOME: TEN OF CUPS—OUTCOME

You will gain the support of others and will be visualizing ideas in order to mold a new future; your wish for fulfillment or a successful outcome will be granted.

> NOTE: The Ace of Swords indicated the season (Winter), the Knight showed the ending of one phase of your life and the beginning of another, and if a Court card had fallen in the third, fourth, or fifth position, it would have told you the type of person you became involved with. Note also that there were a lot of Swords, indicating both strife and action, and the Ten of Cups in the last position, indicating a cyclical rebeginning (the number 10) in the area of love (Cups).

THE ZODIAC SPREAD

There are two ways to use the Zodiac Spread. One method is to use it in predicting events (similar to the Keltic Cross and Category layouts) and the other is to use it for a Month-by-Month Forecast, where each astrological house is assigned a month of the calendar year. The first method will be referred to as a Zodiac Spread and the second, a Zodiac Month-by-Month.

Since the Zodiac Spread represents your future in different areas of your life, I've designated one or more categories to read for each astrological house. You can use them all or only the ones you feel apply.

LAYOUT AND PROCEDURE:

Shuffle the cards while thinking about what the various areas of your life will have in store. Then, lay out thirteen cards face up in the positions shown in the diagram.

Each position (or astrological house) has its own significance which is explained below. Begin by reading the category suggested in the first house and continue on throughout all 12 houses to the 13th and final card, the summation.

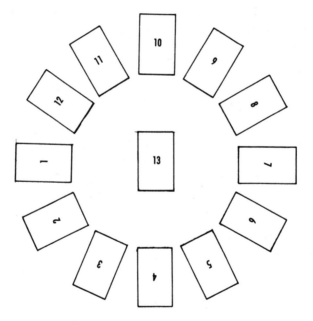

SIGNIFICANCE OF THE CARD POSITIONS:

1. FIRST HOUSE:

This deals with your self-expression, identity, or how you see yourself. (Read the Focus category.)

2. SECOND HOUSE:

This represents tangible assets, personal income, and earning capacity. (Read Finances.)

3. THIRD HOUSE:

This house governs intellect and communication, mental expression, letters, writings, and relatives. (Read Papers, Mail, News, Family.)

4. FOURTH HOUSE:

This rules your home, property, environmental experiences, and domestic affairs. (Read The Home.)

5. FIFTH HOUSE:

This is associated with pleasurable pursuits, romance, entertainment, and speculative ventures. (Read Romance, Pleasure, Fortune.)

6. SIXTH HOUSE:

This pertains to working conditions, job efficiency, obtaining or holding a job, and one's relationships with other employees, as well as matters associated with health, sickness, and nutrition. (Read Work/Career, The Physical Body.)

7. SEVENTH HOUSE:

This refers to partnerships, agreements, and mergers, as well as marriage, divorce, business relationships, and close personal relationships. (Read Unions.)

8. EIGHTH HOUSE:

This house governs death, rebirth, legacies, and inherited assets. (Read Endings, New Beginnings, Inheritance.)

9. NINTH HOUSE:

This is a very important house in that it governs spiritual guidance and teachings which work toward developing self-knowledge. It also refers to travel and lengthy journeys. (Read Special Guidance/Esoteric, Best Course of Action, Travel.)

10. TENTH HOUSE

This house describes your goals, ambitions, achievements, and worldly attainments. (Read Desire, Success.)

11. ELEVENTH HOUSE:

This house is associated with friendships and/or affiliations which help to advance your personal objectives. (Read Friends, Others.)

12. TWELFTH HOUSE:

This is also a significant house in that it represents a blind spot in your makeup that could cause limitation or unnecessary suffering. (Read Anxiety.)

13. SUMMATION:

This is the final result of all the preceding cards. (Read Outcome.)

You can always use clarification cards if your answer is unclear (see Tips on Doing Readings).

THE ZODIAC MONTH BY MONTH

With this layout, you can read simply the Focus category for each month, which gives you a capsulized version of each month's events or you can pick several categories of interest and read them all.

LAYOUT AND PROCEDURE

1. Shuffle the cards while thinking about what's ahead for you during the next twelve months.
2. Lay thirteen cards face up in a circle as shown, starting with the month with which you want your forecast year to begin and ending with the General Atmosphere, i.e., if you want to start in January, the first position would be read as January, the second, as February, and so on (see diagram example).
3. Read just the focus category for the General Atmosphere, but on the month positions, read as many categories as you wish.

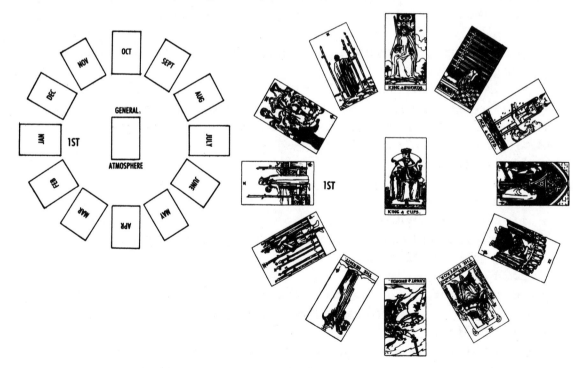

Example:
Let's assume you started your year in January. The first card read would be the General Atmosphere which in this case would be the King of Cups. Reading the Focus, you would find that your major thrust would be on "activities centered around the home; financial independence; day-dreaming about love and romance; and/or a person with a Cancerian-type of temperament." The next position you would read is the Two of Wands. Begin your reading for January with the Focus, and if more information is desired, read as many categories as you choose. Continue reading for February, March, April, etc., until your calendar year is complete.

Take special note of Major Arcana cards falling on a particular month because that month will be important. Watch for Aces because they signal fresh starts or new beginnings in the suit they represent and for multiples (three or more) of numbers indicating numerological trends.

REMEMBER: If you don't know what categories to choose you can always refer to the category definitions in Part One. If you want to clarify a category you can always use a clarification card (see Tips on Doing Readings).

THE CATEGORY SPREAD

This is a general "all-purpose" reading *that can be used when there are no particular questions in mind* and you just want to know what's coming up in your future. It can be used every week, month, or year.

It's called a Category Spread because 32 cards are used to represent each of the thirty-two categories of interpretation, and only one category *per* card is read.

PROCEDURE
1. Shuffle.
2. Lay out one card for each of the 32 categories, as shown.
3. Proceeding in order, read the appropriate category for each card. For the first card read the first, or Focus category. Then go to the second card and read *only* the Desire category, then to the third card and read *only* Romance, and so on. Continue reading each consecutive category until you reach the last card and category, which would be the Outcome.

FOCUS	DESIRE	ROMANCE	THE UNEXPECTED	OTHERS	THE HOME	TRAVEL	PAPERS
1.	2.	3.	4.	5.	6.	7.	8.
WORK/ CAREER	UNIONS	EMOTIONAL STATE	PLEASURE	NEWS	FAMILY	THE PHYSICAL BODY	FINANCES
9.	10.	11.	12.	13.	14.	15.	16.
TIME	FRIENDS	VISITORS CALLERS	MAIL	ANXIETY	DIS-APPOINTMENT	ENDINGS	NEW BEGINNINGS
17.	18.	19.	20.	21.	22.	23.	24.
INHERITANCE	REWARDS GIFTS	SUCCESS	FORTUNE	BLESSINGS	SPECIAL GUIDANCE	BEST COURSE OF ACTION	OUTCOME
25.	26.	27.	28.	29.	30.	31.	32.

Example:

Let's say you ask: "What's coming up for me next week?" If your first card is the Emperor, your Focus will be on "construction, formation and solidity," etc. That is the only category to be read from that card. If your next card is the Three of Wands, you would read the Desire category for that card and find that "You want a successful partnership or union," etc. Following the diagram, the third card read would be about success. Read only the information given in the Success category and continue on to your next card and category, The Unexpected. Follow the same procedure throughout the remaining 28 cards and categories until your reading is complete.

REMEMBER: You can add clarification cards if you want, but on the new card read only the category about which you are seeking clarification. In other words, if you're reading Papers and you want more information on it, draw another card but read *only* the Papers category.

THE COURT ARCANA

This is the only reading specifically geared to: Who, What, Where, When. The interpretation takes only one card, and is the easiest, most precise way to answer questions about personality, time frame, and vocation. For example:

• What work am I best suited to do?
• What work will I do?
• When would be the best time to start this enterprise?
• What type of person would be best for me?
• What type of person will I marry?
• What type of boss am I working for?
• What type of employee is this person?
• What type of career will bring the most success?

PROCEDURE

1. Take the 12 astrological Court Arcana cards (King, Queen, and Page of each suit) out of the deck and put the rest away.
2. Think about your question while shuffling, then intuitively pick one card or cut the pile from right to left and take the top card off the righthand pile.
3. The answer to your question is found in the qualities and time frame embodied in the astrological sign of the card.

> **Examples:**
> I once asked what area would bring me the most satisfaction and prosperity. The card I drew was the King of Wands (Aries): "TYPE OF VOCATION: Any area where leadership qualities are desired because you can work alone." I then asked what area would I specialize in, and drew the Queen of Cups (Scorpio), which read: "TYPE OF PERSON: Spiritual, psychic, clairvoyant ,... TYPE OF VOCATION: Occult work, counselor. . . . "

If you wanted to know *when* an event would occur, and drew the Queen of Cups, which is Scorpio, you would know the time frame was October 23 through November 21.

If more information on an astrological sign is desired, there are numerous books on the subject of astrology that go into lengthy detail.

SPIRITUAL GUIDANCE

I developed this spread to guide you along your spiritual path. The eight questions posed are designed to give a better understanding of the underlying or motivating factors involved. This layout is especially useful when your question concerns your spiritual growth, or problems that can't be answered through the mundane spreads.

PROCEDURE

One card is drawn for each of the eight questions. I've found that in order to give the most accurate and comprehensive reading possible, you must shuffle the cards *before* each question and then draw the card instead of arranging the entire layout at once.

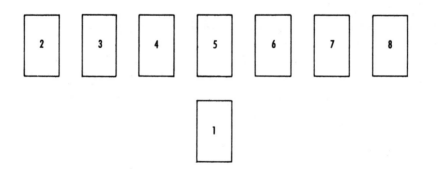

(Shuffle the cards and ask:)

   1. WHERE YOU ARE NOW, OR THAT WHICH CONCERNS YOU:
Cut the deck once toward the left, then turn up the top card on the right and read the Focus and Desire for your answer.

   (Shuffle again and ask:)

   2. WHAT IS THE FORCE OR MOTIVATION BEHIND YOUR DESIRE:
Cut the pile again toward the left, take the top card off the right, and read the Focus category on that card.

(Shuffle again and ask:)

3. WHAT IS THE UNDERLYING PROBLEM:

Follow the same cutting procedure and read both the Anxiety and Disappointment categories.

(Continue to shuffle and cut the cards throughout the next five questions, asking:)

4. WHAT YOU NEED TO UNDERSTAND THAT YOU'RE NOT AWARE OF:

Go to the Special Guidance category and read the Esoteric first, then read the Mundane.

5. WHAT YOU NEED TO DO TO COME TO TERMS WITH YOUR PROBLEM:

Read the Best Course of Action category.

6. WHAT'S THE BEST WAY TO PROCEED IN ORDER TO CARRY OUT THE ADVICE GIVEN:

Read the Best Course of Action category again.

7. SPIRITUAL GUIDANCE CONCERNING YOUR FUTURE:

Read the Esoteric portion of the Special Guidance category.

8. YOUR ULTIMATE ATTAINMENT:

Read the Focus and the Outcome categories.

Example:

This is a reading I did for myself when I was going through a particularly difficult and confusing time both in my personal life and with the sales and management of my first book, and I wanted to know if things were going to improve.

1. WHERE YOU ARE NOW, OR THAT WHICH CONCERNS YOU: SEVEN OF CUPS—FOCUS/DESIRE

The focus is on the search for truth, gut-wrenching experiences, and life-altering events related to your family, friends, work, or love; feelings of powerlessness, inadaquacy, or confusion; cosmic contact and spiritual experiences.

You wish things weren't so hard and you'd like to become less reactive, to cut off anyone or anything that elicited a negative emotional response.

2. WHAT IS THE FORCE OR MOTIVATION BEHIND YOUR DESIRE: THE DEVIL—FOCUS

You're going through an adverse cycle of events where problems seem to multiply and nothing's going right. Your perception is clouded and you're unable to see clearly, or perceive the whole picture.

3. WHAT IS THE UNDERLYING PROBLEM: THE EMPEROR—ANXIETY/ DISAPPOINTMENT

You're troubled by plodding work and a sordid relationship, and are disappointed in a partnership that seemed carved in granite but has turned to sand.

4. WHAT YOU NEED TO UNDERSTAND THAT YOU'RE NOT AWARE OF: THE STAR—SPECIAL GUIDANCE/ESOTERIC

In *The Autobiography of a Yogi*, Paramahansa Yogananda states: "The Karmic Law requires that every human wish finds ultimate fulfillment." Could it not follow then that your desire is the thing itself knocking at your door?

It's the call of destiny that motivates you or compels you to go on. Your desire is *not* in vain and that which you are yearning for will ultimately find fulfillment.

5. WHAT YOU NEED TO DO TO COME TO TERMS WITH YOUR PROBLEM: THE HIEROPHANT—BEST COURSE OF ACTION

Don't allow yourself to be pulled under or overcome. Learn to operate in new ways and develop more strength of will or character.

6. WHAT'S THE BEST WAY TO PROCEED IN ORDER TO CARRY OUT THE ADVICE GIVEN: THE CHARIOT—BEST COURSE OF ACTION

Look to your inner world, change the way you *react* to events, and choose to be happy. When you let go of fear or doubt, success will come.

7. SPIRITUAL GUIDANCE CONCERNING YOUR FUTURE: THREE OF PENTACLES—SPECIAL GUIDANCE/ESOTERIC

The goal is worth the suffering.

8. YOUR ULTIMATE ATTAINMENT: JUDGEMENT—FOCUS/OUTCOME

The focus will be on new personal relationships, new business ventures or partnerships, beneficial help, improved conditions, and a complete change in habit, consciousness, or purpose.

And, after a period of suffering or failure to find happiness, the past will begin to fade and you will experience a regeneration of mind or spirit which will be directed toward new ideas, new areas, and new beginnings.

REMEMBER: You can always clarify a question by using a clarification card (see Tips on Doing Readings).

◆ CREATING YOUR OWN SPREAD ◆

At some point, you might think of a spread that is even easier than the ones I've described, so I would like to give you some pointers that could help you get started.

One of the best ways I've found to create a spread is to look over the categories to find the ones that are best suited to answer the questions you have in mind. Once that's been established, think about the possible progression of events (or order of priorities) that would be in accord with how you imagine the answer to your question could evolve, i.e., near future, unseen elements, underlying motivation, outcome, etc. For instance, when I created the Spiritual Guidance Spread, I wrote each question down, then searched the categories to find the ones that answered them most thoroughly. I continued the process until I had categories to answer all my questions. The order of that particular layout wasn't important. In the Category Spread, I wanted an in-depth reading, and the best way to go about it was to read all thirty-two categories from thirty-two different cards. The Simplified Keltic Cross came about because I found that more times than not the full Keltic Cross contained information extraneous to the answer of my question.

It's as simple as that, really.

REMEMBER: Clarification cards can also be used here (see Tips on Doing Readings).

PART 4

INTERPRETATION OF THE CARDS

THE
MAJOR
ARCANA

THE MAGICIAN.

◆ THE MAGICIAN

A Major Arcana always indicates an important event, category, or month, and will overpower all other cards in both impact and effect.

IN A READING

Many 1s would indicate that a situation is about to begin or is in the beginning stages.

NUMBER 1

The focus is on new beginnings, manifesting desires, love's urgings, houses or property, finance, and the future.

FOCUS

You want to begin something new, to "do, act, or go forth," and/or are hoping for a miracle in your life or affairs.

DESIRE

Though you don't think so now, a new romantic beginning or rekindled affair is at hand and a great love affair is imminent.

ROMANCE

You will suddenly become more goal-oriented or motivated and will have the wherewithal to attract whatever it is you need in your work environment, and/or you will receive a considerable increase in salary or income.

THE UNEXPECTED

You'll be struggling to assert yourself or your work, but that is going to change dramatically.

OTHERS

It would be better to stay where you are than to go on a "wild goose chase," and if you've been concerned about the sale of a home or property, an offer will be accepted and it will be sold.

THE HOME

If you are planning a trip or vacation, you will have to cut it short or postpone it.

TRAVEL

You'll begin a new project or venture similar to something you just finished (but better), and papers will be involved. If you have to take a test, you'll pass with flying colors. Or, a transfer of ownership will be processed and completed.

PAPERS

Expect a new beginning and a fresh start. A new partnership could also be in the making.

WORK/CAREER

If you can't have your relationship the way you really want it, you won't be sure you want it at all.

UNIONS

EMOTIONAL STATE   You will be wound up and ready to go, ambitious, and in a state of positive expectancy, but at times you'll be too headstrong and impatient.

PLEASURE   A new love or strengthened old one will have some happy surprises in store. This could also indicate a pleasant social event or get-together.

NEWS   You are going to have to wait a day or so before you can resolve a dilemma, find what you need, or get a problem corrected.

FAMILY   A new course of action will ensue with a relative or there will be a change of existing plans with a family member and/or you will feel slighted by a relative.

THE PHYSICAL BODY   You will experience stress and/or will find it difficult to ascertain the problem or obtain the correct medication.

FINANCES   You will do very well financially or in your business transactions.

TIME   In time, you will experience a new beginning and attain that which you asked for, wanted or envisioned.

FRIENDS   You will get some much-needed help, advice, or counsel from a friend.

VISITORS/CALLERS   Expect a rewarding financial transaction, call for work, and inquiry.

MAIL   Someone will try to deliver a package but you won't be home to receive it, or you will receive a letter regarding a financial transaction that will need to be acted on.

ANXIETY   You are going to have trouble maintaining a consistent attitude.

DISAPPOINTMENT   You will be disappointed because your romantic desires will be unfulfilled at this time, or you will have problems related to the sale of a home or property. Don't worry, it's not going to last.

ENDINGS   The old way is going to die and the new way begin. "The king is dead, long live the king!"

NEW BEGINNINGS   Expect a change in your love life because an aura of romance is going to prevail, bringing a new love or strengthening an old one.

You are going to realize that in the fulfillment of one desire lay the **INHERITANCE**
seeds of another.

You will be feeling that you're doing all the giving and that it's **REWARDS/GIFTS**
being taken for granted, or that what you're giving is unappreciated.

You will be successful in money matters, creative pursuits, new **SUCCESS**
projects or ventures, and any endeavor that you can do on your
own.

Luck will be with you in landing a new job or employment oppor- **FORTUNE**
tunity and/or beginning a new business.

You will be grateful for a lucky financial break or transaction, or **BLESSINGS**
the manifestation of an idea.

Mundane: A situation has been (or soon will be) presented that has **SPECIAL GUIDANCE**
all the inherent components of the manifestation of your desires.
Take the best from it or move on it, because it is through this that a
new potential will emerge.
Esoteric: You are only at the very first stage of your development
and you must understand your place in the Cosmic Scheme of
things. The Universe always gives more than you can conceive of or
ask for . . . all you have to do is accept more. "Thou shall decree a
thing and it shall be established unto thee."

The result will be up to you. It depends entirely upon your intention, **BEST COURSE**
and desire, or how much you want it. **OF ACTION**

You are going to begin again on a new foot, or with a new partner. **OUTCOME**

THE HIGH PRIESTESS

◆   # THE HIGH PRIESTESS

A Major Arcana always indicates an important event, category, or month, and will overpower all other cards in both impact and effect.

IN A READING

Many 2s indicate a waiting period where there will be partial success but more to be revealed later. They can also indicate a reconciliation, a reunion, and/or an element of surprise.

NUMBER 2

The focus is on positive and negative polarities; waiting, learning assimilation, and application; trade, finance, and negotiations; and public activities or public relations.

FOCUS

You want to follow through with a course of action and/or to utilize an idea, skill, or philosophy.

DESIRE

You will be putting love, or the one you love, out of your thoughts in order to avoid emotional entanglements or the pangs of desire.

ROMANCE

You will be surprised about an incident involving a car, and be bombarded with memories from your past.

THE UNEXPECTED

You will be cold toward those who are insinuating, or who operate unethically or under false pretenses, but others will provide unexpected assistance or aid, and your ideas, requests, or presentations will be well received.

OTHERS

You are going to have an unexpected and very welcome surprise.

THE HOME

You will take a short trip or travel for work, but if planning a long-distance trip or move, it will probably be postponed or canceled.

TRAVEL

You will be discussing finances, payments, or time schedules where papers are concerned, and/or will profit through things involving papers.

PAPERS

Business will be very slow in the beginning, but will pick up greatly later on, and you will make very good money, or more than others. You may even receive an unexpected bonus or two.

WORK/CAREER

You will be at a crossroad and will wonder if you are going to come

UNIONS

together or split apart once and for all, but you'll have to wait before the answer will be revealed because only time will tell.

EMOTIONAL STATE   At times you'll be impatient, but for the most part detached, withdrawn, uninvolved, or removed, and your discerning abilities will be quite acute.

PLEASURE   You'll be pleased about a financial arrangement, and will have a pleasant surprise concerning a problem that's been bothering you.

NEWS   A message or communication will require a decision or necessitate action on your part.

FAMILY   You will communicate with your relatives, but will feel detached, alone, or on your own.

THE PHYSICAL BODY   If you have been ill, you'll have a swift recovery.

FINANCES   You will be waiting for results or for the arrival of someone or something. Patience will be needed but ultimately you'll be successful.

TIME   There will be a few stops and starts and some "stuff" to push through, but after that, things will begin to flow more smoothly. A surprise is also in store.

FRIENDS   A friend or relative will call that could benefit through your guidance, so keep a positive outlook; and if you've been waiting to hear from a friend, you soon will and an invitation will be extended.

VISITORS/CALLERS   Someone from a distance will call to see you. Some form of worry or anxiety over a visitor or caller could also be indicated.

MAIL   You will receive a financial statement or form that will need your endorsement.

ANXIETY   You will be troubled, frustrated, and upset over a tedious, time-consuming, or unpleasant job situation, or an encounter with sexual overtones.

DISAPPOINTMENT   You'll be disappointed in having to wait, and in people who promise and then don't deliver.

You will no longer accept that which is counterproductive, nor will you sacrifice what's fundamentally right for momentary satisfaction, so you will direct your actions accordingly or take steps to correct problem areas.

ENDINGS

A new product or future business endeavor may come into view, or you could seek a new agent.

NEW BEGINNINGS

You will "inherit" a sense of self-worth and a learning experience.

INHERITANCE

You'll be undecided about the purchase of a product and/or will be gifted with the ability to look at yourself or others objectively.

REWARDS/GIFTS

You are going to attract an unlooked-for job opportunity or secondary occupation, and will benefit personally, professionally, or financially through a wise career decision.

SUCCESS

You will be lucky in *all* financial transactions or negotiations.

FORTUNE

You will be grateful for a release from tension and the opportunity to work, make money, or expand in your field of endeavor.

BLESSINGS

Mundane: Once you make a decision or decide upon a goal, make a commitment to it and let nothing divert you from it or keep you from attaining it. Recognize the patterns that have sabotaged you in the past and cut them off.
Esoteric: This is a gestation period. Changes are taking place on the inner planes, and at the appropriate time, these new energies will be released and you will spring back into full force.

SPECIAL GUIDANCE

Visualize the desired result as an accomplished fact, and *act* as if you are *already* what you want to be and you shall be.

BEST COURSE OF ACTION

Help will come if you need it, and things are going to turn out quite differently than you anticipate. You can also expect a pleasant surprise or two.

OUTCOME

◆ THE EMPRESS

A Major Arcana always indicates an important event, category, or month, and will overpower all other cards in both impact and effect.

IN A READING

Many 3s indicate group activities or situations involving more than one person. They can also indicate delay, but with the promise of future success.

NUMBER   3

The focus is on passive rather than active activities; feelings, emotions, inner promptings, and intuition, self-expression, socializing, or connecting; short- or long-distance trips; and "being" rather than "doing."

FOCUS

You are discontented because something is missing or lacking in your life, or because you want to find something creative, meaningful, or fulfilling to do, but you don't know what.

DESIRE

You will long for love and affection and want very much to express the things in your heart but cannot and will not be content to be just a surface lover.

ROMANCE

You are going to be surprised by a sudden flirtation or romantic possibility.

THE UNEXPECTED

It will be a strain communicating with some people because you will feel scattered, intolerant, or critical, yet it will motivate you to get your intention clear and to take action to resolve the difficulty.

OTHERS

You will want to take it easy, be outdoors, travel, or move, but if you considered moving to a new locale or living with another, you won't go through with it because it won't feel right.

THE HOME

You will travel for work or pleasure and will look at or discuss property to buy, rent, or purchase for a new home.

TRAVEL

You will experience problems connected with papers. Don't gloss over documents; read them carefully or define them more clearly . . . you may need someone else's input.

PAPERS

You will try to put off work for awhile and/or schedule business appointments for a later date, or you will want to work in a human-

WORK/CAREER

potential profession that motivates others through self-actualization or creative interaction.

UNIONS
You will be examining your relationships with others and trying to sort out your feelings.

EMOTIONAL STATE
You will feel taut, troubled, or out of sorts because you'll want to create something but won't know what, and your thoughts and feelings will be unruly or discordant.

PLEASURE
You will find peace, comfort, and inspiration through nature, rest, or relaxation, social gatherings, and small trips or pleasurable pursuits.

NEWS
Something inside is trying to tell you something. Get in touch with your feelings.

FAMILY
Your relatives will be concerned with the sale of or purchase of a home or real estate venture. Expect communication problems.

THE PHYSICAL BODY
Your upper back could bother you, and a rest or vacation would do wonders. Get in touch with your body and see what it wants or needs . . . you'll be happy with the results if you do.

FINANCES
Expect a postponement or delay in affairs concerning finances, but the money is forthcoming.

TIME
In time, you will intuitively sort things out and come to the conclusion that it's better not to give problems any (more) thought or attention, and to relax and start enjoying yourself.

FRIENDS
You're not saying what you really want to say, or expressing the things you really feel, or doing what you really want to do. Female friends are also indicated.

VISITORS/CALLERS
If you planned to unite with someone, your plans will be canceled or delayed . . . at least for now.

MAIL
Something that's been overlooked is going to cause an upset or delay, but it will arrive shortly.

ANXIETY
Communicating with others will be a strain, and you will be frustrated because you'll feel you're in a "holding pattern" and unable to make the kind of changes you want to see happen in your life.

You will be unhappy because you won't be able to manifest the things of your heart.

DISAPPOINTMENT

Stress or strain will come to an end.

ENDINGS

You're going to make a very important or significant connection with someone and though it's only the initial stage of an action or union, the gears will be set in motion.

NEW BEGINNINGS

You will "inherit" the ability to intuitively synthesize information and grow as a result.

INHERITANCE

You will give someone a gift in appreciation or exchange for a service he/she provided for you, or one will be given to you.

REWARDS/GIFTS

Your success will come through a positive change in your attitude, trusting your intuitive resources or inner promptings, and doing what the heart dictates, and in anything pertaining to nature, organics, or "the great outdoors."

SUCCESS

Luck will be with you in finding an emotional or physical outlet that will resolve tensions and ease your mind or soothe your soul.

FORTUNE

You'll be thankful for an intellectual respite and healing of emotional ills.

BLESSINGS

Mundane: This is not a time to think, act, or do. You're already overloaded and mental pursuits won't give you what you need. Further attempts to follow your intellect or reasoning mind will only cause frustration or lead you astray.
Esoteric: You are in a reorientation period. If you have neglected to heed your feelings or intuitive faculties, you will be prevented from utilizing your intellectual resources until the balance is restored. Thought must learn to unite with feeling, and in this case, feelings must lead.

SPECIAL GUIDANCE

Heed your feelings or instincts and not your intellect, and learn to trust your feelings more.

BEST COURSE OF ACTION

Expect delays or postponements . . . but there is a promise of future success.

OUTCOME

◆ THE EMPEROR

A Major Arcana always indicates an important event, category, or month, and will overpower all other cards in both impact and effect.

IN A READING

Many 4s indicate fruition or the manifestation of an idea, along with the foundation or "space" where things can grow.

NUMBER 4

The focus is on construction, formation, and solidity, and the appearance of someone or something that will change the status quo or present an opportunity to enter into a new partnership, relationship, or life-style.

FOCUS

You want to see your ideals manifested on the physical plane in the form of material gain or accomplishment.

DESIRE

You'll be thinking about the one you love and will want to be with him or her again, and he/she will be thinking the same about you. When you hear from him/her, you'll make plans to get together.

ROMANCE

You will be surprised by your unexpected progress, good fortune, or "arrival" in business or financial matters, or you'll surprise yourself by making a major "yes" decision you've been putting off.

THE UNEXPECTED

You'll be happy about a social invitation that will soon be presented, as it contains unexpected joy or good fortune.

OTHERS

You will be doing a lot of thinking about one who exerts a strong influence or dominant force over you.

THE HOME

A plan or rendezvous will be temporarily postponed due to a time-consuming work schedule or a legal matter.

TRAVEL

You can expect financial gain or profit through papers or mail.

PAPERS

You will have discussions concerning contractual agreements, profit sharing, subsidies, or management.

WORK/CAREER

You and a partner or loved one will unite and discuss plans for the future.

UNIONS

Someone or something will lift your spirits, provide a new founda-

EMOTIONAL STATE

tion for your future, and change the course of your experience for the better.

PLEASURE

You'll be pleased about consenting administrators, and/or will enjoy sensual pleasures or a rewarding personal relationship.

NEWS

You will soon hear something that will shed new light on your present outlook or financial status which will come as a great relief, and if you ask for backing on an idea you'll probably get it.

FAMILY

If planning to visit the home of a relative, the visit will be postponed because of another; or, someone could be lying to a relative or misrepresenting facts.

THE PHYSICAL BODY

You will be worried about a physical condition (yours or that of another) and your teeth may need attention. Also, if you were concerned about a tumor, it will be benign. Sex will be much better the second time around.

FINANCES

You can expect an increase in your finances which will allow you to spend money on gifts or luxuries, and if you had a problem collecting money on an account of NSF check, it will be resolved.

TIME

You will embark on a new line of work or money-making enterprise, new thoughts, conditions, or actions will replace old, *and* someone will want to develop a future with you or to legally cement your relationship.

FRIENDS

Friends will surround you, and you will have the kind of foundation or support that fosters further growth and development. Male friends are also indicated.

VISITORS/CALLERS

A caller will not arrive or call as anticipated.

MAIL

You will be involved with letters or papers that can open new doors, or facilitate growth in a new direction, and if concerned about a bad check or payment due on account, it will be made good or paid.

ANXIETY

You will be troubled by plodding work, a sordid relationship, or an extramarital affair.

You will be disappointed in a partnership that looked as if it was carved in granite but turned to sand.

DISAPPOINTMENT

You will make a decision to forget an unsatisfactory or disappointing relationship, and to discipline your mind to keep the person out of your thoughts.

ENDINGS

Someone or something will appear that will enable you to actualize a concept you devoted a lot of thought, time, work, or love toward.

NEW BEGINNINGS

You will "inherit" a new line of work and earn interest on an account.

INHERITANCE

You will wine and dine someone, or he/she will wine and dine you.

REWARDS/GIFTS

You will prosper in all financial transactions, complete every task you set out to do, and accomplish much more than you thought you would; and/or you will succeed in launching great plans, building new platforms, and making executive decisions.

SUCCESS

Luck will be with you in material affairs or employment matters through the entry of a "take-charge" type person (or attitude), and a turning of the tide in the romantic department for the better.

FORTUNE

You'll be grateful for the elimination of that which was oppressing you, for improved conditions, and for a thought's turning into reality.

BLESSINGS

Mundane: An opportunity will arrive that could well be the foundation of a very successful future. This will be a very propitious happening.
Esoteric: If your foundation was built correctly, the manifestation will follow. If not, you will have to rebuild or start over.

SPECIAL GUIDANCE

Accept that which is coming your way and don't delay.

BEST COURSE OF ACTION

You will achieve most, if not all, of your desires, and someone (perhaps a man) will be very beneficial to you or to that which you seek.

OUTCOME

◆ # THE HIEROPHANT

A Major Arcana always indicates an important event, category, or month, and will overpower all other cards in both impact and effect. **IN A READING**

Many 5s indicate change, challenge, and fluctuations (lucky or unlucky). They also indicate material prosperity but spiritual poverty if not properly balanced or understood. **NUMBER 5**

The focus is on establishments, organizations, groups, or structures (including the family structure), key or critical figures you align yourself with, the search for truth or understanding, new thinking, and new opportunities. **FOCUS**

You want to establish a deeper bond with someone or to unbind the bonds that block, restrict, or keep you from having what you want. **DESIRE**

Romance will enter your life, but the relationship won't get off the ground because you want an elevated love and will not settle for less. You will sacrifice love altogether rather than have a relationship that isn't right. **ROMANCE**

You'll be surprised by a business venture or presentation that fails, but on a more positive note, an unexpected romantic opportunity will arise. **THE UNEXPECTED**

Someone will call for a decision on your part, like "How should I proceed?" or "What should I do now?" **OTHERS**

You will try to connect with a business establishment in order to get an idea off the ground, but won't have much luck; or, if work needs to be done around the home, you will make a good deal with a contractor or dealer. **THE HOME**

Travel may be necessary in order to exchange ideas or communicate needs; strength of will will be needed, and/or there will be confusion over travel plans caused by too many variables. **TRAVEL**

You will question the value of your work and will find it very hard to continue to do it when faced with so many overwhelming adversities; you will want to give up, but you won't. **PAPERS**

WORK/CAREER

You may have run up against unforeseen obstacles in the past, but you will soon find a better opportunity . . . something more aligned with what you want, or through a different source than that which was previously established.

UNIONS

You will not be fulfilled in your relationship because it is either non-productive or dissatisfying at a very deep level.

EMOTIONAL STATE

Your feelings of anxiety will cause you to turn within to find the answers that you need, and if that doesn't work, you will seek the aid of others in an effort to find a solution.

PLEASURE

You will get a great deal of pleasure or satisfaction through regrouping forces and/or gaining insights into situations through new and unusual sources.

NEWS

Someone in a business where money changes hands is going to give you a hard time or the runaround.

FAMILY

You will want to keep the peace with your family and not make waves.

THE PHYSICAL BODY

You will experience chest pains, shortness of breath, or respiratory problems.

FINANCES

Someone will forget or neglect to pay or mail money that is owed you, but on the whole your financial position will be stable.

TIME

You are going to run into many unforeseen obstacles or conflicts with medical institutions, working establishments, organizations, or family structures that will put a wedge between you and another.

FRIENDS

You will have a conflict with a friend or loved one; or you will be confronted with a situation you would rather not deal with, but you will handle it.

VISITORS/CALLERS

You are going to get a very unexpected and upsetting phone call, and if you were anticipating the arrival of a loved one, you are going to be disappointed.

MAIL

A letter or bill will upset and annoy you, a letter from a doctor, healer, or teacher will be required, or a letter from a friend will arrive.

You are going to have some conflicts with "key" or critical people in your life and will find it difficult to communicate effectively or get your ideas across.

ANXIETY

You will be disappointed in an idea, program, or communication that didn't come across as you thought or hoped it would.

DISAPPOINTMENT

Complications regarding incorrect work methods or programs will end, but so will the possibility of merging with another in a business venture or personal matter.

ENDINGS

Industrious ideas toward a new line of work will occupy your thoughts and mental preparations will be made.

NEW BEGINNINGS

You will be gifted with spiritual insight, prophetic dreams, or an innate ability to teach or counsel others.

INHERITANCE

You will be given something that involves paper, food, or furnishings.

REWARDS/GIFTS

You are going to attain great insight into a situation that was previously obscured, and some of your best achievements will come through unestablished sources or foreign cultures.

SUCCESS

Through luck you will gain insight into something that's been a mystery, or get unexpected assistance from an unexpected source.

FORTUNE

You will be thankful for a shift in mood or attitude, the opportunity to teach others, or a move into a less demanding atmosphere.

BLESSINGS

Mundane: It's better to endure suffering or abstention than to be in a position where you'll have to compromise yourself or your values. *Esoteric:* If your mind is filled with all the things it thinks it wants and needs, there can be no room for betterment. For the Higher to enter, some of the debris must be cleared away. Let go of your attachment to the past, feelings of loss, or your old routine; move into the new and unknown. That is where you'll find your opportunities now.

SPECIAL GUIDANCE

Don't allow yourself to be pulled under or overcome. Learn to operate in a new way and develop more strength of will.

BEST COURSE OF ACTION

You will be prevented from moving forward or advancing at this time by the "powers that be."

OUTCOME

THE LOVERS.

◆ THE LOVERS

A Major Arcana always indicates an important event, category, or month, and will overpower all other cards in both impact and effect. **IN A READING**

Many 6s indicate adjustments in thoughts, attitudes, or conditions. They can also represent the ability to transcend difficulties. **NUMBER   6**

The focus is on sudden and unpredictable changes, interesting experiences, love, friendship, newness, unions, meetings, examination, choice, reorganization, travel, personal property, or domicile. **FOCUS**

A dilemma will be presented demanding an action or decision, and you will want to figure out the best way to proceed or make the right choice. **DESIRE**

A separation from a loved one is going to cause great feelings of frustration and alienation. **ROMANCE**

You are going to be surprised by a very fortunate adjustment in your love life (could be a call from an admirer), and by something that looked negative on the surface related to your work or field of endeavor turning out to be an unexpected blessing. **THE UNEXPECTED**

You can expect many social calls and invitations but past failures will make you leery of making the same mistakes all over again. **OTHERS**

You will be very productive, with several projects going at the same time, as well as domestic, social, and business activities to attend to, but you could run into some problems with faulty equipment or appliances. **THE HOME**

A choice will be presented which will call for a decision on your part, like whether you should go or not. **TRAVEL**

Ideas will flow easily and unexpected good fortune or prosperity will come through things involving papers. Also, a "failure" now will prove to be a blessing later. **PAPERS**

You will find that some people are not interested in the work you normally do, or what you have to sell, but this will be a blessing in disguise, because new avenues will open up offering unexpected gains in a different direction. **WORK/CAREER**

UNIONS   You will be feeling trapped in a dead-end situation or marriage.

EMOTIONAL STATE   Your emphasis will be on your work, studies, and reaching your goals rather than on social activities, and you'll tend to be a loner, but be prepared for the unexpected because that is going to change considerably.

PLEASURE   You are going to be very pleased about a beneficial product or project, the restoration or reparation of something you considered a failure or loss, and new social or romantic interests.

NEWS   There will be unexpected family problems, or you will hear that someone who owes you money is not going to pay or is going bankrupt. A call from a lover could also be indicated.

FAMILY   Your relatives will be experiencing problems concerning their home, real estate, or property, or too many family responsibilities are being heaped on you and the load is creating a rift that needs to be communicated and resolved.

THE PHYSICAL BODY   You will be physically productive or sexually active, and will be in the process of building a healthier body or mind.

FINANCES   Money will be coming in through commissions, trade, or skills, and/or through a mortgage, loan repayment, or unexpected source, and if a need arises, money will come to cover it.

TIME   You will have to make a choice; to continue on or move in a different direction.

FRIENDS   You're going to have a much-needed confrontation with someone you consider to be a friend . . . don't go easy on him or her.

VISITORS/CALLERS   You're going to get an unexpected call and/or visit from a friend, lover, or admirer.

MAIL   Money will come in through the mail or a mail-order business.

ANXIETY   You'll be troubled that things are not going to go according to plan, and though you are (or will be) separated from your lover, you will not be able to put him/her out of your mind.

You will be very disappointed in the sudden ruin of a project, plan, or business venture and your inability to exert any influence over the situation.

DISAPPOINTMENT

You are no longer going to be alone. Social separateness or alienation is going to end.

ENDINGS

You will embark on many social excursions or gatherings with friends, but will run into unexpected problems in business or romantic unions, and may have to meet later than expected.

NEW BEGINNINGS

You're going to "inherit" unexpected good fortune and a "saving grace."

INHERITANCE

A social invitation or introduction will arrive, and you'll receive or buy a gift.

REWARDS/GIFTS

Your success will come through unexpected places, social situations, or amorous suitors, and/or pulling off a financial coup.

SUCCESS

Something that once looked like a loss will prove to be the opposite.

FORTUNE

You will be grateful that you have enough money to pay your bills and cover your needs, or that a new product you purchased worked out the way you wanted.

BLESSINGS

Mundane: Something is going to change your plans or the course of your experience, something that may look negative on the surface but will later prove to be a blessing in disguise.
Esoteric: Things don't have to go according to plan in order for you to benefit from them. It's time to drop "support" systems and depend on the Universe.

SPECIAL GUIDANCE

Look beneath what appears to be . . . Fate will bring serendipity.

BEST COURSE OF ACTION

You may suffer through unavoidable consequences or predicaments (or as a result of another), but you will do the right thing or come to the right conclusion and someone or something will correct the problem or remove you from it.

OUTCOME

THE CHARIOT.

◆ THE CHARIOT

A Major Arcana always indicates an important event, category, or month, and will overpower all other cards in both impact and effect.

IN A READING

Many 7s indicate a period of introspection or solitude. They can also indicate unlooked-for advantages or gains through things that come unexpectedly.

NUMBER 7

The focus in on introspection, reevaluation, and decisions of passion; confusing issues that make you reexamine your affairs and ask questions such as: "Should I do this or that?" "Is it this or that?" "Will it work out or won't it?"

FOCUS

You don't know what you should do or where you are going, and are afraid of losing control. You want to force a resolution, but don't know how.

DESIRE

You will want to share your deepest feelings but will keep them to yourself because you can't find an "outlet" or won't want to run the risk of being vulnerable; and/or you'll have superficial involvements or fast flings with strangers.

ROMANCE

You're going to receive an unexpected gift (spiritual or actual), and a call from a loved one, admirer, or sweetheart.

THE UNEXPECTED

You will be uncomfortable around others because of confusing situations, and will find yourself going through the motions or exchanging social pleasantries but not really participating or meaning it.

OTHERS

There will be many unexpected problems to combat, but you will overcome them all and attain a sense of deep satisfaction. Events concerning real estate, property, or a new home will take a surprising twist.

THE HOME

Your thoughts will be on someone who is away; you will want to be with him/her and when you talk, the two of you will make plans to get together.

TRAVEL

If you had intended to write a book or presentation, or take new action on an old idea, you won't want to because it will be too much

PAPERS

trouble. Something will cause you consternation because it wasn't your fault, but *you're* the one who will have to deal with it.

WORK/CAREER   You will wonder if you should pursue a plan or continue a project, but will be driven to do so, and a perplexing dilemma will be resolved for the time being. You could also have an opportunity to be filmed or taped, or to work with film or tape.

UNIONS   Passions will be strong or grow quite fast in your dealings with others, and you'll be thinking about what the future holds in terms of your relationship.

EMOTIONAL STATE   You will be frustrated, confused, and upset, and the more you try to push or resist, the worse it will get. Only when you let go, will peace come.

PLEASURE   You will enjoy flirting, partying, or being out with "the gang" as well as an unexpected business opportunity or increased income, but real happiness will come through surmounting your weakness, doubts, or fears.

NEWS   Someone will call and invite himself/herself over, or someone will call and come over.

FAMILY   Plans or schedules will be discussed with your relatives, but you'll feel pressured by time or other commitments.

THE PHYSICAL BODY   If you don't slow down or take it easy when you feel you should, you will get sick, catch a cold, or suffer from mental strain or physical exhaustion.

FINANCES   You will have to confront someone over a money issue, but your arguments will be successful and the money will be paid to you.

TIME   Situations are going to become very confusing or disquieting, and you will find it difficult to "keep the faith" or continue on without becoming overwhelmed.

FRIENDS   In no time at all, things are going to work out between you and a friend or relative ... don't worry, arguments or disagreements won't last.

Though events will be confusing, they will work out the way you want, or in the perfect way, and if someone agreed to come, he/she will. You can also expect a late-night phone call from an admirer. **VISITORS/CALLERS**

News you've been waiting for will finally arrive, but it won't be what you expected. **MAIL**

An upsetting condition, confrontation, or conversation with or regarding another is going to trouble you a great deal and you won't be able to get help or comfort when you think you need it. **ANXIETY**

You will be disappointed in the sudden collapse of an idea or valued object, disillusioning mental, spiritual, or emotional pursuits, or past failures, and you will want to give up on everything. **DISAPPOINTMENT**

A fixed attitude, unworkable involvement, or unpleasant experience will come to an end and in its place will come a new perspective, sudden insight, or uplifting turn of events. **ENDINGS**

You will be considering the possibility of a union with someone you like or love . . . what would it be like? **NEW BEGINNINGS**

Business or financial matters will cause confusion as to the best way to proceed or action to take, but you will "inherit" the ability to surmount the difficulty or correct the problems. **INHERITANCE**

You will receive a flash of spiritual illumination that will uproot a deep-seated psychological problem, and/or you will be in a quandary over a gift. **REWARDS/GIFTS**

Your best success at this time will come through continuing on or "going for it" in spite of obstacles, discouragement, or disappointments and taking a rest when one is needed. **SUCCESS**

Someone will present you with a very enticing opportunity concerning your home or place of business that could open up a whole new vista or increase your income substantially. The choice will be up to you. **FORTUNE**

You'll be grateful that things are working out better than anticipated and of their own accord. **BLESSINGS**

Mundane: You will soon have a new perspective and attain great peace or satisfaction.

Esoteric: All paths lead to the same place and we are all doing what we are supposed to be doing even when we're wondering if we should or shouldn't be doing it or think we're making mistakes or going astray. The real issue is, will you overcome or be overcome. Will you choose "aliveness" (even if there are no safe spaces) or will you choose "deadness"?

SPECIAL GUIDANCE

Look to your inner world, change the way you react to events, and choose to be happy. When you let go of fear or doubt, success will come.

BEST COURSE OF ACTION

Though nothing may have changed significantly in your outer world, you'll have changed dramatically, and you will be revamping your objectives or your approach to life as a result.

OUTCOME

◆   STRENGTH

A Major Arcana always indicates an important event, category, or month, and will overpower all other cards in both impact and effect.

IN A READING

Many 8s indicate a positive change of mind or status because the beneficial qualities of the number 8 are rarely diluted.

NUMBER 8

The focus in on challenging situations pertaining to business and finance, family matters and things that stemmed from the past, spiritual fortitude, and results or reward for persistence and effort.

FOCUS

You want positive results in business or love, and to overcome the obstacles to the attainment of that goal.

DESIRE

You will not be ready to commit to or become totally involved in a new relationship . . . this could be because of an emotional attachment to the past.

ROMANCE

An unexpected upset, challenge, or confrontation with another will

THE UNEXPECTED

arise. This could be concerning a financial matter, or it could be a run-in with the law.

OTHERS

You will feel challenged by others who directly or indirectly oppose you or your ideas; and, an encounter with someone will leave a lasting impression on you.

THE HOME

You will be involved with consciousness-raising books, studies, methods, or groups, and you will do your work or chores without argument or complaint.

TRAVEL

You will take several short trips or jaunts, and a friend or relative will be planning to go on a trip. A dispute over a traffic ticket or moving violation could also be indicated.

PAPERS

You'll be enmeshed in paperwork, or working with philanthropic or self-help material, all of which will be complicated and time-consuming; or, you will be angry that the work you did was not acknowledged or appreciated. This will pass, however.

WORK/CAREER

Results may be slow in coming, but you will hold your own, get a lot accomplished, and summon up enough energy to do what it takes to get the job done; and in some way, you'll be recognized or rewarded for your efforts.

UNIONS

You'll be contemplating a union or discussing marriage and will begin to see things in a more positive light. You will also make a decision to forgive and forget the past, and to get on with the future and the now.

EMOTIONAL STATE

You're going to be troubled by the past or something stemming from the past.

PLEASURE

You will be pleased by the recognition of spiritual assistance as it makes its presence known in your life and affairs. You will also enjoy your personal freedom, and having the "space" to do what you want to do.

NEWS

You're going to get some unexpected news (could be through a phone call) concerning your work that will dispel some of your doubts, put a new slant on your work, or increase your earnings.

There will be altercations stemming from an imagined slight or unexpressed resentment.   **FAMILY**

Your energy will be dynamic, and if there should be a problem, you will have the strength to overcome it. No physical disability or handicap will keep you down.   **THE PHYSICAL BODY**

Financial troubles will be handled effectively, or money that was held up, promised, or expected will arrive and all debts will be paid.   **FINANCES**

In time, things will clear up and your efforts will begin to show results.   **TIME**

A friend from the past will return, causing a renewal of activity in the present or future . . . this will be a very positive encounter.   **FRIENDS**

Someone from your past is going to call or arrive, or you will make a call on one you haven't seen in a while.   **VISITORS/CALLERS**

You're going to mail a letter or card that concerns a new product (could be a warranty), or you will send away for a license or membership.   **MAIL**

You'll be troubled by the "seeming" lack of results in your affairs.   **ANXIETY**

You will be very disappointed in love, business, or spiritual affairs that just seem to be stagnating. But this is only a temporary condition and things will soon take a turn for the better.   **DISAPPOINTMENT**

Restraints will come to an end, and positive changes in your business affairs in the form of recognition or promotion will at last come your way. You can also expect improved conditions in your finances and love life.   **ENDINGS**

A situation will arise with one who will exert a great deal of power or influence over you, but you'll be steadfast in your goals or intention and if challenged, will take up the gauntlet and *win*. Nothing will defeat you.   **NEW BEGINNINGS**

Things are going to come up to be cleared up once and for all, and positive changes will bring a renewed feeling of power, accomplishment, or control.   **INHERITANCE**

REWARDS/GIFTS You will receive good news, praise, or recognition for your work and efforts, or a gift of money or flowers.

SUCCESS Adversity will evoke even greater effort on your part, enabling you to achieve results, succeed in overcoming opposition, and win others over to your point of view.

FORTUNE You'll be fortunate in money matters, and in resolving business or emotional dilemmas.

BLESSINGS You will be grateful for spiritual help, intervention, or assistance.

SPECIAL GUIDANCE *Mundane:* There are powerful spiritual forces at work and obstacles to your success will be overcome . . . you will be given the power to succeed.

Esoteric: This is an important Karmic period, and actions taken during this time will be the needs of your tomorrow. If you are feeling challenged, it's because you are harboring a deep-seated mis-understanding, mistrust, or resentment toward someone (perhaps even God), and you are being given the opportunity to resolve it once and for all . . . remember, love conquers everything, even Karma.

BEST COURSE OF ACTION Put aside the notion that your prayers can only be answered by striving or personal effort, and if you pray, pray with conviction . . . don't be fearful.

OUTCOME You will overcome all obstacles, and nothing will keep you from advancing toward your goals because you will have the kind of inner fortitude that nothing can defeat.

THE HERMIT

A Major Arcana always indicates an important event, category, or month, and will overpower all other cards in both impact and effect. **IN A READING**

Many 9s in a reading mean that situations or events are nearing completion or have just been completed and another plateau awaits. **NUMBER 9**

The focus is on seeking and finding, problem-solving, perfecting or completing; the final stage, summit, or pinnacle of experience in one phase of your life and the dawning of the next; and/or people from the past who reenter your life. **FOCUS**

You want to change your destiny or get back together with the one who's been estranged. **DESIRE**

An old flame or romantic interest will reenter your life, but you may still be strangers. **ROMANCE**

An admirer from the past will reappear and then disappear, and/or you will find an article written about you, or be given the opportunity to write something . . . perhaps a column for a magazine. **THE UNEXPECTED**

Though you have suffered deprivation, loneliness, or enforced isolation, you are about to make a major transition into a new lifestyle. **OTHERS**

The completion of a cycle will end depression and ensure success. If the problem concerns the sale of a home, it will be sold. If not, it will be the result of a movement that takes you out of the home and into the mainstream. **THE HOME**

You will travel for work or study or will hear that someone you care for is going on a trip; or a friend from the past will call with a vacation invitation. **TRAVEL**

You will deal with papers connected with insurance, health, or home, and/or something that involves papers will make you very happy. **PAPERS**

In a very short time, productivity will increase and people will seek **WORK/CAREER**

THE HERMIT.

you out for your talent, knowledge, or wisdom. You can also expect recognition, acclaim, and financial success.

You will want to bridge estrangements and share your heart with someone, and some special communication will be implemented.

UNIONS

You will experience sadness, apprehension, or trepidation due to a sudden development that evokes a sense of loss; but don't worry, that is going to change into a feeling of great relief, joy, and accomplishment.

EMOTIONAL STATE

You are going to have a change of heart brought about by someone or something. This could be the result of a new business venture, or it could be someone who will unexpectedly assist you, acknowledge you, or bring good tidings.

PLEASURE

Expect a call for work and a message from an admirer.

NEWS

You will talk to a relative long distance, or spend time with a friend who comes to visit, and if you've had a falling out with a loved one, you will soon make up.

FAMILY

There will be checkups, tests, or health-related problems on the horizon, but all will end well.

THE PHYSICAL BODY

You are going to receive some money for "work well done," and have enough to spare for pleasurable pursuits, products, or gifts.

FINANCES

In time, a new cycle will commence (a much happier one), and you will feel that the worst is over.

TIME

A friend from the past will return bearing good tidings, and/or will bring the solution to a problem if you let him/her help.

FRIENDS

Someone from your past whom you haven't seen in a long while will call and you will make plans to get together.

VISITORS/CALLERS

You will be waiting for an important letter, document, or package to arrive.

MAIL

You will be troubled by the fact that there are no real answers or solutions to your questions, and/or that the advice you do receive is unwanted.

ANXIETY

DISAPPOINTMENT   You are going to be very disappointed in the "things" of the earth —i.e., life, love, and the pursuit of happiness.

ENDINGS   Isolation, restriction, or suppression will come to an end.

NEW BEGINNINGS   You will begin to see the light at the end of a very dark tunnel and the future will start to look much more promising.

INHERITANCE   You will "inherit" an omen of better days to come.

REWARDS/GIFTS   You will be gifted with the ability to teach or enlighten others, and someone will give you a nice gift . . . something you need or want.

SUCCESS   You will be successful in bridging estrangements, beginning a new business, or making good money through metaphysical or commercial enterprises.

FORTUNE   Luck will be with you in reaching positive solutions, and in achieving most of your goals in a relatively short time.

BLESSINGS   You'll be grateful that the one who's been away or estranged has returned, or that a strong desire or fervent wish has been granted.

SPECIAL GUIDANCE   *Mundane:* You *will* attain that which you are seeking.
Esoteric: You've reached a point in your evolution where you should *know* that you don't have to have all the answers, or know the future in advance, in order to ward off failure. Reservations and distrustful thoughts are barriers that stand between you and the Source, and they must be worn down and eliminated.

BEST COURSE OF ACTION   Don't strive to overcome a situation or force a resolution. Take a modest or reticent approach with dignity and unassuming grace.

OUTCOME   You will accomplish most of your goals and emerge into a new plateau of potentiality, yet you will know that this is only the first step of your unfoldment and there's much more ahead to be achieved.

◆ THE WHEEL OF FORTUNE

A Major Arcana always indicates an important event, category, or month, and will overpower all other cards in both impact and effect.

IN A READING

Many 1s would indicate that a situation is about to begin, or is in the beginning stages.

NUMBER 10
(1 + 0) = 1

The focus is on controversial matters, conflicts of interest, unexpected or unforeseen developments that change your plans or alter your course, important news or information, and an idea whose time has come.

FOCUS

You want information or insight; to pin something down or to resolve a dilemma.

DESIRE

Someone from your past is going to return, but you will be undecided about the relationship, or the way it's going to go.

ROMANCE

You are going to have a very unexpected change in your affairs.

THE UNEXPECTED

Though you will interact with others both personally and professionally, you will be "on guard" or apprehensive, and your opinion will be the deciding factor in a very important career decision.

OTHERS

Expect an increase in your financial obligations, living expenses, or rent; or, service people will have to come back because their work wasn't completed.

THE HOME

You will be considering a major trip or move, and will discuss the possibility with others.

TRAVEL

You will uncover some valuable information, receive important financial news, or get a "winning ticket."

PAPERS

You will make some profit, but your work will still be unsatisfactory, and new elements will make it necessary to effect changes or make new arrangements.

WORK/CAREER

A negative condition is going to end, followed by an important decision.

UNIONS

You will have fluctuating moods caused by job-related and/or per-

EMOTIONAL STATE

WHEEL of FORTUNE.

sonal problems and will find it very hard to keep your emotions under control.

You will derive pleasure through good friends, good books, or new groups, unions, or partnerships. **PLEASURE**

Some distressing information will necessitate a decision on your part . . . this could be concerning your career. **NEWS**

Someone in your family will be a tremendous burden or constant source of agitation to you, and you will wish you could be free of him/her; or, someone you love will not need medical treatment or surgery, and you will be grateful. **FAMILY**

One minute you will feel fine, and the next minute you won't. You will tend to eat too much sugar or starch, and suppressed emotions will cause a negative physical reaction. **THE PHYSICAL BODY**

You'll be worried that your resources are dwindling, or that your profits won't make up for your losses or initial investment, but important news will shed new light on the issue. **FINANCES**

Some advancement will be made, but your position will still be unstable. **TIME**

Sudden and unexpected ill health will befall a friend or loved one, and he/she could wind up in the hospital; or, you will hear some very unexpected news. **FRIENDS**

All plans will be unpredictable. Expect many unforeseen changes or vicissitudes (good and bad). **VISITORS/CALLERS**

You're going to get an important letter, package, or document. **MAIL**

You'll be troubled by upsetting news, incidents, or actions on the part of another; or you will worry about maintaining your financial position or a sudden loss of income. **ANXIETY**

You will be disheartened about your unsatisfactory love life, job, or career. **DISAPPOINTMENT**

Whether you see it coming or not, a problematical situation is about to end. **ENDINGS**

NEW BEGINNINGS   A new cycle in your affairs is about to commence, followed by the arrival of some very important news or information, and you will make permanent changes in business or health . . . a change for the better.

INHERITANCE   A cycle is going to be completed through the progression of circumstances, and good news concerning your finances will arrive.

REWARDS/GIFTS   You're going to have to purchase something you'd rather not have to buy.

SUCCESS   Your success will come through preordained changes that will alter your present circumstances, ease tensions, and better your conditions.

FORTUNE   Through luck, a new cycle is at hand and the end of a problem is approaching.

BLESSINGS   You will be grateful that a negative condition has finally come to an end.

SPECIAL GUIDANCE   *Mundane:* Situations will be out of your control (your premonitions will probably be right). Get ready for a new way of life because one is about to commence.
Esoteric: What's happening in your life will soon turn into something much better. This apparent havoc is actually the beginning of a new order which was destined to commence at this time and if events had not convened in just this way, you'd still be where you were and you would miss the turn of fortune that fate has in store for you.

BEST COURSE OF ACTION   Don't get stuck on "plans" . . . letting things go the way they will, will bring good fortune.

OUTCOME   Events are going to sum up in such a way that it will be impossible to miss the result . . . but a new start in a new direction will work out in your behalf, and give you the chance to begin anew.

◆ # JUSTICE

A Major Arcana always indicates an important event, category, or month, and will overpower all other cards in both impact and effect.

IN A READING

Many 2s indicate a waiting period where there will be partial success but more to be revealed later. They also indicate a reconciliation, a reunion, and/or an element of surprise.

NUMBER 11
(1 + 1) = 2

The focus is on wanting to reach your goals, settlements, legal matters or income, health, investments of time, cause and effect, and trying to understand the workings of destiny in your life or affairs.

FOCUS

You want an emotional level of expression, to rejuvenate or correct a problem area, or to perfect an idea so that it can be put to good use.

DESIRE

You will review the quality of your love life or relationship(s) and will realize that's exactly what you want—quality, not quantity—and so far it's been the other way around.

ROMANCE

You will be surprised by the arrival of money, or news that money will be arriving sooner than anticipated.

THE UNEXPECTED

Others will make you feel insecure, vulnerable, or defenseless.

OTHERS

Your present living quarters will no longer appeal to you because it has outlived its purpose or you've outgrown it, and you will want to move to a new home or begin a new life elsewhere; and/or you (or a relative) will sell your home and move.

THE HOME

You will move into a new situation or environment, and though spending time away from home will fulfill some needs, you will still be intrinsically dissatisfied.

TRAVEL

A new element will be just what you need to take the wrench out of a stalemated endeavor or unsatisfactory method of operation that was slowing down progress; and/or a lawsuit will be settled in your favor or a contract signed.

PAPERS

Someone will displease you, unearth hidden insecurities, or make you feel that your work is inferior or that your job is in jeopardy.

WORK/CAREER

One cycle is going to end and a new one begin, and a tense situation will become more flexible. **UNIONS**

There will be a lack of fulfillment on a personal or emotional level of expression because an essential ingredient is missing. **EMOTIONAL STATE**

You will enjoy buying new clothes or products or mentally preparing for future events, and because of this, productivity will be stimulated in all areas. **PLEASURE**

You will hear some distressing or upsetting news about your work. **NEWS**

A relative will be experiencing problems with his or her mate and may be considering a separation or divorce. **FAMILY**

Your teeth will need attention, and if you should speak to a new physician you will find him/her to be a charitable or valuable ally, and/or an earlier prognosis will prove to be correct. **THE PHYSICAL BODY**

You will be feeling a definite crunch in your pocketbook and will wonder where your next dollar is coming from; and to make matters worse, every time you turn around another expense will arise. But your finances are about to improve. **FINANCES**

In time, your accounts will be squared, problems solved, and bills paid with money to spare, but something else will still be up in the air, unresolved, or missing. **TIME**

If problems are to be resolved or cleaned up, you're the one who will have to resolve them or bring the relationship back to a healthier status. **FRIENDS**

You will find out something to your benefit through a phone call or caller, and you will have the opportunity to teach or learn something yourself. **VISITORS/CALLERS**

There will be messages, letters, or mail concerning an impending injunction, lawsuit, or litigation. **MAIL**

You'll be troubled by an unresolved dilemma or business issue, and will have no recourse but to wait it out. **ANXIETY**

DISAPPOINTMENT   You will be disappointed in the apparent unfairness of the workings of destiny in your life.

ENDINGS   Bogged-down commercial activities and annoying financial conditions will come to an end.

NEW BEGINNINGS   Change will come, but a shadow of isolation or unhappiness will remain because some personal or essential ingredient is still missing.

INHERITANCE   You will "inherit" a business lead or opportunity to make money.

REWARDS/GIFTS   Someone will do a charitable deed or act of kindness.

SUCCESS   You will succeed in recognizing what's wrong and coming to the right conclusions or decisions.

FORTUNE   Through luck you will find a rejuvenating product, unsolicited assistance from others, and a valuable piece of information.

BLESSINGS   You'll be glad that you have the courage to stand up for your rights and to confront and resolve disputes or complications.

SPECIAL GUIDANCE   *Mundane:* You have just completed a cycle of destiny, and a brand-new cycle is about to commence. The present will have to evolve before it can be weighed or judged and time will provide the key to the understanding that you need.
Esoteric: Let tomorrow take care of itself.

BEST COURSE OF ACTION   Wait for time to take its course.

OUTCOME   Problems will be resolved one by one, and a turbulent time is coming to an end.

◆ THE HANGED MAN

A Major Arcana always indicates an important event, category, or month, and will overpower all other cards in both impact and effect.

IN A READING

Many 3s indicate group activities or situations involving more than one person. They can also indicate delay but with the promise of future success.

NUMBER 12
(1 + 2) = 3

The focus is on your life, values, and way of thinking, caused by a complete reversal in your affairs. Your dreams will no longer seem valid and everything that's been before now looks hopeless, obsolete, or meaningless.

FOCUS

You want to release a problematic or painful situation and let a higher wisdom handle your affairs so that you can let go of discouragement, striving, or trying to figure things out.

DESIRE

You will be waiting to see what a lover will do. This could also indicate a sudden flight from home, but not a permanent one.

ROMANCE

You will be surprised by an unexpected financial opportunity that is going to come your way, and by suddenly having the wherewithal to handle a rough situation effectively.

THE UNEXPECTED

You will wonder if the work you are doing, or the relationship you are in, has become obsolete and you're trying to whip a dead horse.

OTHERS

You will experience remorse or sadness brought about by a lover or family member.

THE HOME

You will take a short trip to a new environment, or you will be stranded without means of transportation.

TRAVEL

You will be examining the small print, and will want to define it more clearly. You will also be concerned about the response of others regarding documents, legal matters, or probates.

PAPERS

You'll have repeat clients, and some financial increase or profit, but will be waiting for something to happen or turn up, and will fear the work you're doing has little value or that you won't be able to sustain yourself in the future.

WORK/CAREER

You will experience suffering or martyrdom in your marriage and in your career because you can't have the one you really love, and/or are bound by financial restrictions.

UNIONS

Impending situations and existing conditions will cause much suspense and anxiety, and you will search your soul for a feeling of self-worth or purpose, but you will make it through this turbulent time, by grace of God!

EMOTIONAL STATE

A fresh direction will begin to emerge that will give new meaning, purpose, and inspiration to your life.

PLEASURE

You will be waiting for (or hoping that) a friend or lover will call.

NEWS

You will soon spend time in the home of a relative or dear friend that you haven't seen in a while, and it will be very pleasant.

FAMILY

You need to get more rest, and to get rid of those who "zap" your energy or take all and give nothing in return.

THE PHYSICAL BODY

Financial problems will arise over someone who will stick you with the bill or try to take more than their share, but you will have enough to get by.

FINANCES

Unsettled conditions will begin to resolve themselves or work out on their own accord, but it will be difficult to keep an open-minded outlook due to your intense emotional reactions.

TIME

A friend or loved one will help you get something you're after or accomplish what needs to be done, or will offer assistance in a new plan or venture of yours . . . all you have to do is ask.

FRIENDS

You will be examining other people's thoughts or actions, and after a great deal of consideration, will come together on mutually beneficial terms.

VISITORS/CALLERS

You will be tired of waiting for news or money because you sense deception and distrust the party involved. But on the other hand, an awaited letter will arrive.

MAIL

Not knowing where you are going or what you're going to do, and waiting for someone to make a move or do something, will make

ANXIETY

you feel that your life is out of your hands and there's nothing you can do to change it.

DISAPPOINTMENT — You will know that a friendship, love affair, or partnership is not working out or has become obsolete, but you will feel powerless to get out of it, change it, or do anything about it.

ENDINGS — Emotional problems, physical handicaps, or poverty will come to an end.

NEW BEGINNINGS — You will hold off on an idea because you won't be ready to commit, or will feel the time isn't right or that there's too much hard work involved.

INHERITANCE — You are going to have a complete reversal in your thinking.

REWARDS/GIFTS — You will receive a beneficial gift or an attractive job offer.

SUCCESS — A new business proposal will come to the fore that will ease financial tensions or inject new life into a situation that's fallen into a rut.

FORTUNE — You will be fortunate in money matters, and luck will be with you in reversing a negative trend.

BLESSINGS — You will be grateful that conditions are improving, and that a better way of life is beginning to emerge.

SPECIAL GUIDANCE — *Mundane:* There is a greater hand steering your course than yours. *Esoteric:* Let it be "Not my will but Thine." In time you will understand why you had the experience you had, and to what ultimate purpose you were being led.

BEST COURSE OF ACTION — Surrender control to the Higher Powers and take your hands off it.

OUTCOME — Problems will be resolved one by one, and a turbulent time is coming to an end.

◆   # DEATH

A Major Arcana always indicates an important event, category, or month, and will overpower all other cards in both impact and effect.   **IN A READING**

Many 4s indicate fruition or the manifestation of an idea, along with the foundation or "space" where things can grow.   **NUMBER 13**
(1 + 3) = 4

The focus is on endings and new beginnings in career, partnerships, or status quo . . . new conditions, new opportunities, and a new life-style.   **FOCUS**

You feel you can't go on with the status quo and want things to change radically.   **DESIRE**

Your relationship is going to come to an end (if it hasn't already), but your love for that person will continue to burn like a lone candle in the window of a deserted home.   **ROMANCE**

Though you don't think it possible now, you can expect a sudden change in your affairs . . . a release and a reconstruction.   **THE UNEXPECTED**

You will realize that you must forget the past (or your lover) and all that was and try to rebuild your life. Or, you will be overly concerned about what others think of you.   **OTHERS**

A new idea, plan, or action will be implemented (could be connected with your work), and/or you will want to move or relocate.   **THE HOME**

Expect a slight delay in travel plans. You may start to go, then have to wait or pull back, and then go later, but a change in conditions will work to your benefit or open new doors.   **TRAVEL**

It will be virtually impossible to carry on with a plan or course of action involving papers. You will have to look for an alternative.   **PAPERS**

Things are not going to go as planned, and there will be a lot of unexpected changes or obstacles to confront.   **WORK/CAREER**

You will come to the full realization that your relationship, as you have known it, has come to an end . . . and it's over.   **UNIONS**

You will be very unhappy, depressed, or overwhelmed by the events   **EMOTIONAL STATE**

DEATH.

that unexpectedly conspire to change your course or status, but hold tight because things will soon take a turn for the better.

Happiness will come through good friends and reuniting with those who have been absent.   **PLEASURE**

Someone is about to go out of your life temporarily and you will hear about it. This news could come through as a psychic prediction or message.   **NEWS**

A happy gathering of family and friends is in store.   **FAMILY**

You'll have discussions about health, death and dying, and the ability to transform the quality of life by changing your attitude or the way you think.   **THE PHYSICAL BODY**

You will be worried about your finances because of a sudden loss or severance of income.   **FINANCES**

In time, it will become very obvious that events are not going to go according to plan or work out the way you wanted them to.   **TIME**

Things are not going to continue as they were because an unforeseen event will make it impossible to carry on. Don't worry; you'll make amends or pick up where you left off later.   **FRIENDS**

A call will come concerning a dubious proposition, and you will soon have to travel whether you want to or not, because you'll feel obligated.   **VISITORS/CALLERS**

Expect a disappointment. Something you counted on will not come through or come to pass.   **MAIL**

You will be very troubled about your future, finances and making ends meet.   **ANXIETY**

You'll feel "short-changed" in a romantic situation or career endeavor because you hoped for so much more than you received.   **DISAPPOINTMENT**

A hoped-for or promised venture connected with your profession or livelihood will come to an end, or a monthly income will be severed.   **ENDINGS**

NEW BEGINNINGS   You are going to have a new direction, focus, or plan. Everything you're experiencing at the present time is going to change, and something you thought was a lost cause will be reinstated or will begin to flourish again.

INHERITANCE   You will "inherit" inner growth and the realization of Divine Order in the face of what once appeared to be a negative condition.

REWARDS/GIFTS   You will have discussions about a gift that is about to be given or received. This could also indicate the arrival of a package containing books, music, or tapes.

SUCCESS   Your greatest success will come through your ability to rise up again in a different form or a different way and begin anew.

FORTUNE   You will have luck in a new business enterprise, and income thought lost will be retrieved, revived, or reinstated.

BLESSINGS   You'll be grateful that a negative situation has finally come to an end.

SPECIAL GUIDANCE   *Mundane:* Many changes are going to take place and in three to six hours, days, weeks, or months a new direction will emerge and the "dead" shall rise again.
Esoteric: A habit or pattern has become difficult to break and you have not been able to correct it alone. You have no recourse now but to step aside and let the Higher Powers move in and lead you out of the difficulties. You must accept this "death" in whatever form it takes if a resurrection is to occur and the situation restored to its rightful or proper condition.

BEST COURSE OF ACTION   Let go of situations that no longer serve a purpose in your evolution. If you try to pursue them, you will advance only to have to pull back, or find that you have no one around to help or guide you.

OUTCOME   A new order will be established, and like the Phoenix, you will rise up out of your own ashes and begin again.

◆ TEMPERANCE

A Major Arcana always indicates an important event, category, or month, and will overpower all other cards in both impact and effect.

IN A READING

Many 5s indicate change, challenge, and fluctuations (lucky or unlucky). They also indicate material prosperity but spiritual poverty, if not properly balanced or understood.

NUMBER   14
(1 + 4) = 5

The focus is on all the things you thought you had completed or had a handle on—old friends, lovers, habits, desires, health, money or business problems—resurfacing for the sole purpose, it seems, to "test" you to your very core.

FOCUS

You want spiritual assistance in producing the solution to a problem.

DESIRE

You are going to have an unexpected call from or "encounter" with an admirer, someone you were attracted to or involved with in the past who's returned as if to have a last go-around or to close that chapter in your life for good.

ROMANCE

You will be surprised at your ability to turn a negative situation into an extremely positive one simply by redirecting your energies. This could also indicate a deeply penetrating spiritual experience.

THE UNEXPECTED

If you trust in the right outworkings of your affairs, they will work out exceptionally well.

OTHERS

You're going to feel that you're being "tested" and will be under a lot of pressure trying to understand or rise above the events that are happening to you. In addition, an appliance will burn out, short out, or go on the fritz.

THE HOME

Because you've been extremely busy and are in need of a rest, you'll postpone activities involving travel to another day.

TRAVEL

Papers will contain only partial solutions; something will still be missing, and anger will arise with others if facts are not readily available.

PAPERS

You'll feel that if you continue on the path you're on without relief or gratification, you will absolutely explode, and the desire for change will be so intense that it comes, bringing the very thing you want.

WORK/CAREER

You will feel hurt or slighted because your partner is ignoring you or not including you in his/her plans, being completely honest with you, or living up to his/her promises or commitments.

UNIONS

You'll feel nervous, agitated, frightened, or confused, and will have a difficult time maintaining emotional balance.

EMOTIONAL STATE

Happiness will come through a new "toy," like-minded people, and improved health or finances (after a period of worry or suffering).

PLEASURE

You'll have to confront someone in order to collect money that should have been paid to you, or to regain ownership or get the paperwork moving, and it will be a delicate situation.

NEWS

Your relatives will be very understanding and always there with the right word or gesture.

FAMILY

Upsetting conditions or pressures are going to cause a previous health problem to resurface, and that problem will probably need medical attention.

THE PHYSICAL BODY

You're going to experience a chain reaction in money matters with only a partial response at first, and then one thing will lead to another and a moderate degree of success will be attained.

FINANCES

It's going to take a lot of discipline or genuine wrath to not let yourself be overcome and to manifest the things you want.

TIME

Diverse elements are going to stir up old wounds or deep-seated problems and you'll be caught off-guard by the emotional on-slaught.

FRIENDS

Someone from the past will say hello and good-bye—will come into your life and then go right out.

VISITORS/CALLERS

Some news or information regarding finances will cause a chain

MAIL

reaction, as it will necessitate another action which in turn causes another.

ANXIETY
You're going to have an unforeseen problem to confront. This could also indicate unwanted advances from a suitor.

DISAPPOINTMENT
You'll be distressed by health problems, financial worries, and business discouragements, or the fact that you can't or won't make the compromises necessary to keep your relationship going with another, even if it means a loss.

ENDINGS
You will no longer be subject to limitation, anger, frustration, or emotional pressure.

NEW BEGINNINGS
Everything on every level is going to be transformed into something else, and you will find yourself moving in a completely different direction . . . this will be a vast improvement.

INHERITANCE
You will "inherit" spiritual encouragement and positive changes by looking beyond your limitations.

REWARDS/GIFTS
Someone who likes you a great deal will give you something or lavish his/her generosity upon you. This could also indicate a spiritual gift of some sort.

SUCCESS
Your best success will come through your ability to maintain control over volatile conditions and utilize ideas in order to bring forth the kind of results you want.

FORTUNE
Luck will be with you in transforming negative situations into positive ones.

BLESSINGS
You will consider it a blessing that you have a friend or boss that favors you or loves you.

SPECIAL GUIDANCE
Mundane: Many unforeseen or unexpected events are going to come up, but these elements will chemicalize, neutralize, or transform situations, all with a positive end in view.
Esoteric: What you're experiencing is a clash between the old and the new, a chemical reaction in mind, body, and affairs caused by a reaction to a new action. There is nothing to fear; it's part of the process and without it change could not occur.

Work on yourself, and don't be afraid to air your fears or let your "demons" surface. Confront them head on, and if you need verification or more understanding, ask for it!

BEST COURSE OF ACTION

The right ideas or actions will be provided, but it will take special effort or concentration on your part to use them to your advantage.

OUTCOME

◆ THE DEVIL

A Major Arcana always indicates an important event, category, or month, and will overpower all other cards in both impact and effect.

IN A READING

Many 6s indicate adjustments in thoughts, attitudes, or conditions. They also represent the ability to transcend difficulties.

NUMBER 15
$(1 + 5) = 6$

The focus is on an adverse or negative cycle of events where problems seem to multiply and nothing goes right. Your perception will be clouded and you will be unable to see clearly or perceive the whole picture.

FOCUS

You want to shake off adversity or end a negative condition.

DESIRE

You will still carry a flame for the one you love, and hope to recover what was lost and begin again.

ROMANCE

To your great relief, a weird or unpleasant event will turn into a lucky break.

THE UNEXPECTED

You will be extremely irritated or angry with an associate and you will either let him/her know it or take action on it; or you will feel overworked, overtired, unappreciated, and on your own.

OTHERS

This is not a good time to push for results, scrutinize situations, or move to a new location. Others will have the upper hand, so don't make waves or force confrontation.

THE HOME

A trip or outing will be postponed due to unavoidable circumstances.

TRAVEL

THE DEVIL .

You will be overwhelmed by the amount of work that must be done in order to achieve your goals, and the effort it will take to complete the task will seem insurmountable. **PAPERS**

You are going to be working very hard but for little or no profit and as a result, you will feel frustrated and thwarted from capitalizing on your potential. Things will seem so bad they're almost a joke. **WORK/CAREER**

All attempts at union or reconciliation are going to be blocked, but because of this, you'll begin to realize what works for you and what doesn't. **UNIONS**

You will be depressed or in a negative state of mind, or will feel that there's no escape from your workload, life-style, or undesired fate. **EMOTIONAL STATE**

An unusual and/or depressing condition will take the pleasure out of a situation you would normally find rewarding. This could also indicate a sexual aberration or some kind of bondage or illicit or dead-end love affair. **PLEASURE**

You will have an upsetting conversation with someone regarding your work or place of business and you will take it very much to heart. **NEWS**

You will feel like an emotional garbage dump and will be unable to get an idea across or attain that which you want or need, but in time you will find an equitable solution. **FAMILY**

You will be tired or run-down because you have become a slave to your work or are burning the candle at both ends, and you will have problems sleeping because you have too many things on your mind. **THE PHYSICAL BODY**

You will have major financial difficulties and unexpected losses resulting from bad checks, bad investments, or adverse conditions, but you'll soon have the opportunity to make more money, so don't worry. **FINANCES**

You will be in a state of "suspended animation" and will have no recourse but to wait things out. The past will no longer give pleasure and the future is yet to be. **TIME**

FRIENDS

You will know that a friend or loved one is making you unhappy yet will feel bound to that person and find it difficult to free yourself of his/her influence.

VISITORS/CALLERS

You will have a negative confrontation or phone call. This could be with someone you really dislike or who has "done you wrong."

MAIL

An unexpected expense or bill will arise, something you had not considered or budgeted for.

ANXIETY

You'll experience unexpected complications or devastating conditions concerning a project or endeavor, as well as an unexpected bill or expenditure that you weren't prepared for or really can't afford.

DISAPPOINTMENT

You're going to be disheartened by the never-ending battle to succeed and will feel blocked or stymied at every turn.

ENDINGS

A business merger or large-scale plan will fall through because circumstances will impede any further progress or development.

NEW BEGINNINGS

You will be fed up with the lack of results for your efforts and trying to keep your "chin up" through setbacks and reversals, and will decide to withdraw your energy or give up.

INHERITANCE

You will run into unexpected complications and have the sudden realization that what you have been pursuing cannot be continued.

REWARDS/GIFTS

Being released from bondage, burdens, and physical or mental oppression will come as a much deserved reward.

SUCCESS

It will be a battle to succeed, because your success or advancement is going to be blocked for the time being.

FORTUNE

Luck will be with you in attaining pertinent information concerning your situation.

BLESSINGS

In spite of everything, you will have learned something from the experience, and for that you will be grateful.

SPECIAL GUIDANCE

Mundane: This is not a propitious time for *any* venture, and a rash decision could result in loss. It will also be very hard for you to keep the faith and not get sucked into negative thinking or race-conscious beliefs.

Esoteric: When you seek the reason for a negative situation, it only serves to amplify the condition and heighten the frustration, because "where thoughts go, energy flows." When you are in tune with God, the right answers come . . . you need more perspective.

Don't forge ahead blindly. Slow down, plan carefully, and proceed with caution. Get a second opinion if necessary.

BEST COURSE OF ACTION

You won't be able to shake off adversity or conclude matters to your satisfaction, but will realize that "to everything there is a season, and a reason."

OUTCOME

◆ THE TOWER

A Major Arcana always indicates an important event, category, or month, and will overpower all other cards in both impact and effect.

IN A READING

Many 7s indicate a period of introspection or solitude. They can also indicate unlooked-for advantages or gains through things that come unexpectedly.

NUMBER 16 (1 + 6) = 7

The focus is on unexpected events or devastating conditions, financial problems, business problems, conflicts, separations or divorce, drastic measures, bizarre encounters, and loss of faith in one's self or one's world.

FOCUS

You are past hope, but pray that the worst is over and conditions will begin to improve.

DESIRE

An unexpected event, like a lie, infidelity, or abandonment, will destroy your trust in the one you love or your love for that person.

ROMANCE

You'll be unprepared for the emotional havoc that will be brought about by uncontrollable situations, upheavals, and communications or altercations with others.

THE UNEXPECTED

You will feel abandoned, betrayed, or deceived by others.

OTHERS

Household appliances will act up, break down, or give you problems and your energy level will be very low.	**THE HOME**
Watch for car problems or sudden accidents; slow down and use caution. Also, plans could change unexpectedly or have to be postponed.	**TRAVEL**
You will discuss finances or contracts with someone in an effort to collect money that is owed, readjust a contractual agreement, reinstate funding, or get paper articles back.	**PAPERS**
You'll be concerned about the lack of business or money and may begin to feel that you've made a mistake, but you will try to take a positive point of view and wait for the final verdict.	**WORK/CAREER**
You will feel betrayed or abandoned by your partner and a divorce or parting of the ways in your relationship is imminent.	**UNIONS**
You'll feel insecure, uncertain, and filled with doubt or fear.	**EMOTIONAL STATE**
You're going to experience a new beginning and improved conditions which will help you to regain a sense of peace, emotional balance, and/or power in your life or career.	**PLEASURE**
Some unexpected or surprising news is going to overthrow existing conditions and bring a new opportunity . . . go for it!	**NEWS**
Your relatives will be worried about an impending action (this could be a court action) and what the outcome will be.	**FAMILY**
You'll need to rest before commencing any new ventures. Money may soon be received for an accident or incident involving pain or suffering, and medical expenses may be more than expected.	**THE PHYSICAL BODY**
You'll be very upset or concerned about financial conditions, bills, or medical expenses. A sudden loss of income, a cancellation of funding, or a company going bankrupt or out of business could also be indicated.	**FINANCES**
You will find yourself fighting for "your rights." This could be an internal rather than an external battle.	**TIME**
You'll soon hear some very unexpected, disheartening, or disaster-	**FRIENDS**

ous news. This could also indicate a betrayal, abandonment, or parting of the ways in a relationship.

VISITORS/CALLERS   You will have to wait before you can reach someone you wish to contact, and/or you will make a call on someone who is upset or impossible to console (or he/she will call on you).

MAIL   Expect a delay or foul-up with money matters or contractual agreements, but the receipt of a certain letter will tilt the scales in your favor.

ANXIETY   You'll be confronted with an issue in your relationship with another that will cause you to wonder if you've been deluding yourself or operating under a false sense of assurance.

DISAPPOINTMENT   You will be disappointed in an unresolvable business or technical problem.

ENDINGS   Suffering, grief, or discord is going to come to an end.

NEW BEGINNINGS   You'll be working on new projects and something thought lost or impossible to recover will suddenly be found or reinstated. This could even be a love affair.

INHERITANCE   You will "inherit" a new business opportunity.

REWARDS/GIFTS   Someone is going to help you to correct or resolve a problem.

SUCCESS   Your financial position will improve considerably, and success will come through improved business, new opportunities, and recognition for your talents.

FORTUNE   You'll consider yourself fortunate because you've overcome the problems that were plaguing you and were given a fresh start, or because you've suddenly come into an abundance of money or love.

BLESSINGS   You're going to be grateful for a resurrection in your affairs, improved conditions, and unexpected luck or good fortune.

SPECIAL GUIDANCE   *Munacne:* More disruption, misfortune, and bitter experiences lie ahead and even your home life will be affected, but you must remember that you're not seeing the whole picture, and what looks absolute or hopeless is *not* final.

Esoteric: What is right, essential, or meaningful will be preserved. It's time to discern what *is* meaningful.

Remain calm in the face of unexpected changes or "assaults" and listen to the inner voice that assures you that everything *is* going to be all right.

BEST COURSE OF ACTION

In some way, something will be given or done that will make up for any loss or injury.

OUTCOME

◆ # THE STAR

A Major Arcana always indicates an important event, category, or month, and will overpower all other cards in both impact and effect.

IN A READING

Many 8's indicate a positive change of mind or status because the beneficial qualities of the number 8 are rarely diluted.

NUMBER 17
(1 + 7) = 8

The focus is on faith, the future, and what *could* be.

FOCUS

You want to find (or regain) a sense of meaning, inspiration, or purpose to your life and hope your future will be better than your past.

DESIRE

You will be feeling the lack of love or fulfillment in your life and will dream of, or hope to meet, someone special, and something will occur that will inspire you or encourage that wish.

ROMANCE

You will go on a spontaneous buying spree and will like what you purchase, or have unexpected financial breaks. Or, you will win money in a lottery, sweepstakes, or bingo game.

THE UNEXPECTED

People will like you very much, and will offer insights into the possibilities of expanding your business; or, they will advise you on what you need to know.

OTHERS

Someone or something will give you an insight into what your future might hold . . . a very positive and inspiring disclosure. And, if

THE HOME

in real estate or are concerned about a property, you will sell or lease-option it.

Someone will travel to see you or will call on you upon his/her return home.

TRAVEL

You will be involved in paperwork that connects the past with the present and fills in the gaps or elaborates on the original concept.

PAPERS

You will be unhappy with the status of your work and will want things to change or improve.

WORK/CAREER

You'll feel that you're bound to another through an emotional link or Karmic tie and that even if you wanted to let go, you couldn't.

UNIONS

Someone (or something) new is going to inspire you and give new hope or meaning to your life and affairs.

EMOTIONAL STATE

You will be pleased about a new and promising opportunity or the birth of a new talent or career potential.

PLEASURE

Expect news, calls, or letters related to financial gain or profit.

NEWS

A relative will have problems with reservations, confirmations, or legal documents.

FAMILY

You will gain insight into the root of a problem and take steps to correct it. This could also indicate medical tests or workups in the offing.

THE PHYSICAL BODY

Don't worry about your finances. You'll make money in the long run and your prospects for the future look even better.

FINANCES

In time, you will begin to feel that things are going to work out after all, and that your quest has *not* been in vain.

TIME

Someone close is going to provide a feeling of "safety" or substance, a respite from the cares of the world.

FRIENDS

You will reassess your options and possibilities for your future as a result of a call or caller.

VISITORS/CALLERS

You can expect money in the mail or news that someone has some money for you and wants you to pick it up.

MAIL

ANXIETY   You will be troubled by a yearning heart—can't have, and can't let go. A health flare-up or malady is also indicated.

DISAPPOINTMENT   You will be hurt or disappointed by harsh words, "enforced estrangement," and circumstances that impede further growth or development for the time being.

ENDINGS   Misdirected energies will be discontinued.

NEW BEGINNINGS   You will receive help or guidance from a teacher, friend, or other.

INHERITANCE   You are going to receive a gift of money, kindness or love . . . and also a sign from the Universe that your wish *is* possible.

REWARDS/GIFTS   You are going to receive a generous offer or charitable gift.

SUCCESS   You are going to discover a new method, talent, or ability that you can bring into your work or the work that you'll be doing in the future.

FORTUNE   You will make great strides in your long-term professional goals and be showered with gifts, assistance, and business calls; also, good news will arrive offering new hope and the promise of future success and fulfillment.

BLESSINGS   You will be grateful for spiritual assistance, inspiration or guidance, and/or money or means.

SPECIAL GUIDANCE *Mundane:* It's the call of destiny that motivates you or compels you to go on. Your desire is *not* in vain, and that which you are yearning for will ultimately find fulfillment.
Esoteric: In the *Autobiography of a Yogi*, Paramahansa Yogananda states: "The Karmic Law requires that every human wish finds ultimate fulfillment." Could it not follow, then, that your desire is the thing itself, knocking at your door?

BEST COURSE OF ACTION   Follow what you know to be true for yourself with deep sincerity and a firm resolve, and in due time your star shall shine.

OUTCOME   Things will work out better than expected, and your faith in the future will burn brightly once more.

◆ THE MOON

A Major Arcana always indicates an important event, category, or month, and will overpower all other cards in both impact and effect.

IN A READING

Many 9s in a reading mean that situations or events are nearing completion, or have just been completed, and another plateau awaits.

NUMBER 18
(1 + 8) = 9

The focus is on inner disturbances or disquiet, feelings of foreboding or dread, and a very perplexing, changeable, or deceptive course of affairs in whatever area is most important to you at the moment.

FOCUS

You want your dreams to come true or for things to go smoothly, but have a feeling they are not going to.

DESIRE

You are going to be disillusioned and disappointed in a relationship you thought would work but didn't.

ROMANCE

You will be unprepared for an altercation you'll run into at work.

THE UNEXPECTED

Your response to others will be inconsistent and changeable, but you will want to help them find their inner light.

OTHERS

If you are planning to entertain a friend or get together with someone on a project at home, it will prove to be a very disillusioning experience. This also indicates a period where you will tend to sleep or eat more than usual.

THE HOME

If you go on a trip or outing it will be very unpleasant due to many unforeseen problems or disturbing influences which will cause you to return sooner than expected, or make you wish you hadn't gone.

TRAVEL

If you're looking for answers, the information you receive will be perplexing, inconclusive, or difficult to follow up on; but don't give up, you're closer than you think.

PAPERS

You will run into conflicts which will require a great deal of emotional control, but you will master the situation internally rather than moving into an external fray.

WORK/CAREER

You will experience disunion, disillusionment, disappointment, and subterfuge.

UNIONS

You will be crushed by a huge disappointment. Someone or something you counted on will let you down and you will be completely devastated.

EMOTIONAL STATE

What once looked promising or entertaining will prove to be its opposite, and what you hoped would bring pleasure will turn into a test of endurance.

PLEASURE

Expect an upsetting or disappointing message concerning someone you care for or love.

NEWS

Upsetting conditions will arise making you feel confused, uncertain, or threatened. Too many emotional elements will be imposed upon you.

FAMILY

You could have physical premonitions of that which is to come, or be subject to strange sensations, sleeping disorders, or lumps, bumps, or cysts.

THE PHYSICAL BODY

You will be paid that which is owed or due you, but will feel short-changed or cheated.

FINANCES

After a major crisis, you will break into the light of a new day.

TIME

You will be disillusioned, confused, and uncertain about a friend or lover, and won't be able to sort out your feelings.

FRIENDS

An unexpected caller will arrive or call but you won't be too pleased about it because it will upset or bother you.

VISITORS/CALLERS

You'll be concerned about your mail, or the arrival of something through the mail, or something you're doing that involves mail.

MAIL

Your thinking will be muddled and you will be troubled by feelings of dread, deception, or foreboding, because you can't see your way clear on any level and have a terrible feeling that you will lose out or be disappointed.

ANXIETY

You are going to be very disillusioned by other people's actions, words, or deeds, and you may also be chastised unfairly.

DISAPPOINTMENT

ENDINGS

Strife, conflict, confusion, and despair over old wounds or grudges will cease to exist.

NEW BEGINNINGS

A new trend or group effort will begin and things will work out after all. A new friend may also be found.

INHERITANCE

A challenge will have to be confronted that will take a strong will and strength of character.

REWARDS/GIFTS

You will find that something thought lost, hopeless, or impossible to acquire will be retrieved, revived, replaced, or purchased.

SUCCESS

After a period of devastation and despair, you will achieve success and things will end on a happy note.

FORTUNE

Expect some very fortunate adjustments in your dealings with others, group efforts, and camaraderie.

BLESSINGS

You will have the presence of mind to take the middle road, which will free you from the pendulum of win/fail, have/want, or pleasure/pain.

SPECIAL GUIDANCE

Mundane: There will be many unforeseen changes and unexpected occurrences, and only when you're willing for things to be the way they are, and accept them *as* they are, will they change. You can't run from the problem . . . the only way out is through.

Esoteric: There is a law of balance operating in the universe which demands equality. For every win there must be a loss, for every happiness, a sadness, and for every positive move, a negative challenge. You cannot have one without the other; it would be like trying to separate day from night.

BEST COURSE OF ACTION

Be neutral and follow your inner light.

OUTCOME

Change will bring a new perspective and a new you, and by putting your pessimism or insecurities behind you, you'll become a much stronger and happier person.

◆   # THE SUN

A Major Arcana always indicates an important event, category, or month, and will overpower all other cards in both impact and effect.

IN A READING

Many 1s would indicate that a situation is about to begin, or is in the beginning stages.

NUMBER 19
(1 + 9) = 1

The focus is on people, society and the public, glamour, self-image or keeping up appearances, benefits, charity or spiritual quests, achievement, accomplishment or vindication, marriage, unions or mergers.

FOCUS

You want a union or marriage, or recognition in your field of endeavor; or, you are seeking God or Cosmic Consciousness.

DESIRE

You will not see the one your heart yearns for, but others will vie to take his or her place.

ROMANCE

Someone you were thinking about is going to call (could be a lover or two), and you will be surprised by the high cost of living or an unreasonable bill.

THE UNEXPECTED

You will be putting on a facade, keeping up the illusion of gaiety or well-being when there really is none, because the thing you really want, the essential ingredient or heart's desire, is missing.

OTHERS

You'll be improving your surroundings or appearance, your work or health will take you away from home, and/or, someone will call regarding a new home.

THE HOME

If you go on a trip, it will be disappointing or fruitless and what you hoped to accomplish or attain will not come to pass. If you look back in retrospect, you will wish you hadn't gone.

TRAVEL

You're going to experience problems with legal forms, documents, or contracts and will be confused and uncertain about how to proceed or what you should do.

PAPERS

Things will be very slow, but you won't want to work anyway. You need a new element to boost your inspiration or enthusiasm and one will come.

WORK/CAREER

Partnerships will have to be put on ice, and the future will look very uncertain. **UNIONS**

You'll be drained emotionally or spiritually, and because of this will feel very tired, lackluster, or blah. **EMOTIONAL STATE**

Good friends and social activities will offer simple pleasures. **PLEASURE**

You'll have discussions about upcoming mergers and business projects. A public-speaking job may also be offered. **NEWS**

You will talk with a relative but will feel that they aren't really with you. **FAMILY**

You're going to be feeling tired, run down, or uninspired, and your psychic ability will be impeded. You will also think you don't look very good and may do something to change your appearance, like cut your hair or buy new clothes. **THE PHYSICAL BODY**

New money is going to come in, funding will be reinstated, or you will successfully settle a financial or contractual issue that's been a constant source of aggravation to you. **FINANCES**

You're going to be exhausted in your working environment and in dire need of a respite or healing of the heart or spirit. **TIME**

Mixing business with friendship could prove to be a bad idea now. **FRIENDS**

Existing plans will change due to a call or caller, and/or you'll make a call on someone with "bag in hand." **VISITORS/CALLERS**

Expect good news concerning your finances. **MAIL**

You will be troubled because things for all intents and purposes should be good, but they are not because your heart is so unfulfilled. **ANXIETY**

You will not be able to get together with the one you love or want to be with. This could also indicate a broken engagement. **DISAPPOINTMENT**

The possibility of starting something new or merging with another in an enduring relationship will not be realized at this time. **ENDINGS**

Ideas for a new line of work will begin to formulate, a tempting **NEW BEGINNINGS** business offer or partnership will be proposed, and/or a possible court action could be discussed.

INHERITANCE

You're going to have to put a business project on ice for now, but money will come in through an appeal that was won.

REWARDS/GIFTS

A huge favor will be given that will save you a lot of money, and/or a promotional opportunity will come your way that will put you or your work more in the public eye (this could come through a celebrated or media event).

SUCCESS

A man is going to propose a new direction, project, or enterprise for the future that concerns a possible union or partnership.

FORTUNE

You'll be lucky in overcoming financial difficulties or adversities, and/or getting out of a sticky situation or "wrong move" in a legal matter.

BLESSINGS

You will be grateful for a "second chance" or reprieve, and for the things of true value in life that you do have.

SPECIAL GUIDANCE

Mundane: Don't judge conditions by "appearances". . . remember that Shamballa lies in the Gobi desert.
Esoteric: You've triumphed over the events and lessons of the past and are molding a new persona which is not yet strong enough to hold its own. The space you're in now can be likened to a womb which is protective and nurturing, and when this embryonic stage or metamorphosis is complete you will be strong enough to face the world, and/or spiritual integration will be attained.

BEST COURSE OF ACTION

Keep an open mind and you will be able to see or hear the truth that will lead you out of the desert and set you free.

OUTCOME

At this point, nothing is going to be clear or resolved and business mergers or personal unions will not come to pass or work out as you had envisioned. But the right actions were taken so the sun will shine tomorrow.

◆ JUDGEMENT

A Major Arcana always indicates an important event, category, or month, and will overpower all other cards in both impact and effect.

IN A READING

Many 2s indicate a waiting period where there will be partial success but more to be revealed later. They can also indicate a reconciliation, a reunion, and/or an element of surprise.

NUMBER 20 = 2

The focus is on new personal relationships, new business ventures or partnerships, beneficial help, improved conditions, and a complete change in habit, consciousness, or purpose.

FOCUS

You want to bury the past and start fresh, and/or to know whether or not to invest time or money in a new relationship or enterprise.

DESIRE

Someone's actions or attitude will make you think twice about seeing him or her again, starting up again, or continuing the relationship.

ROMANCE

A situation will present itself that will suddenly change your thoughts, feelings, or plans. This could be concerning a romantic matter.

THE UNEXPECTED

Personal endeavors like love or romance seem to be impeded, but business affairs or spiritual matters will be rewarding.

OTHERS

New action and decisions will be required of you, and an unexpected caller will arrive.

THE HOME

A short trip or jaunt will prove to be very beneficial because you will inadvertently meet a new admirer, or one who will help you in your work. Whatever the case may be, it will be a significant encounter.

TRAVEL

You will come up with new methods or innovative ideas in your paperwork, or someone you've worked with will direct more business your way.

PAPERS

The resolving of inner or outer conflicts will mark the end of suffering and bring improved conditions, or a change in consciousness

WORK/CAREER

through spiritual evolvement or self-development will bring new purpose, meaning, or motivation to your work.

UNIONS You will be in the process of breaking away from the past. In business-related affairs, you'll be very glad, but in matters of the heart, very sad, because you'll feel that you will never forget or stop loving that person.

EMOTIONAL STATE You will be remembering an old love and feeling very nostalgic for the way things were or how you used to feel when you were in love, and will wish with all your heart that you could feel that way again.

PLEASURE Some very uplifting news and a positive turn of events will be a turning point for you.

NEWS You are going to hear a voice from out of the past.

FAMILY You are going to get some good news from or concerning a relative.

THE PHYSICAL BODY You will hear that someone you care very deeply for has become very ill (could be a heart attack), and/or you will have dizzy spells or health problems caused by stress or your diet.

FINANCES You will experience improved conditions in the form of a money judgment, payment on an investment, or profit sharing.

TIME In time, things are going to turn out much better than you thought or hoped for, and you are going to experience a feeling of improvement, upliftment, and a new beginning on a much higher and happier turn of the spiral.

FRIENDS Your friends and loved ones will be supportive and nurturing, but your relationship with one in particular must improve or end.

VISITORS/CALLERS A lover will call, and an important decision will be made as a result of that call.

MAIL Projects will be a "go." Expect a positive response or "yes" answer. A letter containing money from the past could also be indicated.

ANXIETY You will be troubled by an unexpected confrontation or argument over money or legal rights.

DISAPPOINTMENT — You'll be disappointed in something that did not, or is not, working out as anticipated . . . but it's only temporary.

ENDINGS — Suffering, regret, or pain are going to end, followed by a complete and total change of consciousness.

NEW BEGINNINGS — A new partnership or personal relationship is about to be established.

INHERITANCE — You will "inherit" upliftment and inspiration, which will bring about new purposes or ambitions.

REWARDS/GIFTS — There will be a new avenue or "escape" brought about by another, or you will receive a gift of roses.

SUCCESS — You are going to get paid for long-standing debts, find out something you need or want to know, and receive new inspiration in a stalemated, dead-end, or abandoned endeavor.

FORTUNE — You will receive beneficial help and luck will be with you in resolving arguments or dilemmas.

BLESSINGS — You will be grateful for a new lease on life and the receipt of money.

SPECIAL GUIDANCE — *Mundane:* Things are going to be different and you'll have a change of consciousness for the better.
Esoteric: Cosmic forces are going to correct the situation, but this is only the first step. There is still the possibility of defeat unless your cooperation is continued. What's meant by cooperation is your determination to persevere without immediate results, and to allow the power of the Infinite to penetrate your consciousness and steer you into that which you desire or to change your Karma for you.

BEST COURSE OF ACTION — Accept what is going to be offered . . . it could change your life.

OUTCOME — After a period of suffering or failure to find happiness, the past will begin to fade, and you will experience a regeneration of mind or spirit which will be directed toward new ideas, new areas, and new beginnings.

◆ THE WORLD

A Major Arcana always indicates an important event, category, or month, and will overpower all other cards in both impact and effect.

IN A READING

Many 3s indicate group activities or situations involving more than one person. They can also indicate delay, but with the promise of future success.

NUMBER 21 = 3

The focus is on world issues or world-shaking events, encounters, and gatherings; travel, change, sports or physical concerns, organizations, risks, and new opportunities; but also restrictions, walls, or blocks.

FOCUS

You want to succeed in all areas of your life—your work, your dreams, everything—and you'll have an obsessive desire to liberate yourself from restraint.

DESIRE

What has been must be let go of for the time being, because the world must take a turn before a new day can emerge, bringing with it the possibility of beginning again on a new foundation.

ROMANCE

Someone's irrational behavior will hurt or upset you very much, and you won't know how to contend with it. This will be someone close like a friend, lover, or relative . . . it could even be a pet.

THE UNEXPECTED

You will feel like everyone in the world has what they want but you, and you will want to go away, leave everything behind, and begin a new life or start all over somewhere else.

OTHERS

You are going to be feeling pressured and troubled due to insurmountable problems and will be about ready to explode, leave the country, or move to some remote beach so that you can be left alone.

THE HOME

An unscheduled, unplanned, or "must-go" trip is in the offing. Go . . . it could change your luck.

TRAVEL

New information or helpful hints will be applied to your paperwork, and you will be happy with the finished product.

PAPERS

You will experience temporary blocks to your progress with nothing

WORK/CAREER

THE WORLD.

really going on, or you may be unemployed at the present time, but things will improve considerably and you'll have more work than you can handle (or want).

You'll wonder if you'll ever have the relationship you want because in your mind, it seems that no matter what you try to do, you never manage to achieve results.

UNIONS

You are going to run the gamut of your emotions with heights of bliss and depths of despair, but in the final analysis, you will come out on top.

EMOTIONAL STATE

You will be happy about the sudden acquisition of money and the opportunity to advance in your profession.

PLEASURE

You are going to have some unpleasant communications regarding your finances, family, or health and could also talk about the loss of a loved one or a separation or divorce.

NEWS

Your inlaws will be a burden you won't want to deal with, or a separation in the family will cause unhappiness.

FAMILY

You will be recuperating from an illness, injury, or infection and should slow down and take it easy. Also, if you're seeing a doctor, you may have to switch to another.

THE PHYSICAL BODY

You are going to acquire money from more than one source. This could also indicate a tax refund or interest gained on an account.

FINANCES

As time goes on, you'll think that your situation is hopeless.

TIME

You and a lover will not unite due to obstacles or adverse conditions, and if you give a friend an inch, he/she will take a mile; and/or, you will make a call on a sick or needy friend or one will call on you.

FRIENDS

You will be upset with another who will call and break an appointment, or you won't want to deal with the people who call you on the phone.

VISITORS/CALLERS

You will think about mailing a letter to a company but will put it off, and/or a letter will arrive that will make you angry.

MAIL

ANXIETY

You will want to liberate yourself from limitation and lack, other people's problems, negative attitudes, and forced confrontations.

DISAPPOINTMENT

You will be disappointed in your inability to break free of the restrictive influences that are blocking you from manifesting any of your goals.

ENDINGS

You will no longer be content to go along with the status quo, or accept a subservient or compliant fate, and will be "mad as hell and not going to take it anymore."

NEW BEGINNINGS

You'll feel that you've transcended the obstacles, difficulties, or disappointments you had to face, and it will be a very good feeling.

INHERITANCE

You will "inherit" praise for your work or more work and money.

REWARDS/GIFTS

A box or package will arrive.

SUCCESS

You will be successful in your dealings with others (be it in social situations or large groups), and you will realize a new method of operation that could make your work a lot easier.

FORTUNE

You can expect fortunate changes in business and finance—new opportunities, expansion, and increase.

BLESSINGS

You will be glad that you have the ability to utilize special skills and to "brave the storm."

SPECIAL GUIDANCE

Mundane: Your obsession (or preoccupation) with the past is hindering your ability to see what is really going on, but no matter how bound you're feeling now, you can still break free. Facts can change. *Esoteric:* The key to liberation is to find the path to inner peace and thereby transcend choice or result.

BEST COURSE OF ACTION

It's going to take genuine "wrath" to rent the fabric or free yourself from the oppression you're feeling, yet this must be done if transformation is to occur or a lost opportunity be regained.

OUTCOME

Eventually you'll surmount limitations or obstacles and come out on top.

◆ THE FOOL

A Major Arcana always indicates an important event, category, or month, and will overpower all other cards in both impact and effect.

IN A READING

The "0" represents the God force and is an ancient symbol for the number 22. Since the number 4 (2 + 2 = 4) represents manifestation on the earth plane, I see the fool as the spirit of God ("0") linking with man (4).

NUMBER   0 or 22

Many 4s indicate fruition or the manifestation of an idea, along with the foundation or "space" where things can grow.

The focus is on faith, hope, trust, and contentment; high ideals and the possibility of a brighter tomorrow; choice, personal effort, and the Cosmic play of the Universe in your life and affairs.

FOCUS

You want to be happy and are searching for the thing that will bring happiness; or, you want to better understand the workings of God or the way in which He answers.

DESIRE

You will have mixed emotions regarding another, who will want more than you're ready to give or commit to. Part of you will want to enter the relationship with complete abandon, while another part will hold it at bay.

ROMANCE

You'll be surprised by the unexpected arrival of something you wanted *before* the desire was expressed. This could be anything from a call from one you wanted to see to money you hoped to receive.

THE UNEXPECTED

You will live life as you see fit without the need for "votes," and your friends and business associates will be friendly, loving, and supportive . . . old wounds will begin to heal.

OTHERS

An unexpected guest or caller will arrive.

THE HOME

If planning to meet with someone on a business matter, you will probably conduct it over the phone instead, and/or you will be considering a major move or "disappearing act."

TRAVEL

There will be a considerable amount of paperwork to be processed

PAPERS

or handled which will require a great deal of concentrated effort and application, but you will see it through to completion, and after a brief respite, will take on more.

WORK/CAREER

You'll begin a new enterprise which will afford you the opportunity to work with or teach the public on a grander scale, and if you've been thinking about leaving your current job or taking a leave of absence, in time you will.

UNIONS

If your relationship serves you or your growth, you will stay together. If it does not, you'll let it go and move on.

EMOTIONAL STATE

You will begin to feel discontent or uneasy because of a subtle intuition or inner dedication to a better way of life that will be propelling you forward . . . kind of a "divine discontent."

PLEASURE

The unexpected arrival of a desired situation *before* the desire was expressed is going to make you very happy. This could be in connection with your work, finances, or love life.

NEWS

A question will be posed that will need exploration (could be concerning travel plans) and you won't know what to do.

FAMILY

A relative will be job hunting, or a major decision will be required from you that can be put off no longer. If it concerns a change of residence or extended trip, you'll decide against it.

THE PHYSICAL BODY

You'll feel as though you are not running at your peak ability. You may also speak with someone in the healing arts or visit a friend in the hospital. Also, if a health decision concerns you, you'll probably wait it out rather than go through something that may be unnecessary.

FINANCES

A decision concerning your career and finances will be made soon, and if you have been expecting some money, it will arrive.

TIME

As time goes by, you'll be waiting for all the pieces to fall into place.

FRIENDS

Someone is going to make you feel like a fool for allowing yourself to be cheated, deceived, or abused.

VISITORS/CALLERS   You're going to profit through a caller (or callers), and a business plan or new proposal will be enacted or confirmed.

MAIL   You will get into a scuffle concerning letters or papers with someone who won't be willing to extend himself/herself.

ANXIETY   You're going to feel that you won't be able to complete a project now that it's begun, or that it will take far more work than you're equipped to handle, or that you've gotten in way over your head.

DISAPPOINTMENT   You will be disappointed in your inability to maintain control over uncontrollable situations, in having to be the harbinger of bad tidings, or that you made a mistake because you didn't follow your own counsel.

ENDINGS   You will no longer be attached to the way you think something should go or wish it would have gone, and you will drop it, quit, or put it behind you.

NEW BEGINNINGS   You'll have the conviction that no matter what life hands you, it's going to be all right. You will also embark on a new program or creative endeavor involving papers, methods, or studies that will be very rewarding or gratifying.

INHERITANCE   You will "inherit" the sustaining power of *grace* in your life or affairs.

REWARDS/GIFTS   You will give your services to another free of charge, or vice versa.

SUCCESS   Your success will come through terminating the areas in your life that no longer serve you or your growth.

FORTUNE   Luck will be with you in correcting a mistake.

BLESSINGS   You'll be acutely aware of the presence of God in your life, and thank Him for giving you the kind of spiritual understanding it takes to let Him decide your course.

SPECIAL GUIDANCE   *Mundane:* Of yourself, you don't know what you need, or what will bring happiness in the long run. If you let go of all you *think* you want or need, "want" will also go, and in its place you'll find its objective . . . happiness.

Esoteric: "The kingdom of heaven is within you." Talk things over with God. The more you do, the more clearly you'll understand His guidance (as a natural inner urging) and the way in which He responds.

Release wants, cares, or worries and "let go, let God." Don't hang on to an idea or support system out of fear of failure or loss.

BEST COURSE OF ACTION

That which you are in need of will be given or come to pass, although it may not come in the form you think you want or need.

OUTCOME

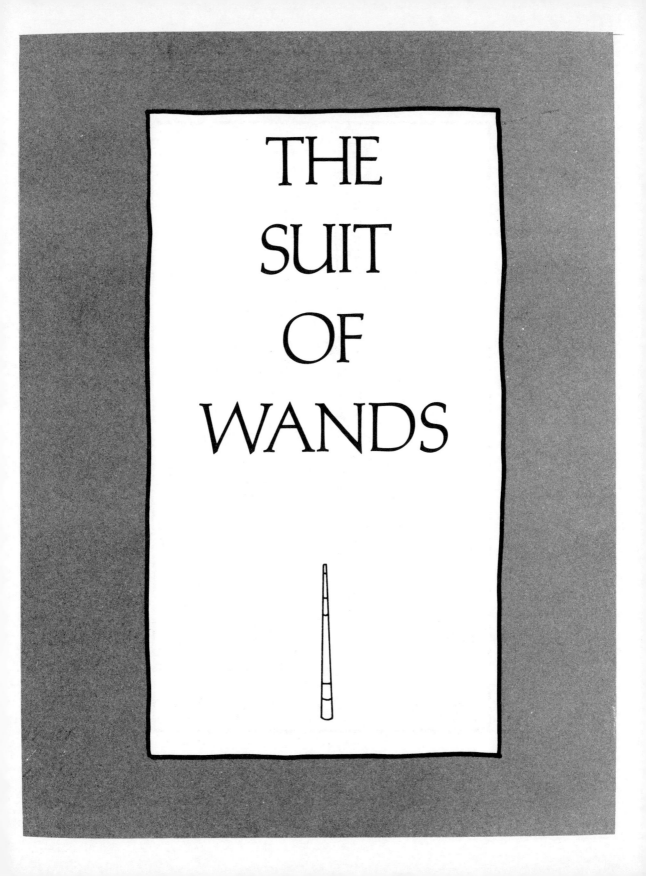

THE
SUIT
OF
WANDS

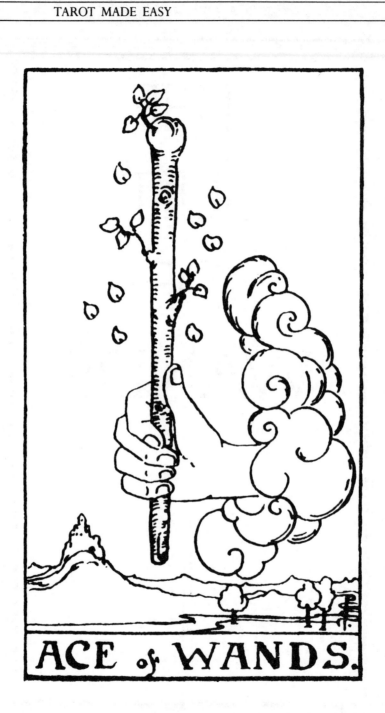

◆ THE ACE OF WANDS

An Ace marks a fresh start. The Ace of Wands foretells the dawning of a new beginning in the area of ideas, growth, ambition, and expansion.

IN A READING

AUTUMN (September—October—November)

SEASON

Many 1s indicate that a situation is about to begin or is in the beginning stages.

NUMBER 1

The focus is on potential, that which could be or is about to be, increased business and social activities, and new avenues of fulfillment or promise that come in from out of the blue.

FOCUS

You want a new beginning or fresh start in business or love.

DESIRE

You won't want to experience life alone or have a "part-time" relationship; you will want a full-time partner and though you will be receptive to those who advance, the time won't be ripe to reap the full harvest.

ROMANCE

You will be surprised by a "must go" trip, good news in a card or letter, and a sudden flirtation or romantic invitation.

THE UNEXPECTED

You will be considering a new partner for future ventures rather than sticking with your current one.

OTHERS

You will start a new project or venture, something that you can do out of your home, and you will have discussions about moving into a new home.

THE HOME

A financially rewarding excursion or business trip is in the offing.

TRAVEL

You will be writing a book or working on a new concept or project.

PAPERS

Ideas concerning a new business or enterprise will begin to formulate and you will have several options to consider, all of which look promising.

WORK/CAREER

You can expect a happy union, and if you've had problems in the

UNIONS

past, tensions or misunderstandings will be resolved. This could also indicate a marriage or live-in arrangement.

EMOTIONAL STATE   You will be analyzing your relationships, taking another look at your possibilities, and your outlook will be good.

PLEASURE   You will derive a lot of satisfaction through being productive and in writing, creating, or innovating new projects.

NEWS   You will hear good news about your work or a new business concept that will mean more money or publicity for you. This could also indicate news from a romantic interest.

FAMILY   You are going to have a phone call from a relative or will be discussing relationship problems.

THE PHYSICAL BODY   You will begin a new treatment, purification, or cleansing program. You could also see a new doctor.

FINANCES   Money will soon be received for artistic, creative, or inspired ventures.

TIME   You are going to experience a new beginning. An innovation in ideas and activities will be the start of a brand-new direction and way of thinking for you.

FRIENDS   Things are not going to go as anticipated, and if you had planned a trip or outing with a friend, you may have to go alone, meet later, cancel the trip, or cut it short.

VISITORS/CALLERS   You will have discussions about new ventures, business projects, artistic ideas, manuscript sales, teaching, or lecturing.

MAIL   A package will arrive or be delivered.

ANXIETY   You will be worried that your product (or project) is not in demand or that no one wants it, and so you will lack the determination to carry on or see it through to its completion.

DISAPPOINTMENT   You will be disheartened about good work that's gone unnoticed, or the lack of business or clientele.

Dwelling on the past when it doesn't serve you and blocks to productivity or romantic endeavors are going to end. **ENDINGS**

Productivity in the area of innovative ideas or a business of your own will increase, and a new and useful product will be realized or in demand. **NEW BEGINNINGS**

You are going to be inspired by a new idea, direction, or clear-cut way to proceed. **INHERITANCE**

You will discuss a gift, or someone will ask you what you would like in the way of a gift, or your previous business efforts will be rewarded by cash and sales. **REWARDS/GIFTS**

Your success will come through new concepts, innovative ideas, and the rejuvenation of a declining business or decadent property investment. **SUCCESS**

You will have luck in new beginnings or fresh starts. This could also indicate a breakthrough of some kind. **FORTUNE**

You will be glad that you are busy or able to proceed with your work or creative ideas with renewed energy. **BLESSINGS**

Mundane: You've got to make a move or take the first step. *Esoteric:* What is unconscious or unmanifested will soon take form. New elements are being conceived, whether they're perceived at this time or not. **SPECIAL GUIDANCE**

Do something different, and be alert or receptive to new ideas. Act on the *alternatives* that will be presented. **BEST COURSE OF ACTION**

A new start or way of life will be realized and you will be hoping that things will continue to pan out in the future. **OUTCOME**

◆ THE TWO OF WANDS

Many 2s indicate a waiting period where there will be partial success but more to be revealed later. They can also indicate a reconciliation, a reunion, and/or an element of surprise.

IN A READING

Many Wands (three or more) indicate that conditions are primarily in the realm of thought, or in the very first stages of development.

The focus is on your career or working environment; directing your energy toward changing or improving yourself or your image or status. That will be most important and everything else will come second.

FOCUS

You are hoping that something good is about to happen and want to see it materialize.

DESIRE

A lonely or unhappy soul is going to enter your life who will offer to take care of you, or propose some type of living arrangement. This *could* be someone who is already married.

ROMANCE

Good fortune or tidings will come through the entry of an admirer or benefactor.

THE UNEXPECTED

You will be well liked and appreciated, and a chance encounter is going to bring an unexpected blessing or profitable gain.

OTHERS

You will buy or get something for the home or for use within the home, something you've been waiting for or wanting.

THE HOME

You will take an unexpected trip, or your transportation will be out of the ordinary (or in a different car than yours), and there will be a few stops and starts along the way. This could also indicate a boat trip.

TRAVEL

You will examine papers for accuracy (remember, quality takes time), or you will transfer information or accounts. If considering or preparing a business proposal, check the small print.

PAPERS

You will be in a position of power, expansion, and surprising success, and because of this, your attitude will be improved and your determination renewed.

WORK/CAREER

UNIONS

Good news will brighten your spirits . . . someone you've been estranged from or who closed you out or cast you aside is going to try to win you back.

EMOTIONAL STATE

No matter what ensues, you will not let yourself be overcome or dragged under because everything will be back in perspective, and whatever fears or dread you've had in the past will be assuaged.

PLEASURE

You will enjoy the validation you receive for your skills and applying yourself to your work or career goals, but love and friendship will be the heart's reward.

NEWS

An idea for a new project or business venture will arrive but it will be a questionable endeavor.

FAMILY

If you are at odds with someone in your family, you will soon reconcile your differences. You will also hear some surprising news.

THE PHYSICAL BODY

You should increase your vitamins, or eat more fish, fruit, or nuts, because doing so will give you more energy.

FINANCES

Finances or financial arrangements will be discussed and mutually agreed upon and business profits will begin to increase.

TIME

Your routine will undergo a change from business to romance through the entry of a good-humored and easygoing person.

FRIENDS

Someone will call on the pretext of business when, in fact, it's a personal interest.

VISITORS/CALLERS

You are going to get a call and/or visit from a very ardent lover or admirer.

MAIL

Expect good news concerning your business or finances and/or the arrival of an important business letter or package.

ANXIETY

You'll be worried about a course of action you took or a major purchase that was made.

DISAPPOINTMENT

You will be disappointed in a delayed payment, loss of income, or cancellation of funding.

ENDINGS

Your plans for a busines merger or get-together are not going to go through because the timing will be off.

An ardent admirer, business referral, or benefactor will come into view and initiate a much-needed change or overdue promotion. **NEW BEGINNINGS**

A well-thought-out plan of action will come to you, and a new business idea and potential partnership will be in the making. **INHERITANCE**

You are going to receive a gift (could be money or clothes), and a get-together or party will create a quandary over a gift . . . what to do? **REWARDS/GIFTS**

Your work will be well received, and you will be praised for its quality and thoroughness. You will also be afforded the opportunity to advance your position or make more money, and your romantic life will take a surprising turn. **SUCCESS**

You will have luck in obtaining facts which were hidden, making new business connections, and hearing from the one you hoped would call. **FORTUNE**

You will thank God that everything is back in order, set straight, or righted, and for like-minded friends and professional camaraderie. **BLESSINGS**

Mundane: An offer is about to be presented. If you don't feel right about it or it isn't enough, don't sell yourself short or settle for less. There *is* something better on the horizon.
Esoteric: What you need to know will be intuitively given and later confirmed. **SPECIAL GUIDANCE**

Proceed in a step-by-step manner, doing only that which is required, and don't do anything you're not completely sure of or that you don't want to do, or you will end up regretting it. **BEST COURSE OF ACTION**

You will find a way through, but not yet be completely established. **OUTCOME**

◆ THE THREE OF WANDS

Many 3s indicate group activities or situations involving more than one person. They can also indicate delay, but with the promise of future success.

IN A READING

Many Wands (three or more) indicate that conditions are primarily in the realm of thought, or in the very first stages of development.

The focus is on faith-testing or evoking situations, checking theories or beliefs, promising unions, business ventures, or partnerships, large or small companies, contracts or documents, and unexpected "wins."

FOCUS

You want a successful partnership or union and to overcome the nagging feeling of fear or apprehension concerning it.

DESIRE

A difficult decision (like "Should I or shouldn't I?") will soon be made regarding a new relationship.

ROMANCE

You will be surprised by a very successful business or financial transaction and/or start of a new enterprise, and a flattering remark or proposition from an admirer or potential suitor.

THE UNEXPECTED

You will have mixed emotions regarding some, and be complimented, well liked, and enriched by others.

OTHERS

You will leave your home in the hope of manifesting your desires, or to meet someone that can help you attain them.

THE HOME

You will be talking to a loved one who's been away or lives in a different city or state, and if traveling for work, you'll do very well, both personally and professionally.

TRAVEL

Some of your paperwork will be put off or left unfinished for the time being, because you'll need a break from mental activity or because your mental resources have been exhausted.

PAPERS

Your business will begin to flourish and practical help will be offered in whatever area concerns you.

WORK/CAREER

UNIONS — This is an excellent time for unions, and in spite of your fears, you will unite, form a new partnership, or marry.

EMOTIONAL STATE — You will feel apprehensive or distrustful, but this feeling will soon pass.

PLEASURE — You will overcome a "testy" situation, and will get a great deal of satisfaction through your talents, skills, or natural abilities.

NEWS — You are going to get a call from a loved one and a lover.

FAMILY — A relative or close friend will be expressing his/her concern over the signing of a contract or settlement of a business deal.

THE PHYSICAL BODY — You will be concerned about the health of another, but you yourself are in need of a rest . . . you're the one who's working too hard.

FINANCES — Business and finance will begin to improve through increased trade or commerce, and friends will prove to be a great help or asset. Also, the conclusion of a business deal will bring an unexpected bonus.

TIME — You will be indecisive or afraid to move ahead for fear that if you do, you'll be hurt or suffer the consequences.

FRIENDS — You will be considering a new venture with someone and making accurate predictions for others.

VISITORS/CALLERS — Someone coming to visit will necessitate a change of plans or create more work for you to do; or, you will put off an appointment so you can spend more time together.

MAIL — Money will come through the closing of a business deal and/or a previous agreement.

ANXIETY — You won't know whether to "go with the flow" of what's being offered or not.

DISAPPOINTMENT — You will be discouraged about a trip or venture that is not panning out as anticipated or going according to plan.

ENDINGS — Having to "go it alone" will end. Someone will arrive who will help eliminate your apprehension or give you something that could turn an idea into a reality.

Your love life will improve greatly, new partnerships will be established, and/or an existing relationship will be strengthened. **NEW BEGINNINGS**

You will "inherit" a situation wherein your faith will be tested or evoked. **INHERITANCE**

You will be happy with something you recently purchased, or someone will help you get something you want. **REWARDS/GIFTS**

You will gain the respect, cooperation, or admiration of others, take the right action, or make the right decisions. **SUCCESS**

Luck will be with you in turning a thought, idea, or dream into a reality. **FORTUNE**

You will be very grateful for the manifestation of an idea, profitable returns from a new enterprise, or the successful completion of a goal. **BLESSINGS**

Mundane: Put your energies into constructive ideas or cooperative partnerships that are aligned with you or what you want, and have more faith.
Esoteric: When your heart speaks, listen. If something doesn't serve you, drop it. If there's something you *can* do, do it; if you can't, drop it. **SPECIAL GUIDANCE**

Trust that your ideas *can* be realized, and expect the best. **BEST COURSE OF ACTION**

New partnerships will be established, successful conclusions will be reached, and your apprehension will dissolve. **OUTCOME**

◆ THE FOUR OF WANDS

Many 4s indicate fruition or the manifestation of an idea, along with the foundation or "space" where things can grow. **IN A READING**

Many Wands (three or more) indicate that conditions are primarily in the realm of thought, or in the very first stages of development.

The focus is on a "mulligan stew" of experiences, with special energy directed toward interpersonal relationships, communications, participation, short or long distance trips, and/or the quest for enlightenment. **FOCUS**

You want to quit or give up. **DESIRE**

You are going to be disappointed, as plans to unite with the one you want to see or be with will fail or be canceled, at least for now. **ROMANCE**

An old friend or lover is going to return or call when you least expect it. **THE UNEXPECTED**

You will let no one get the upper hand or put you in a vulnerable position. **OTHERS**

You will be feeling irritated, coerced, or victimized by harassing conditions, relationship problems, and being everyone's garbage dump, or you and another will have an unpleasant tête-à-tête or confrontation. **THE HOME**

A profitable or beneficial trip is upcoming. **TRAVEL**

You will have a tremendous amount of paperwork to process but it will flow easily (you'll meet your deadline) and you'll be very pleased with the results. You may redefine or revise some of it, however. **PAPERS**

A business partner or associate will upset or irritate you. Steer clear . . . you can't win anyway. **WORK/CAREER**

You will be confronted with unexpected problems and will wonder if you or your partner is being totally honest or portraying a situation to be other than the way it is. **UNIONS**

EMOTIONAL STATE   At times you will feel very self-conscious and want to run and hide, but at other times you will meet issues head on. You will also be quick to anger and fly off the handle easily.

PLEASURE   You will enjoy a social outing or reunion with a friend or loved one and/or going on a buying spree.

NEWS   You will be upset by a conversation with a relative and/or will be hurt that you haven't heard any news from a friend or loved one.

FAMILY   There will be family problems, fights, or upheavals, but blood is thicker than water and peace will prevail.

THE PHYSICAL BODY   You will feel tense, anxious, or easily irritated and subject to muscle aches, neck or backaches, and general physical discomfort, and/or sex with your partner will be unrewarding.

FINANCES   Your income will come in chunks rather than in small, stretched-out amounts, and you will do much better than you thought.

TIME   You are going to practice a philosophical or metaphysical approach. Be more open or involved with others, and as a result, you'll find the way a lot easier.

FRIENDS   You will feel obligated to make a commitment you're not ready for, or someone will try to coerce you into doing something you don't want to do, but you will not be swayed or intimidated. You will put them in their place or say *"no!"*

VISITORS/CALLERS   You will unexpectedly see or hear from a friend or loved one and you will make tentative plans to get together.

MAIL   A letter will arrive concerning travel, transportation, or your car, or you will write a presentation in order to sell or introduce a new idea, project, or product.

ANXIETY   You will be troubled by too many things to do, unavoidable commitments, or a friend, lover, or family crisis.

DISAPPOINTMENT   You will be disappointed in a reunion or get together with another because you won't connect on any real or satisfactory level.

You may have thought you were going to get out of an engagement or end a situation, but you are going to continue on. Your plans to quit will not come to pass.   **ENDINGS**

You will feel disorganized or upset, but you will implement a new action that will enable you to detach yourself from a problem or free you from your obligation.   **NEW BEGINNINGS**

You will realize that your conception of a situation was in error, or that you made a mistake in judgment.   **INHERITANCE**

A small gift will be given or received.   **REWARDS/GIFTS**

Your success will come through areas of work that deal with communications, teaching, lecturing, or public exchanges.   **SUCCESS**

Through luck you will meet, talk to, or run into someone very interesting.   **FORTUNE**

You will be grateful for the fulfillment of an emotional (or spiritual) need, and a healing of ills through the intervention of a friend or associate . . . there really *is* a God.   **BLESSINGS**

Mundane: You will have a struggle trying to get things accomplished, meet your obligations, or ward off the "ghosts" of your past and all the memories associated with them.   **SPECIAL GUIDANCE**
Esoteric: Your first response is to want to quit, run away, or evade the issue but the best response is to deal with it. It is only through participation in all of life (the good, bad, and incomprehensible) that we find answers enabling us to correct ourselves and our problems or better understand the workings of God.

Produce the best you are capable of as effectively as you can and don't try to live up to a conception of how you think you should be . . . or what anyone else thinks, for that matter.   **BEST COURSE OF ACTION**

Action will be taken to correct for losses or mistakes and instead of quitting, you will be participating even more with the knowledge that the Universe *does* know what it's doing.   **OUTCOME**

THE FIVE OF WANDS

Many 5s indicate change, challenge, and fluctuations (lucky or un-lucky). They also indicate material prosperity but spiritual poverty if not properly balanced or understood.

IN A READING

Many Wands (three or more) indicate that conditions are primarily in the realm of thought, or in the very first stages of development.

The focus is on business and romance, inner conflicts arising from unexpressed desires, analysis of win/lose factors in exercising your intention or personal integrity, change, and reformation.

FOCUS

You want to clear things up in your mind and handle situations (or communications) effectively.

DESIRE

Love or romance will find you, but your feelings will be "sus-pended" because your mind will be on other things.

ROMANCE

You will be surprised because the one you want to hear from calls, and/or at the eleventh hour, when you least expect it, a miracle happens.

THE UNEXPECTED

You will feel as if you're making a trade-off or compromise, but you will not let that happen. Instead, you will take steps to assert your-self and to correct the situation.

OTHERS

You will be upset or agitated or feel "out of control" due to what seem to be insurmountable problems caused by others and/or be-cause of a phone call. Vandals or malicious mischief around your home or property could also be indicated.

THE HOME

There will be a departure from home for business, health, or social reasons; or, you will get off cheaply if car repairs are needed.

TRAVEL

You will be involved with papers pertaining to the formulation of ideas, contracts, or release forms, and will benefit through them.

PAPERS

You're going to be considering a major change, and something will need to be handled or approached honestly that will take a lot of courage, but will be resolved and you'll get what you want. Also, the completion of a project will bring unexpected gain.

WORK/CAREER

UNIONS

One of the loves you had cast aside or "suspended" is going to come back, and you are going to spend some very sensual and passionate moments together.

EMOTIONAL STATE

Someone or something is going to cause you to take a very serious look at where you are in your life, or where you hope to go.

PLEASURE

Change, reformation, and improvement in paperwork, finances, and business matters will give you a great deal of satisfaction, and on a more personal level, a budding romance or love affair is indicated.

NEWS

An uplifting message from a lover, loved one, or business associate will arrive.

FAMILY

Your family and friends will support you or help you to see a different point of view, and if they were experiencing problems, they are in the process of clearing up.

THE PHYSICAL BODY

There are three words to describe your health situation: *improvement, sex,* and *sensuality.*

FINANCES

You will have enough money to pay your bills or meet your needs and if involved in a litigation, fight, or debate over finances, you will come out victorious.

TIME

Unresolved personal affairs or business matters will weigh heavily on you.

FRIENDS

A friend from the past will return or call and your friendship will be renewed, deepen, and blossom.

VISITORS/CALLERS

An unexpected caller will arrive (this could be one from your past, bearing gifts), and though you don't think it's possible, the two of you are going to be spending some very sensual and passionate hours together.

MAIL

Expect the receipt of money, or a letter containing money, or you will make money through mail order.

ANXIETY

You will experience an undercurrent of inner disquiet because you will feel that you're being forced to make a trade-off or compromise.

You will be disheartened by obstacles, but when you least expect it, everything will turn around and change for the better. **DISAPPOINTMENT**

Confusion, trepidation, or uncertainty regarding another will come to an end. **ENDINGS**

Business will expand, finances will increase, and nonproductive, defective, or negative areas will be cleaned up. **NEW BEGINNINGS**

You will "inherit" the ability to meet a challenge and come out on top . . . a fresh start and a new friend. **INHERITANCE**

A nice gift will be purchased or given. This could be a car, or something for a car, or it could be wearing apparel. **REWARDS/GIFTS**

Your success will come through a revision of attitude, and summoning up the kind of courage or fortitude it takes to get "the job done" or to have what you want. **SUCCESS**

You will be lucky in business, finance, and negotiations. **FORTUNE**

You will get what you asked for, or something thought lost will be found, bringing great relief and gratitude. **BLESSINGS**

Mundane: Are you looking at things as they really are, or are you ignoring the facts and clouding the issue? Ask yourself this: If I could have everything I wanted, would I want this, or continue to do that? **SPECIAL GUIDANCE**
Esoteric: If you're feeling bad, hostile, or angry, it's because you are not being honest with yourself (or another), and are dealing with situations from a "lose" instead of a "win" point of view. When you recognize this, your peace of mind will be restored.

Look at defects and correct them. Reform some of your ideas or attitudes, and choose from a "win" instead of a "lose" point of view. Don't compromise or accept defeat; you're too close to winning. **BEST COURSE OF ACTION**

Improvements will be made, and you will have a more positive outlook on life in general. Though you can't always get what you want, you'll get what you need, and sometimes what you need can turn out to be exactly what you want. **OUTCOME**

◆ THE SIX OF WANDS

Many 6s indicate adjustments in thoughts, attitudes, or conditions. They also represent the ability to transcend difficulties.

IN A READING

Many Wands (three or more) indicate that conditions are primarily in the realm of thought, or in the very first stages of development.

The focus is on a period of frustration, tension, or anxiety caused by intolerable conditions or restrictions placed on you by time or circumstance; also by things that break, snag, fall apart, or just don't gel the way you want them to.

FOCUS

You want to get on with things, to start a new project, way of life, of life-style.

DESIRE

An amorous and impetuous suitor (one who is perhaps younger than you) is going to try to win your heart . . . he/she just might.

ROMANCE

You will be surprised by the action or response of another to something you inadvertently said or did.

THE UNEXPECTED

Both personally and professionally, people will be friendly, cooperative, and supportive, and you'll get unexpected news, assistance, or a beneficial surprise concerning your work.

OTHERS

You will be frustrated in your endeavors or disturbed about your affairs in general, but you will also be planning a trip to the home of a friend or relative—a pleasure trip.

THE HOME

You will hope that a course of action or plan to meet with someone can be put off for the time being.

TRAVEL

You may ask someone to help you with your paperwork, or you will write a letter concerning a new venture, business proposal, or counter offer.

PAPERS

You'll take a break from your work or current project and do something more pleasurable. Something that moves you from behind the scenes to center stage (maybe a workshop or seminar) or mental work will be very successful and a lot will get accomplished.

WORK/CAREER

UNIONS   A new or perhaps diverse element is going to cause you to rethink the issues at stake and/or make changes in your existing situation or status . . . a positive development.

EMOTIONAL STATE You will be extremely edgy or irritable because you will feel locked into a situation you want to get out of.

PLEASURE   You will enjoy a change in venue, or an outing with a friend.

NEWS   You are going to get some great news, something you've been hoping to hear or have been waiting for . . . this could be concerning a sale, book, or literary endeavor.

FAMILY   Your relatives will be having a difficult time, and will be troubled by finances or partnerships that will end up costing you.

THE PHYSICAL BODY You will finally take a much-needed rest, and will be nursing yourself or a loved one back to good health.

FINANCES   You are going to experience tension related to finances, but difficulties will be overcome and a payment or settlement is in the offing.

TIME   In time, pressure will ease off and things will smooth out. You can also expect some good news or professional assistance.

FRIENDS   Friends will be very supportive and/or you will have professional friends.

VISITORS/CALLERS A professional person or a person of influence or from the media is going to call you for business or social reasons, or you will call him/her.

MAIL   You will receive a payment or settlement, and/or information you requested will arrive.

ANXIETY   You will want things to be different and much better than the way they are.

DISAPPOINTMENT   You won't be able to pull yourself out of an emotional slump or get a handle on things.

ENDINGS   A decision will be made that will solve a business or romantic problem, end internal conflict, and put an end to a "predetermined" course along a path you didn't want to be on anyway.

What seemed like a lost cause will suddenly work out in your favor due to a "preordained" sequence of events which add up and force a resolution. There will also be unexpected growth and assistance in your work or trade.

NEW BEGINNINGS

You are going to "inherit" an unexpected gain in a new direction . . . perhaps romantic.

INHERITANCE

You will benefit through helping others, and something you wanted will be given to you when you least expect it. A gift of silver could also be indicated.

REWARDS/GIFTS

You will succeed in overcoming difficult situations, and in obtaining the help of a professional.

SUCCESS

You will have luck in gaining unexpected help in a time of "crises," and in attracting love or romance as well.

FORTUNE

You will be grateful for a fortunate adjustment in your business affairs and love life.

BLESSINGS

Mundane: Conditions of renewal are approaching and when that happens, things will come together.
Esoteric: Think of life as an interwoven pattern where all parts work together to make a whole. You are not apart, but part of the tapestry. You can overcome your resistance to this experience by observation and a gentle acceptance of "what's so."

SPECIAL GUIDANCE

Persevere in spite of the trials you have to endure and don't resist "what is" or try to force results, because that will only cause frustration and make matters worse.

BEST COURSE OF ACTION

Negative conditions will end and positive ones will be established, but your success will be well earned.

OUTCOME

THE SEVEN OF WANDS

Many 7s denote a period of introspection or solitude. They also indicate unlooked-for advantages or gain through things that come unexpectedly.

IN A READING

Many Wands (three or more) indicate that conditions are primarily in the realm of thought, or at the very first stages of development.

The focus is on love affairs, timing, trips, clarity, and finance, and pressure related to work, schedules, and personal commitments.

FOCUS

You want a clear-cut direction or a "yes" or "no" answer and/or a commitment on the part of another.

DESIRE

You will think about love and what it would be like to live with someone or get married.

ROMANCE

Problems concerning your family, finances, business plans, or schedules will take you by surprise.

THE UNEXPECTED

You will be involved with groups, teachers, writers, publishers, or professional people of all kinds.

OTHERS

You will juggle your work, appointments, and social affairs successfully, and if business calls you away from home you will handle it over the phone instead. You could also give someone a set of keys . . . maybe a lover.

THE HOME

You will be planning a trip with a sweetheart, or a vacation with a loved one.

TRAVEL

You will resolve things quickly and effortlessly. A contract in hand could also be indicated.

PAPERS

You will handle your affairs skillfully and complete all projects or financial matters successfully . . . but love will be more important than work.

WORK/CAREER

You will want a marriage, union, or serious commitment but will have a "tug-of-war" between your head and heart; if the heart wins, a sacrifice will have to be made.

UNIONS

EMOTIONAL STATE You will feel that no matter what "stuff" gets in your way, you're on a roll that nothing can thwart.

PLEASURE You will enjoy liberating yourself from exacting schedules, work demands, or stalemated business affairs.

NEWS Someone is going to tell you he/she loves you, or someone very taken with you will call or propose a union.

FAMILY Relatives will call with good news about their home or finances or you will call on them.

THE PHYSICAL BODY You will try to accomplish too many things at once, and will feel pressured to take on more than you care to handle, and that will affect your health adversely. Also, do not ingest food you're not certain of.

FINANCES Financial obstacles will be surmounted, and a check, subsidy, commission, or settlement is in the offing.

TIME If you haven't fallen in love yet, in time someone's going to come along and sweep you off your feet.

FRIENDS Your friends will be loving, kind, benevolent, and supportive, and you will see (or hear from) a friend you haven't seen in ages.

VISITORS/CALLERS You will call on someone for something and you will get what you want (it may take time but you will get it), and someone will call that you'd rather not hear from.

MAIL Expect to receive a check or money in the mail, and an R.S.V.P. from a company or client.

ANXIETY You will want to be with the one you love, but won't be able to surmount the obstacles imposed on you by others or by time and circumstance.

DISAPPOINTMENT The lack of commitment on the part of others or people who don't show up, follow through, or drop the ball will be a big disappointment to you.

ENDINGS Exciting news or an important decision will bring about a feeling of great satisfaction or accomplishment, and put an end to problems, stress, or strain.

All obstacles or vicissitudes will be overcome and you will be in a much more positive frame of mind.

NEW BEGINNINGS

You are going to receive a special consideration, financial break, payment, or advantage.

INHERITANCE

You can expect a very unselfish gesture on the part of another who will give you something you want even if it means a sacrifice for him/her. The end result, however, will be that you both benefit.

REWARDS/GIFTS

You will be successful in all of your negotiations, agreements, or financial transactions. Money that is owed will be paid, and/or money for a subsidy or grant will soon be given.

SUCCESS

Luck will be with you in regaining something thought lost or forgotten and/or in concluding business matters successfully.

FORTUNE

You will be grateful for financial increase through a business of your own, and/or that you have concluded a business trip, deal, or venture, successfully.

BLESSINGS

Mundane: You will get more satisfaction through self-improvement than by trying to change external conditions.
Esoteric: There's a movement stirring within that's causing much apprehension, but this movement is actually progressive. You must realize that not only must the outer change, but the inner as well. Fortunately, you have the innate ability to turn a challenge into a useful commodity and some of your greatest achievements were born out of your frustration.

SPECIAL GUIDANCE

Ignore opposition and let nothing make you veer off from your course. Straighten out your affairs, make steps toward commitment, and refuse to accept less than what is essentially right . . . be true to yourself.

BEST COURSE OF ACTION

In the end you will triumph, and all matters will conclude successfully or to your satisfaction.

OUTCOME

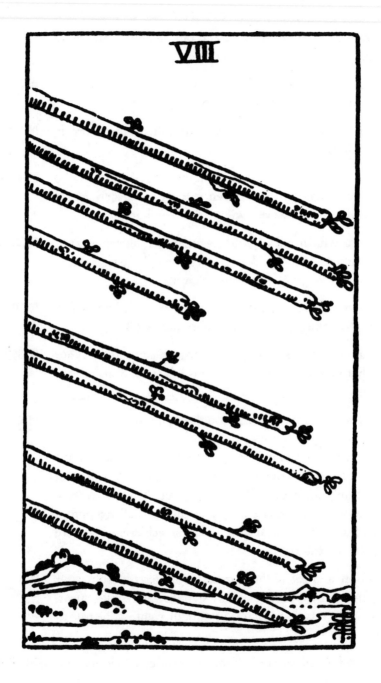

THE EIGHT OF WANDS

Many 8s indicate a positive change of mind or status because the beneficial qualities of the number 8 are rarely diluted.

IN A READING

Many Wands (three or more) indicate that conditions are primarily in the realm of thought, or at the very first stages of development.

The focus is on expansion, movement and time spent away from home, romance, meetings and gatherings, new opportunities, and long-distance communications.

FOCUS

You want to speed things up, settle a matter of concern, or branch out on your own.

DESIRE

This is a positive time for romance and if a significant love affair doesn't begin (a very warm and enchanting one), you'll at least be charmed by an admirer or two.

ROMANCE

A romantic introduction, invitation, or proposition will take you completely by surprise (a positive development) and/or an invitation will be extended and accepted.

THE UNEXPECTED

Someone will cause you to make changes in your thinking or current plans (a positive development) and a better arrangement will be made.

OTHERS

Expect a lot of calls, messages, and activity. You could be away from home more than at home, and may also have the desire to move or to live by the water.

THE HOME

You will travel for work, pleasure, or a journey home. This also indicates that a problem concerning travel arrangements will be settled in a positive or fortunate way, or that a trip could lead to a new way of life.

TRAVEL

You will run into unexpected complications or legal problems with papers or paperwork that will cause a frustrating delay.

PAPERS

You will be very enterprising, and can expect good fortune in business, profitable returns, and sudden progress or "boom."

WORK/CAREER

UNIONS — You won't be able to get what you want out of a relationship. A business loss or setback is also indicated.

EMOTIONAL STATE — You'll be in a positive frame of mind and unusually light or confident due to a new discovery or enterprise; or, your thoughts will be turned toward love and romance.

PLEASURE — Sudden activity, unusual correspondence, and movement in your affairs and in the lives of others will lift your spirits and change your frame of mind.

NEWS — You will correspond with another who is out of state, and a very persuasive suitor will call who will want to see you or romance you.

FAMILY — You're going to hear some good news from a relative (this could be regarding a court case), and will soon be spending time in the home of another family member.

THE PHYSICAL BODY — You will have a healthy sex life, sexual release, or encounter.

FINANCES — You can expect a sudden improvement in your financial affairs, lots of activity and correspondence related to your work, or proceeds from a new enterprise that's just beginning to yield a profit.

TIME — You're going to have a change for the better. Expect some very good news or positive correspondence *and* a beginning or renewed friendship or romance.

FRIENDS — An unpleasant occurrence will arise with a friend over something that was misrepresented or misunderstood.

VISITORS/CALLERS — Expect good news concerning your finances, and a business opportunity over the phone (could be long distance).

MAIL — There will be letters pertaining to license agreements, purchase orders, or legal documents, or you will mail letters to companies or clients.

ANXIETY — You'll be feeling pressured to get things done, and there will be too many activities or responsibilities to handle all at once. You will also have problems with travel plans or your family.

You will be dissatisfied with your business and your love life because it isn't going well, isn't enough, or isn't what you want. **DISAPPOINTMENT**

Unhappiness, displeasure, and feeling alone will come to an end. **ENDINGS**

New ideas or opportunities concerning your business will put a new slant on your life or open new doors. **NEW BEGINNINGS**

You will "inherit" a just reward or a positive revision in your finances. **INHERITANCE**

You will give someone a gift because of his/her kindness or because you like him/her very much. **REWARDS/GIFTS**

You're going to overcome stagnation and move back into the flow of life. You will also achieve a great deal of satisfaction through trips, movies, or entertainment and/or in attracting the attention or admiration of others. **SUCCESS**

Conditions are going to change for the better due to some good fortune or turn of fate, or luck will be with you in finding the best product to suit your needs. **FORTUNE**

You'll be grateful for the end of stagnation or delays, renewed activity in your career, and a new outlet for your talents. A new agent or promoter could also be indicated. **BLESSINGS**

Mundane: You're approaching your goal, but your affairs will not be completely set, decided, or determined. **SPECIAL GUIDANCE**
Esoteric: You needn't be anxious about your affairs. The Universe knows what things you are in need of. What you want has *already* been established and you will be led into it or it will come to you.

Take more responsibility, initiative, or accountability for results. Leave home if necessary, or do some shopping around, and don't be afraid to take a chance or make yourself more available to others. **BEST COURSE OF ACTION**

Things will be set in motion though not settled or "grounded," but these new conditions will eventually lead to success. **OUTCOME**

◆ THE NINE OF WANDS

Many 9s mean that situations or events are nearing completion, or have just been completed and another plateau awaits.

IN A READING

Many Wands (three or more) indicate that conditions are primarily in the realm of thought, or at the very first stages of development.

The focus is on character, stamina and self-discipline, courage, faith or conviction, doing your best according to the circumstances you find yourself in, gathering strength, biding time, or awaiting the right moment to act.

FOCUS

You want efforts to bear fruit, to socialize, circulate, and be out with others, and your health (or that of another) to improve.

DESIRE

There will be two loves vying for your affection and you will be trying to sort out the dilemma or find the answer that will quell the conflict, but the solution you come to will either break your heart or be impossible to carry out.

ROMANCE

You will be surprised by the cancellation of an appointment and/or a call that never comes. Or, an "enemy" could turn into a friend.

THE UNEXPECTED

You will be waiting for something to pan out, or for someone to arrive, or if someone in your home is ill, a doctor or friend with a medical background will call or come to call.

OTHERS

An old friend, lover, or admirer will call, and if he/she arrives, will want to stay.

THE HOME

You will travel for business or social reasons and have a glorious time because you will have much charisma, make friends easily, and attract many admirers.

TRAVEL

You will be tied to paperwork, and what at first glance looked relatively easy will turn into a major production.

PAPERS

You will make money at your craft and promote yourself and your business. If you are involved in or considering a metaphysical venture or profession, it will prove to be very lucrative and rewarding.

WORK/CAREER

UNIONS   If you want to unite with someone and your intention wavers, you could miss your chance, because while you're dallying, he/she could move in a different direction.

EMOTIONAL STATE You will experience displeasure and dissatisfaction caused by confusing issues, delay, or adversity.

PLEASURE   You will enjoy giving to another, or being in the arms of someone who is extremely engaging and quite a bit different from the others you've known.

NEWS   You will be waiting for a call or response from someone, and will soon have one.

FAMILY   One of your relatives will be experiencing financial difficulties and will be looking for a way out of the dilemma.

THE PHYSICAL BODY You'll be feeling run-down or sick and may seek medical attention, and/or a change of physicians could correct a misdiagnosed problem.

FINANCES   You will make enough money to get by and will have an opportunity to make more.

TIME   In a very short time, you can expect a major change in your activities, attitude, and love life.

FRIENDS   You will be waiting to hear from a friend (or lover) and there will be a lot of nervous energy around that. You may wind up calling him/her.

VISITORS/CALLERS You will get many calls and could be constantly on the move.

MAIL   You will mail a document or manuscript and be awaiting a reply.

ANXIETY   You'll be upset that you have no choice but to wait before your efforts bear fruit, or will worry that another isn't communicating all the facts or is seeing someone else.

DISAPPOINTMENT You will be disappointed in having to wait before further progress can be made.

Both waiting around for something to happen and the way you have habitually dealt with situations in the past are going to end. **ENDINGS**

An old friend or lover will suddenly appear, bearing a new opportunity that could be just the thing you want or need. **NEW BEGINNINGS**

You will "inherit" new ideas or seeds for the future that promise a brighter tomorrow. **INHERITANCE**

You're going to get or give some sound advice concerning health, and will also get a respite from a current struggle. **REWARDS/GIFTS**

Financial transactions and social activities will bring success and rewards. **SUCCESS**

Good fortune will come through social connections, work done in the past, and/or in the arrival of something very much appreciated or needed . . . could even be money. **FORTUNE**

You'll be grateful for the opportunity to do what you want to do after a long period of hard work or exacting labor. **BLESSINGS**

Mundane: If you don't succeed at first, try again. Also, expect good news concerning business, love, or finances. **SPECIAL GUIDANCE**
Esoteric: You're going to have to go it alone for the time being, fighting your own battle your own way, and the past will provide nothing to lean on or sustain you. If you fall down, get back up and dust yourself off. Refuse to be beaten by life and you won't be.

Stay on purpose with your intention and what you want. **BEST COURSE OF ACTION**

There's no getting around it . . . you're going to have to wait for the final prognosis. **OUTCOME**

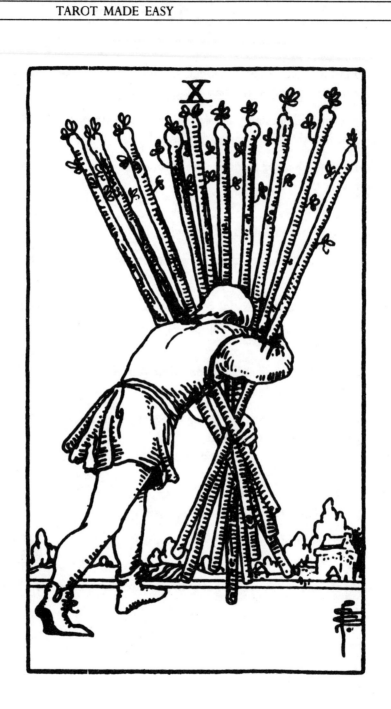

THE TEN OF WANDS

Tens are read the same as a number 1. However, they also signify a cyclical rebeginning, and a time when you must come to terms with something you may have avoided in the past.

IN A READING

Many Wands (three or more) indicate that conditions are primarily in the realm of thought, or at the very first stages of development.

The focus is on a major change or move from one thing or place to another, planning, executing, plodding through, and meeting practical difficulties in order to bring a·new way into being; also, new projects and taking steps toward progress.

FOCUS

You want to tie up loose ends or complete projects that need to be done in order to move on to something else.

DESIRE

You will be in the dark about your love life, or wonder what is going on with your lover and wish he/she would contact you or let you know.

ROMANCE

You will be unprepared for the added responsibilities brought on by another person's words or deeds.

THE UNEXPECTED

Someone will cause you to change your plans or move in a new and different direction, and the adjustment will be difficult.

OTHERS

You're going to be overworked and overtired but will complete the project(s) you set out to do successfully. This could also indicate a change of residence if other cards support it.

THE HOME

You're going to go on a short trip or journey, or will leave your home in an effort to escape from burdens, responsibilities, or problems. A residential move could also be indicated.

TRAVEL

Paperwork will become an overwhelming chore, but you will persist and see it through to its completion. If you intend to market a project, legal rights will be considered or discussed.

PAPERS

You will change your routine or wrap up the work you are currently doing in order to do something else along a different line . . . perhaps another kind of work.

WORK/CAREER

UNIONS

You will hope for a resurrection in your relationship, but will feel as if you are trying to raise the dead.

EMOTIONAL STATE

That which you once loved will become a burden that will no longer give you satisfaction or joy.

PLEASURE

You'll derive a great deal of satisfaction through helping others and completing projects or ventures successfully.

NEWS

A message will come concerning a change of plans and you'll be relieved, or a loved one will call with an invitation to come and visit.

FAMILY

Your relatives will place added burdens on you, or will want you to do something that involves moving, "movement," or manual labor that will take more energy than you feel you can muster up.

THE PHYSICAL BODY

You will be run-down or overtired, and it's probably because you're taking on too much responsibility.

FINANCES

You will be apprehensive about your financial condition due to a setback, loss of income, or something you counted on falling through.

TIME

Time will bring a new slant to what seemed like an impossible situation.

FRIENDS

You're going to have a falling-out with a friend or loved one whom you feel has let you down, or friends will have problems you won't know how to deal with or correct.

VISITORS/CALLERS

You are going to get a call that will entail some work or labor on your part . . . something you'd rather not do.

MAIL

You will complete a project involving papers or letters to your satisfaction, or a letter will arrive containing money.

ANXIETY

You will worry that the energy you're applying to your goals is not enough, or that in the end, when all is said and done, you will fail anyway, and all of your efforts will come to naught.

DISAPPOINTMENT

You will feel that your desire for the things you want will go unfulfilled for a long, long time, and that the "work" you must do in order to pull things together or complete them will take forever.

Physical problems and constricting binds are going to end. **ENDINGS**

You'll have a lot of work to get accomplished because a new way of **NEW BEGINNINGS** life is emerging (both personally and professionally), and you'll have to complete the old and embark on the new simultaneously.

A lot of work is coming your way, as well as a discovery about **INHERITANCE** yourself or your work that can change or revitalize your method of operation.

You will get an unexpected career opportunity. **REWARDS/GIFTS**

Your success will be the result of patient, diligent, and thorough **SUCCESS** research instead of blindly rushing ahead, and of your ability to apply yourself to a goal until it's completed to your satisfaction.

Good fortune will come through a change in your environment, or **FORTUNE** a move from one thing or place to another.

You will be very glad that you've successfully completed a project **BLESSINGS** or task and that the burden is over.

Mundane: Be determined to have what *you* want . . . the goal is **SPECIAL GUIDANCE** within reach.
Esoteric: Don't accept mediocrity. Chip away all that isn't perfect and you will have what is.

In business or material affairs, wait until the proper action becomes **BEST COURSE** evident. Until then, persevere or finish what you started. In matters **OF ACTION** of the heart, don't waste your time on an impossible relationship.

You will persevere in spite of difficulties, burdens, or financial prob- **OUTCOME** lems, until things are resolved, completed, or the way you want, and a new venture will begin that will ease a lot of your previous tensions.

PAGE of WANDS.

THE PAGE OF WANDS

SAGITTARIUS (November 22 - December 21)

Outspoken, direct, charismatic, high-strung, blunt, instinctive, easily bored, sexual, progressive, future-oriented, sportive, subject to wandering, and sometimes edgy or lackadaisical.

Athletics, politics, pilot, instructor, philosopher, professional student, gadget inventor, band member.

The focus is on inventory and analysis; philosophical, spiritual, and work-related ideas, discussions, and activities; the desire for expansion; sexual attraction, new beginnings, and/or a person with a Sagittarian-type temperament.

You want things to change (this could be concerning a loved one), and to break free of oppression or stagnation in business or find a solution to problems.

You will fear that you and your lover are not going to get together, or that even if you did, it would just be a superficial relationship with no real depth or giving of one's self.

You're going to hear something from a friend, loved one, or business associate that will surprise you . . . a happy surprise.

You will want to "move," incite, or motivate others and though you may act distant, indifferent, or contrary to your nature, you will inwardly long for that which is meaningful.

There will be many uncomfortable changes and fluctuating moods.

You will visit with a friend or relative but it will be brief, and you will want to travel or "get away from it all."

You will promote a new enterprise that involves papers and it should be successful because the public will readily accept or purchase your product.

You will find a new approach to your work that could turn into a very lucrative and far-reaching project.

ASTROLOGICAL SIGN	
TYPE OF PERSON	
TYPE OF VOCATION	
FOCUS	
DESIRE	
ROMANCE	
THE UNEXPECTED	
OTHERS	
THE HOME	
TRAVEL	
PAPERS	
WORK/CAREER	

UNIONS   You are going to unite with a business partner or loved one and will hope that a new approach will be successful.

EMOTIONAL STATE   You will be changeable, edgy, and lackadaisical.

PLEASURE   You'll be happy about an invitation to a social event or outing . . . could be to a dress-up affair.

NEWS   Expect messages or mail bringing good news or financial gain.

FAMILY   You will be uninvolved, irritated, or impatient with your relatives and won't want to be bothered.

THE PHYSICAL BODY   A health condition will need attention . . . this could be anything ranging from an upset stomach to a sexual disorder.

FINANCES   Even though your finances are improving in some areas, you will still be worried about money on the whole; and in another area, you will have problems trying to collect money that is owed to you.

TIME   In time, your desires will be realized, your social life will increase, and/or you will meet with or attract a new admirer.

FRIENDS   You and a friend will be discussing a joint business venture.

VISITORS/CALLERS   You will call on a love interest or one will call on you.

MAIL   Someone is going to help you to write or edit a letter, program, or document concerning your career or public relations.

ANXIETY   You will feel repressed because things are not up to par, or as good as they could or should be.

DISAPPOINTMENT   You will be disappointed because you will have to put things off to another day, and also because the one who wants you isn't the one you want.

ENDINGS   Settling for less will come to an end.

NEW BEGINNINGS   You will take inventory and analyze issues from a different angle, but you will think about things, instead of actually doing them, until the right moment to act approaches.

INHERITANCE   You are going to get a business referral or job opportunity.

You will receive an invitation and an offer of friendship, love, or affection from an admirer.

REWARDS/GIFTS

Your success will come through repeat clients, social connections, and business associates and in moving on new ideas instead of trying to "make do" or "stick out" the old.

SUCCESS

You will have luck in attracting romance or meeting a new lover.

FORTUNE

You'll be thankful for business referrals, extra money made at work, and/or good news about your work.

BLESSINGS

Mundane: Change is in the air, and a new approach is at hand. This could come through a friend who will help you "see the light" or attain a new perspective.
Esoteric: Be willing to wait, but don't compromise your self-esteem or avoid "warning" signs.

SPECIAL GUIDANCE

Pursue philosophical or intellectual hobbies, work, or lectures, and get things settled or down on paper up front. That way there won't be any unpleasant surprises, and you won't end up sabotaging yourself.

BEST COURSE OF ACTION

When all is said and done, you will feel that things are just not worth the effort, and/or will avoid situations that frustrate, anger, or distress you.

OUTCOME

KNIGHT of WANDS.

THE KNIGHT OF WANDS

There is no astrological sign associated with the Knights because they indicate situations that are coming in or going out.

When a Knight appears in a reading, a long-term condition will suddenly change.

The focus is on crossroads in life concerning living quarters, business arrangements, partnerships, love affairs, important documents, and impending decisions; there will be stress and difficulty, but eventual success.

You want to set things straight in your mind or affairs or to settle an issue once and for all.

Your heartfelt desires are going to be met through the entry of a kindred spirit (one you've met or feel you've met before) with whom you will establish a deep rapport and mutual feeling of affinity, passion, and trust.

Something concerning your business or career will be provided *before* the desire was expressed, and you will be very surprised.

After a period of tension caused by many difficulties or disappointments, someone will enter the picture that will change things for the better.

You will go on a short trip or jaunt, and will be thinking about moving to a new home or living with someone.

You will soon be missing a family member or a friend who is going on a trip, and/or someone will unexpectedly call or come to call, or you will take a short trip or rendezvous with a lover or admirer.

You will go over documents or contracts with a "fine-tooth comb," and your intuition or inner guidance will tell you everything you need to know.

You will have to deal with very unpleasant people or circumstances in your work, and will feel that you are wasting your time and effort, but eventually the energy will blow off and tensions will vanish.

IN A READING

FOCUS

DESIRE

ROMANCE

THE UNEXPECTED

OTHERS

THE HOME

TRAVEL

PAPERS

WORK/CAREER

UNIONS   You are going to be spending time with one who will awaken your romantic heart and inspire thoughts of love or marriage, and the depth of your feelings for that person will astonish you.

EMOTIONAL STATE   You'll experience stress caused by obstacles and uncomfortable situations, and will have a compulsion to set things straight or fix what's wrong . . . eventually you will.

PLEASURE   Pleasure will come through new vibrations and a change in your life-style, home environment, or attitude toward another.

NEWS   Listen to your intuition, dreams, or psychic impressions. They are right and will prove to be accurate. You could also have prophetic dreams.

FAMILY   Things will not go as anticipated with friends, loved ones, or relatives due to a very unusual or uncomfortable occurrence. There may also be an unexpected illness.

THE PHYSICAL BODY   You will experience a lack of energy (could be due to emotional tensions), and will be subject to clumsiness or small accidents. If planning a trip to the dentist, you will not like the results.

FINANCES   A payment is going to be late or will not arrive at all and it will really aggravate you, but money will come in from a new undertaking or different source.

TIME   After a period of tension or frustration, things will begin to improve greatly. Success *will* come, after difficulty.

FRIENDS   You will experience embarrassment or be extremely self-conscious around your friends or loved ones due to an uncomfortable get-together or faux pas, and someone in your circle of friends could have a drug or drinking problem.

VISITORS/CALLERS   Those that you wish to call or arrive will, and if you have been secretly hoping someone will not arrive, you will get your wish.

MAIL   Letters or documents will need special attention. Rewrite, revamp, or review them, because you could find out something to your benefit.

You will be worried about your finances or will have reservations about another because of financial considerations, and will be aggravated by situations that are not right or are out of sync.

ANXIETY

You will be unhappy about your business or finances in general, and about people in business who give you the runaround or in the end don't come through.

DISAPPOINTMENT

Problems, tensions, or difficulties related to financial settlements, contracts, or partnerships will be resolved on a positive note.

ENDINGS

A lover will call and a sweetheart will arrive, or you will be pursued by many admirers.

NEW BEGINNINGS

You will "inherit" financial increase and a release from tension.

INHERITANCE

A lunch or dinner invitation is coming your way, or a sweetheart will invite you to his/her home.

REWARDS/GIFTS

You will be successful in navigating the straits in difficult business matters or financial negotiations and/or will suddenly come into love or money through the affections of a generous admirer.

SUCCESS

You will have luck in overcoming obstacles or difficulties, and if the card that fell in the Romance category is auspicious, you will also be fortunate in matters of the heart.

FORTUNE

You will be thankful that you were given intuitive insights and/or answers to your prayers and have resolved certain problems concerning business, health, or money, and that a heartfelt desire was met.

BLESSINGS

Mundane: Nothing will seem to jibe, and your attempts to straighten out your affairs will feel like an exercise in futility, but don't let it defeat you because you're very close to reaching your goals.
Esoteric: What are you going to believe in, luck and failure? Or will you put your faith in God and the right outworking of your affairs? You have a choice; which ear will you listen to?

SPECIAL GUIDANCE

Don't try to assess situations and effect solutions in advance. The time will come when you'll know what is true or what to do and if

BEST COURSE OF ACTION

QUEEN of WANDS.

you wait for that moment, you'll leave an opening for the Universe to step in and solve things for you.

In the end, tensions will vanish, things will be righted, and issues will be resolved in your favor. **OUTCOME**

◆ THE QUEEN OF WANDS

LEO (July 23–August 22) **ASTROLOGICAL SIGN**

Affectionate, generous, loyal, adventurous, fun-loving, dramatic, determined, impulsive, daring, passionate, proud, honest, aloof, haughty, egotistical. **TYPE OF PERSON**

Actor, entertainer, creator, artist, musician, fashion figure, confidant, professional sports, and any type of vocation where he/she can be number one. **TYPE OF VOCATION**

The focus is on new avenues or paths, family matters or get-togethers, metaphysical or spiritual pursuits, love affairs, personal fulfillment, and/or a person with a Leo-type temperament. **FOCUS**

You have recently met (or will meet) someone you could have a relationship with and are wondering if you should, or if you will. **DESIRE**

An admirer or sweetheart will suddenly appear, and a very passionate love affair or romance is in store. Or, an enigma will be solved, and you will know how much someone has been thinking of you and how much they care. **ROMANCE**

A sudden surge in your business or career and a call from a lover (one you didn't think would call) will come as a much-welcomed surprise. **THE UNEXPECTED**

It will be hard for you to really let go and let a love affair or personal relationship happen. **OTHERS**

THE HOME
You will be pursuing spiritual interests or a metaphysical career, and/or will entertain a lover or admirer in your home.

TRAVEL
You will stay at home for the most part (or journey home), and/or a major move will be put off for the time being, but you will still be thinking about it.

PAPERS
You are going to be involved with papers or books that teach, entertain, or fulfill you personally.

WORK/CAREER
If you've been off the path, you're going to come back strong. Expect to hear some very good news.

UNIONS
You will no longer accept what was (or the facsimile thereof), and will take a lover, divorce, or end the relationship.

EMOTIONAL STATE
An unexpected stroke of good fortune will cause your spirits to soar.

PLEASURE
Happiness will come through just rewards in your career, a romantic interlude and attracting whatever you need in the way of professional assistance.

NEWS
You will talk with a relative who is experiencing a great deal of tension or adversity due to his/her work, finances, partner, or lover . . . a sad development.

FAMILY
A relative will come to call or you will call on him/her, but it will be a short visit; also, a choice in affections will have to be made . . . could be concerning a lover.

THE PHYSICAL BODY
You will be very health-conscious and interested in quick remedies, New Age-type treatments or methods, vitamins, birth control, or family pets.

FINANCES
You will regret an impromptu expenditure, but it was a wise decision.

TIME
In time, what you are in need of will be provided, and a confusing or upsetting issue will be straightened out for the good of all.

FRIENDS
You will have a run-in with a friend or lover due to a misunderstanding or imagined slight over something that wasn't handled or

communicated effectively, and a friend will bring a change in social activities or a potential romance.

You will get together with your family or friends, or they will call on you. **VISITORS/CALLERS**

Believe it or not, a check *is* in the mail, and you could get it sooner than expected. **MAIL**

A crisis will come up with a family member or one you love that will signal a point of no return, something that makes it very clear that you can no longer coexist or continue the relationship. **ANXIETY**

You will feel as if the last ray of hope has gone out, and that nothing will ever change or get any better. **DISAPPOINTMENT**

A relationship, marriage, or love affair is going to end. **ENDINGS**

You can expect a sudden surge in your love life and the advances of an intriguing foreigner or someone from a different country, culture, or background. **NEW BEGINNINGS**

You will "inherit" a renewed interest in your career, spiritual matters, or literature or books. **INHERITANCE**

You will be directed to a new resource or recourse (this could be in the form of an inspirational book). **REWARDS/GIFTS**

Your success will come through your ability to attract whatever it is you want or need, even if you aren't aware of what that is now. **SUCCESS**

You will have good luck in metaphysical pursuits, mending hurt feelings, and attracting romance. **FORTUNE**

You will be thankful that you are well liked or admired, and that you are back on the path in your career (or spiritual goals). **BLESSINGS**

Mundane: True guidance proves itself, in that it brings with it the action or ability to carry it out ("and by its fruits shall it be known"). If you're in a quandary over what to do, remember that decisions usually make themselves when the time is ready. **SPECIAL GUIDANCE**
Esoteric: Your spiritual development will be resumed, and what was missing will be provided.

KING of WANDS

Ask for assistance or guidance and then follow up on leads, **BEST COURSE**
hunches, or inner promptings. **OF ACTION**

A sacrifice will have to be made because you cannot and will not **OUTCOME**
accept less than the best, or what you know to be intrinsically right.

◆ # THE KING OF WANDS

ARIES (March 21–April 19) **ASTROLOGICAL SIGN**

Ambitious, optimistic, energetic, direct, daring, headstrong, impul- **TYPE OF PERSON**
sive, idealistic, confident, capable; but sometimes self-centered, hot-
tempered, and impatient.

Planning, constructing, developing, building, real estate, or any area **TYPE OF VOCATION**
where leadership qualities are desired, because he/she can work
alone.

The focus is on self-assertion and ambition, business, finance, plan- **FOCUS**
ning, constructing, developing and future unfoldment, contact with
others but standing alone, and/or a person with an Aries-type temperament.

You want to make contact with someone and/or be successful in a **DESIRE**
new business venture.

Problems will cause you to shut down emotionally, but not letting **ROMANCE**
on to what is really going on inside will make the pressure build.
Loosen up and you'll find that love is everywhere.

You're going to be very busy or get several calls for work. **THE UNEXPECTED**

Professionally, you will make many important contacts, but will **OTHERS**
have to wait for things to unfold. Personally, you will be weighted
down with responsibilities and feeling that you have no one to
lighten your load or ease your burdens.

THE HOME

You'll be completely absorbed in projects designed to build, construct, or promote your future or your livelihood, and there will be talks about moving into a new home, or you will get an invitation to stay at someone's home.

TRAVEL

You'll have to leave your home or travel for work, and will get an invitation that involves travel. Accept it . . . you could use a change.

PAPERS

You will be involved with a lot of paperwork and may soon sign a contract or start a new action that will change or alter your life.

WORK/CAREER

Business and finance will take first place and improve, ideas for self-promotion will begin to formulate, and (phone) orders or calls for work will increase.

UNIONS

A new relationship or partnership is about to be established. A marriage proposal could also be indicated.

EMOTIONAL STATE

You will be easily irritated, explosive, or impatient, but that will change because a new vision or romantic opportunity will inspire more confidence or optimism.

PLEASURE

You will enjoy working on a new project, job, or creative idea.

NEWS

You will get a call from a suitor, and a message concerning your work from a business partner; and/or you will hear that you've passed the test, made the grade, or graduated.

FAMILY

There could be some concern about a health problem (but it will be okay) or the sale of a home or property, and if you've experienced problems or feelings of alienation in the past, you're going to have a change of heart.

THE PHYSICAL BODY

You will be watching your health or diet, but may be suffering from tension headaches or lower back aches. You could also begin a new treatment or exercise regime.

FINANCES

You're going to acquire money through new or repeat business contacts, but will want to make more.

TIME

You will make a very important contact and will be looking forward to future unfoldment with this person.

A friend from the past is going to call (someone you recently thought of) and you will also make a new friend.   **FRIENDS**

There will be several business-related calls and news of a delayed or canceled appointment.   **VISITORS/CALLERS**

A mail order or product confirmation will be sent or received.   **MAIL**

You're going to feel that you have no one to lean on for comfort, and nowhere to turn for help or support.   **ANXIETY**

You'll be hurt and disappointed by a friend, loved one, or business associate who has lied to you or played you false.   **DISAPPOINTMENT**

A hope, plan, or "promise" of further unfoldment will not be realized at this time because you won't be ready.   **ENDINGS**

You will face what you have to or the problems contingent thereon, put your chin up, and carry on.   **NEW BEGINNINGS**

Though you will have to be self-reliant, you will have assistance in a time of need.   **INHERITANCE**

You're going to receive a gift (or buy yourself a gift) that you can use in your work, or someone at your job will give you a gift . . . something sweet.   **REWARDS/GIFTS**

Your greatest success will come through new ventures and in your ability to get your concepts across to others. You will also benefit through updating old projects or practices, and through a business that's beginning to show a profit.   **SUCCESS**

You're going to find something that was sought after, like a teaching or teacher. A new love interest could also be indicated.   **FORTUNE**

You'll be grateful for contact with one who's willing to extend himself or herself, who'll provide "means," therapy, or assistance (be it mental, physical, emotional, or spiritual).   **BLESSINGS**

Mundane: Your action, decision, or opinion will be the deciding factor.
Esoteric: If the fruit of the tree is gone, it's time to move on.   **SPECIAL GUIDANCE**

BEST COURSE OF ACTION   Be self-confident, self-reliant, and continue to direct your energy toward your work, research, or ideas, and to any area where leadership qualities are required because that is where your strength lies now.

OUTCOME   You will make contact with people of influence or those you wish to meet or hear from, and will experience gradual expansion and continued unfoldment.

ACE of CUPS.

◆ THE ACE OF CUPS

An Ace marks a fresh start. The Ace of Cups foretells the dawning of a new beginning in emotions, desires, inner experiences, and spirit.

IN A READING

SUMMER (June–July–August)

SEASON

Many 1s indicate that a situation is about to begin or is in the beginning stages.

NUMBER   1

The focus is on affairs concerning the formulation of ideas, love, fresh starts, illumination, inspiration, creative endeavors, pleasure, and satisfaction.

FOCUS

You are searching for clarity or for the truth in a situation where your heart says one thing and your intellect another, and/or you hope an idea will become a reality.

DESIRE

You are going to have a surprise call from an admirer, but not necessarily the one you want to hear from or are attracted to.

ROMANCE

You will be very pleased about the sudden acquisition of a new home or something for the home ... something you wanted or longed for. A surprise from a man could also be indicated.

THE UNEXPECTED

You will be feeling pressured to "perform," or to give more than you are capable of.

OTHERS

You will be analyzing your current relationship with a loved one or admirer, or you will purchase (or get) something you've wanted for a long time.

THE HOME

A profitable or fortunate trip is in store, and you will find something that was sought after, in a way or place you least expect.

TRAVEL

You will be considering a new project (or product) that involves papers ... something connected with your work. You will also ask for and acquire the services of a professional in dealing with a matter concerning papers or documents.

PAPERS

Activity in your work will be renewed. Expect a positive flow of

WORK/CAREER

creative, innovative, or inspired ideas and lots of praise or admiration.

UNIONS

A call, visit, or union with an admirer will bring a refreshing change and a fresh start. A marriage could also be indicated.

EMOTIONAL STATE

Someone or something is going to lift your spirits . . . both personally and professionally.

PLEASURE

Something is going to transpire that you didn't think possible . . . something you want very much.

NEWS

A phone call will clarify a question or concern. You may also hear news of a sudden marriage.

FAMILY

You will get a call from a relative, or visit the home of a relative, in the very near future.

THE PHYSICAL BODY

You will be in excellent condition, mentally, physically, and spiritually.

FINANCES

You will forge ahead in spite of money worries and will begin a new project (or two) that will supplement your income or defray some of your expenses. This could also indicate a pleasant financial surprise and a decision to buy something you couldn't afford before.

TIME

You can expect many positive developments in your finances, love life, and business affairs.

FRIENDS

You will find that you've made a new friend, one who is not only mentally stimulating but kind and generous with his or her help, time, or money as well.

VISITORS/CALLERS

Travel plans will be discussed with a caller.

MAIL

You'll be trying to clear up obscure or ambiguous documents, ledgers, or statements, but will not have much success. More facts are needed. This could also indicate an unexpected letter or payment you'll be pleased about.

ANXIETY

You will be troubled by love or unrequited love, as well as by a product that malfunctions, has to be replaced or repaired, or costs too much to purchase at the present time.

You will be discouraged about something that was said or given (could be unwanted or thoughtless advice), and you will feel used, mistreated, or abandoned by someone you love or care for.

DISAPPOINTMENT

The possibility of seeing your ideas, aspirations, or desires materialize is not going to be realized at this time. However, this is only a temporary condition.

ENDINGS

Happiness and joy will be the order of the day as relationships improve or a wish comes true, because a situation is going to transpire which you never thought would.

NEW BEGINNINGS

Your reactions, moods, or emotions are going to demand analysis. Money coming from work done in the past or a pension plan could also be indicated.

INHERITANCE

A mystery will be solved; or that which was obscured will become clear; or you will get a gift you wanted.

REWARDS/GIFTS

Your best success will come through your creative, inspired, or innovative ideas. This could be anything ranging from books and presentations to the fine arts or useful products.

SUCCESS

You will receive insight, (spiritual) illumination, and an unexpected blessing through a "chance" encounter or disclosure.

FORTUNE

You will be grateful for a fresh inspiration in your work (or a new line of work), renewed creativity, and a new product or fun "toy."

BLESSINGS

Mundane: Your ideas will meet with success.
Esoteric: What you want, wants you, and it's only a matter of time before you get it.

SPECIAL GUIDANCE

Act on new ideas, try new avenues, or say "yes."

BEST COURSE OF ACTION

A heartfelt desire will be realized and you'll be very happy with the outcome of your affairs.

OUTCOME

◆ THE TWO OF CUPS

Many 2s indicate a waiting period where there will be partial success but more to be revealed later. They can also indicate a reconciliation, a reunion, and/or an element of surprise.

Many Cups (three or more) indicate that conditions are felt primarily in the realm of emotion or spirit, but not necessarily as an outward manifestation.

The focus is on relationships, choices of the heart, deep feelings or physical unions, affinity, assistance, support and cooperation, reunions or reconciliations, laughter, joy and pleasure.

You want to be in accord with life and love and/or to resolve problems or estrangements.

There will be no union or total commitment with the one you love or want to be with until you resolve an inner dispute first (like getting clear on what it is that you need and want).

You will hear unexpected good news from or about one you haven't seen in a while and/or gain unlooked-for assistance from influential people or corporate heads in the form of a proposition or proposal that could mean financial gain if you accept.

You will be deeply moved by another, who will display an unexpected act of kindness or chivalry.

You will take a short trip, and/or an admirer will call and want to spend some time with you.

You are going to take a short trip or jaunt and the people you have contact with will be helpful and cooperative. It will be a very pleasant and fruitful journey.

Problems with papers, paperwork, or paper-related projects will be reconciled, amended, or restored to their original condition.

You will want to move out of the proverbial small pond and into the sea, and to reach a larger audience, where visibility or public demand will ensure success.

IN A READING

FOCUS

DESIRE

ROMANCE

THE UNEXPECTED

OTHERS

THE HOME

TRAVEL

PAPERS

WORK/CAREER

UNIONS — Your affections will be torn between two. One is old and one is new and you will have to leave one . . . probably the new.

EMOTIONAL STATE — No matter what you are feeling now, you will soon experience a feeling of great joy, upliftment, love, or concord with another.

PLEASURE — You will enjoy total accord and emotional affinity between yourself and another.

NEWS — Someone will call while you're away or unable to come to the phone and you'll be curious about who it was; or someone will invite you to a celebrated event or special opening.

FAMILY — You will experience love and harmony with your sisters or brothers even if you've had a falling-out in the past.

THE PHYSICAL BODY — You will be concerned about health (your own or someone else's) and will speak to a doctor or nurse; or you will hear of or discuss a malpractice suit or take legal action taken on a personal-injury case.

FINANCES — Money will be coming in through work you like or love or a business partner, and a financial problem that caused you a lot of worry, pain, or aggravation will be resolved or reconciled in a positive way.

TIME — In time, you will back out, refrain, or withdraw from a relationship.

FRIENDS — Expect a reunion (or two) with old friends and loved ones.

VISITORS/CALLERS — You will soon have a very warm reunion, reconciliation, or resolving of arguments with someone you love or care for.

MAIL — You are going to get a love letter, poem, or card.

ANXIETY — You will have problems with business associates and will be troubled by your encounters with them; in matters of the heart, you will fear that things are not going to come together or work out.

DISAPPOINTMENT — You will be disappointed that you were unable to come together with another in a satisfactory or romantic way.

ENDINGS — You will no longer look forward to or plan ahead for the future with another.

When you least expect it, and from a source you least expect, you will be assisted or advanced in your finances, profession, or social life.

NEW BEGINNINGS

You will "inherit" a new possession.

INHERITANCE

A "glamorous" offer or proposal is going to be presented, but it's probably not as good as it seems.

REWARDS/GIFTS

Your success will come through the resolving of arguments or inner conflicts, and in enlisting the aid or support of others in your work or career.

SUCCESS

Luck will be with you in gaining the support of others and in friendships or "passions" beginning or renewing.

FORTUNE

You will be grateful for the care and concern of a newfound friend.

BLESSINGS

Mundane: You will acquire considerable help from others and attain some achievements on your own.
Esoteric: Doubt, fear, or lack of faith can make you turn away from your chosen path. The reason this is so is that you do not trust where you are being led.

SPECIAL GUIDANCE

Communicate your needs, then let go and see what happens.

BEST COURSE OF ACTION

You will be supported in your affairs, and clear up any long-standing debts or "bad feelings," but there will be no union or coming together in a love affair or romantic endeavor at this time.

OUTCOME

◆ THE THREE OF CUPS

Many 3s indicate group activities or situations involving more than one person. They can also indicate delay, but with the promise of future success.

Many Cups (three or more) indicate that conditions are felt primarily in the realm of emotion or spirit, but not necessarily as an outward manifestation.

The focus is on self-improvement, self-healing (nourishment or recovery), self-realization and self-love, social interactions, the effects of others, spiritual awakening, and/or animals or pets.

Since you will be unable to control external conditions, you will realize that you must change internally, and will want to revise your attitude and the way you react or deal with what is happening.

You need to be loved and nurtured, and will want to *be* loving, but need to feel that you are loved and fulfilled first. An empty cup can't quench anyone's thirst.

A personal dilemma is going to work out much quicker and much better than anticipated. An altered-state experience or discussions of marriage could also be indicated.

You'll be oversensitive, overreactive, and overemotional and will feel that no one understands you or really cares. You need to share your feelings and talk about what's bothering you.

Conditions around your home will be upsetting, and if you had planned an outing or made an appointment to see a doctor, you'll change your mind, cancel, or reschedule.

A small outing is in store (or a trip to a doctor or vet), and plans for a family get-together will be confirmed.

You'll be inundated with work that involves researching, organizing, or correlating information and will be antagonistic toward another in conjunction with papers, because his/her actions, words, or deeds will infuriate you.

IN A READING

FOCUS

DESIRE

ROMANCE

THE UNEXPECTED

OTHERS

THE HOME

TRAVEL

PAPERS

WORK/CAREER

Your mind won't be on your work and you will wish you could put it off or take some time off; and you will wonder if you should look for a new line of work . . . something less taxing.

UNIONS

A new beginning will bring great happiness and joy, and problems will be a thing of the past.

EMOTIONAL STATE

You'l be bothered by a conversation with another (could be a close relation) and an unpleasant decision that must be made or communicated.

PLEASURE

Being in the company of others, serving others, or resolving arguments with your friends or family will bring both pleasure and satisfaction.

NEWS

You are going to be upset by a communication breakdown or unsettling conversation with another, but it will be resolved in a happy way.

FAMILY

You're in for a very upsetting or emotionally charged incident where a family member or pet is concerned.

THE PHYSICAL BODY

A period of indulgence, like eating or drinking too much, is indicated. Abuse of pills or alcohol could also be indicated.

FINANCES

Expect to receive payments, checks, or money orders.

TIME

In time, conditions will improve considerably and an animal or pet could be the catalyst that tilts your emotional scales by bringing out your compassionate love nature. Also, a suitor will call and want to spend time with you.

FRIENDS

You will find yourself surrounded by many loving and supportive friends, friends you never thought you had, and you will make many new friends.

VISITORS/CALLERS

You may not know it now, but a friend or admirer is trying to reach you or will call while you're away, and an R.S.V.P. will be required of you.

MAIL

You're going to get some unexpected news regarding a letter, contract, or document that could be a turning point in achieving your goals, and/or you will get tickets in the mail.

You will be overreactive, overindulgent, and overemotional, and could also be troubled by a weight problem. A problem over a pet, or sadness over a cruelty done to an animal could also be indicated.

ANXIETY

You will be very disappointed in the callous, half-hearted, or luke-warm response to something of great importance to you, and in misunderstood words or canceled appointments.

DISAPPOINTMENT

False starts or a sense of alienation from others will come to an end.

ENDINGS

You will experience a renewed feeling of satisfaction about who you are, where you're going, or what you represent.

NEW BEGINNINGS

You will "inherit" something you will like very much.

INHERITANCE

You will have the gift of "grace" in your affairs, and you will buy something for yourself.

REWARDS/GIFTS

Your success will come through friends, social outings or connections and some or all of your expenses will be paid by another.

SUCCESS

You'll be lucky in resolving dilemmas and attaining whatever assistance you want or need. You will also be lucky with wearing apparel.

FORTUNE

You will be relieved about a financial matter or that you were able to sustain yourself thus far, and that light has been shed on an area of great concern that filled you with much fear or apprehension.

BLESSINGS

Mundane: Get clear about what you're striving for or what you want to represent and know the supply will meet the demand. Whatever you choose will be the right choice.
Esoteric: This is a highly impressionable and sensitive time because you're operating on the emotional plane and your body is in tune and susceptible to all kinds of new sensations. But a healing *will* come and a feeling of peace, grace, and gratitude will follow.

SPECIAL GUIDANCE

Be willing to run the risk of failure. Give your ideas a shot and don't allow yourself to be intimidated by others.

BEST COURSE OF ACTION

Great improvements will be made in many areas through your decisive actions, and any strife you may have suffered in the past is going to end.

OUTCOME

THE FOUR OF CUPS

Many 4s indicate fruition or the manifestation of an idea, along with the foundation or "space" where things can grow.

IN A READING

Many Cups (three or more) indicate that conditions are felt primarily in the realm of emotion or spirit, but not necessarily as an outward manifestation.

The focus is on the material aspects of life, such as physical well-being or mortality, and (spiritual) obsessions, desire, want, purpose, ability, and application.

FOCUS

You want or need a job or new source of income, or have an obsessive desire for someone or something.

DESIRE

You'll want your lover and won't be able to stop wanting, and you'll wonder if there's still a chance that you'll get back together and things will work out.

ROMANCE

In the very midst of despair or limbo, something will be offered that you will consider to be a great blessing . . . something related to your work, finances, or love life.

THE UNEXPECTED

In spite of apparent failure or loss, someone's going to help you get what you want, or your ideas will be validated by someone who sees things the way you do.

OTHERS

There will be many things to accomplish. You will also be planning a trip or social call.

THE HOME

You will want to talk to or connect with someone who is out of town, and you soon will.

TRAVEL

You are going to have problems with ledgers, programs, literature, or contracts, and will try to enlist the help of another (or consider legal action) in an effort to get things straightened out or resolved.

PAPERS

Your business will increase and/or a commission, assignment, or offer of employment is on the horizon.

WORK/CAREER

There will either be no union or an unresolved "togetherness" in

UNIONS

your personal affairs; however, business should take a decided turn for the better.

EMOTIONAL STATE   You will feel like a lost soul fighting a lost cause and because of this, you will be unable to find fulfillment in any realm.

PLEASURE   Something will arrive that will bring an avenue of personal or spiritual fulfillment. If you are unemployed and seeking work, this could be a job.

NEWS   You are going to get a call for work.

FAMILY   You will be disheartened by some and supported by others; and a member of your immediate family may soon have to travel.

THE PHYSICAL BODY   You are going to have to let go of a project due to a health or "body" condition, but your health will improve, followed by a change in your mental outlook.

FINANCES   Financial concerns will be dealt with effectively, and you will be very resourceful in acquiring money, means, or sustenance.

TIME   A lucky surprise or turn of fate is in store for you, something very pleasurable that will lift your spirits or change your outlook.

FRIENDS   You have more friends than you know . . . let them in.

VISITORS/CALLERS   A call will bring the solution to a problem or fulfill a deep desire, and you will get a call for work.

MAIL   You will get an unpleasant financial notice (this could be concerning a rent increase), or a very difficult decision will have to be made as a result of a letter.

ANXIETY   You will feel deprived, dissatisfied, and disillusioned because the "things" you wanted out of life have brought you nothing but unhappiness, suffering, grief, or sorrow.

DISAPPOINTMENT   You'll be tired of the world and its hardships and will be at a loss when it comes to dealing with your life because nothing you do seems to work or failure is met at every turn.

ENDINGS   You will put an end to things that serve no purpose or go nowhere.

You are going to have to do some accounting for bills and/or you could go on a shopping spree.

NEW BEGINNINGS

You will "inherit" a positive change in business, finance, or health and/or spiritual guidance or inner rewards.

INHERITANCE

You will receive unexpected assistance in your career area or a call for work.

REWARDS/GIFTS

You are going to get yourself together, clean up your "act," and handle all matters that have been put off or need attention.

SUCCESS

Luck will be with you through your own resourcefulness and you will find that your needs are being answered.

FORTUNE

You will be grateful for the indication of better days to come, heralding the promise of a brighter tomorrow.

BLESSINGS

Mundane: No matter what it looks like now, there is still an avenue for fulfillment.
Esoteric: The Buddha became enlightened only *after* he had done all that he could do and had given up.

SPECIAL GUIDANCE

Take your mind off your work, your lover, or the problem, and do something else. See to your needs first.

BEST COURSE OF ACTION

Some of your material goals will be accomplished, but you will still be "wanting" emotionally.

OUTCOME

◆ THE FIVE OF CUPS

Many 5s indicate change, challenge, and fluctuations (lucky or un- **IN A READING**
lucky). They also indicate material prosperity but spiritual poverty
if not properly balanced or understood.

Many Cups (three or more) indicate that conditions are felt primarily in the realm of emotion or spirit, but not necessarily as an outward manifestation.

The focus is on delays, setbacks, and reassessments; mental, physi- **FOCUS**
cal, or emotional exhaustion. You will be longing for something
interesting to happen, but depressed by obstacles and in no mood
for any further demands.

You want a friend or lover to return, or a *real* relationship based on **DESIRE**
tenderness and mutual enchantment—nothing less. No facsimiles
and no "8 × 10 glossies."

You will seek but not find, and your heart will know that accepting **ROMANCE**
a relationship that is contrary to your nature or being with someone
just to satisfy the urgings of the moment would be an empty victory.

You will be surprised by an unexpected call or meeting with an old **THE UNEXPECTED**
friend or potential lover . . . a very positive encounter.

You will experience a letdown or disappointment, but will have an **OTHERS**
"off" button that will allow you to withdraw from stress rather
than be hurt or emotionally overwhelmed.

You're in for a period of seclusion and/or unavoidable family obli- **THE HOME**
gations.

Travel will be necessary but you won't want to go. **TRAVEL**

Expect delays or setbacks where papers are concerned. Nothing will **PAPERS**
be resolved, settled, or put to rest in your mind.

You will be completely burned out and will want to quit or give up. **WORK/CAREER**
You've done enough and won't want to do anymore.

If married or involved, it will be an unhappy union . . . a union **UNIONS**
without love. You won't want to stick around or contend with it,

but will feel obligated. If single and hoping to meet that someone special, you will not get your wish.

EMOTIONAL STATE   You'll be feeling restless and unhappy due to setbacks, disappointments, or delays, and you won't want to put any more effort into anything.

PLEASURE   The work that you ordinarily love to do will become an unbearable chore and you will be frustrated in other areas as well.

NEWS   You are going to hear very depressing news, and misfortune will befall a friend or loved one and you will hear about it.

FAMILY   You and a relative (or very dear friend) will soon part, and you will be very sad.

THE PHYSICAL BODY   You are going to feel very tired or run down and may also suffer from constipation or hemorrhoids.

FINANCES   You will worry about your finances (every penny will count now) and you'll have to be more assertive or you'll lose out.

TIME   You will try to stay as mentally or emotionally detached as possible.

FRIENDS   You will be discouraged or disheartened by something a friend says or does, and you will soon end a cycle on an outgrown friendship.

VISITORS/CALLERS   A friend or lover will return but you won't be glad because his/her presence, persistence, or drunken behavior will be an imposition or put you off.

MAIL   Expect a delay. That which was expected will not arrive yet, but it will soon.

ANXIETY   You will be troubled by the actions of a friend or lover (or both) and the inability to realize your desires.

DISAPPOINTMENT   You will be sick and tired of problems, obstacles, or delays, and the mere thought of having to do more or putting any more effort into anything will be more than you can bear.

ENDINGS   Your emotional attachment to a situation is going to end.

You will take charge of situations and assume more control or accountability for yourself and your well-being. **NEW BEGINNINGS**

You will "inherit" a valuable lesson. **INHERITANCE**

Instead of asking for payment for services, someone will offer an exchange. **REWARDS/GIFTS**

Your success will come through your own ingenuity and through your ability to apply metaphysical principles to your everyday events. **SUCCESS**

You will suddenly come into more money or money will accrue, and you will have good luck in repairing or replacing damaged objects. **FORTUNE**

You will be grateful for an unexpected gift or service rendered. **BLESSINGS**

Mundane: Something will replace or sublimate the emptiness you feel. **SPECIAL GUIDANCE**
Esoteric: Your desire for the perfect love is in fact a crying out from your very soul to find that which fulfills and rewards you whether there's someone around or not.

Wait until a clear direction is revealed, or what you *really* want arrives. **BEST COURSE OF ACTION**

In time, your desire will be realized and you will know that if someone is to return, he/she will come of his/her own accord. **OUTCOME**

◆ THE SIX OF CUPS

Many 6s indicate adjustments in thoughts, attitudes, or conditions. They also represent the ability to transcend difficulties. **IN A READING**

Many Cups (three or more) indicate that conditions are felt primarily in the realm of emotion or spirit, but not necessarily as an outward manifestation.

The focus is on environmental changes, comings or goings, short trips or jaunts, friends, lovers, relatives, nostalgia, work or employment. **FOCUS**

You are following your own star or listening to your own drummer and have a unique or special wish you want fulfilled, such as phasing something out in favor of another. **DESIRE**

Though you've yearned for only one, you will have a transcendent experience that will open your heart to new possibilities. **ROMANCE**

You will receive support from your boss or superior, a job offer, or an unexpected financial or career opportunity. **THE UNEXPECTED**

Others will lend support and touch your soul, and you will be sought after personally and professionally. **OTHERS**

A relative is going to call from a distance. You will take a short trip or jaunt (could be a shopping trip), and/or a business opportunity will arrive. **THE HOME**

You will have to make many trips back and forth for this reason or that. Also, a friend, relative, or guest will travel to see you, or you will travel to see him/her. **TRAVEL**

Expect good news or a new discovery . . . this could also indicate reward or recognition for literary skills. **PAPERS**

You won't have the strength to keep plodding through with no relief or reward in sight, but a new job or assignment will be presented that will give your spirits a much needed and welcome boost. **WORK/CAREER**

You will long for a future event, but will worry that your plans to unite might fail, or that what you want may not come to pass. **UNIONS**

EMOTIONAL STATE — You will feel very nostalgic as you look back on the past and the way things were.

PLEASURE — You will be pleased about some well-deserved career gratification or unexpected spiritual intervention.

NEWS — You will hear good news from or about a loved one, and also that money will soon be arriving.

FAMILY — There will be much coming and going around the home front, with many departures and arrivals, and a friend or relative you haven't seen in a while is going to call on you.

THE PHYSICAL BODY — You will suffer from health problems or be tired, depressed, or out of alignment with your body, but you will meet your responsibilities or push through it.

FINANCES — You will do well financially and could make more money than you anticipated.

TIME — You will take a short trip, see or hear from an old friend, but will feel nostalgic as you look back over the past and all that has vanished. "You can take the boy out of the country, but you can't take the country out of the boy."

FRIENDS — You are going to get an unexpected offer of love and support from a friend or loved one, but another will soon leave your life and you will be very sad or lonely without him/her.

VISITORS/CALLERS — There will soon be a gathering with family and friends which may also include a love interest from the past.

MAIL — You will be annoyed by a letter or payment. This could pertain to money that should have arrived but didn't. Expect another disappointment.

ANXIETY — You will be doubting your ability to succeed in the work or profession you have chosen and all of its related areas.

DISAPPOINTMENT — You'll be disappointed because you won't be able to manifest your desires as soon as you would have liked or hoped.

A business problem will be solved but a compromise will have to be made. **ENDINGS**

Though you will be surrounded by that which will be satisfying, you will not be fulfilled or content and your heart will cry out for that which will quell your loneliness or fill the void. **NEW BEGINNINGS**

You will inherit the ability to transcend difficulties or problems and an attitude that frees you from wanting what you can't yet have. **INHERITANCE**

A loving word, gift or gesture on your part, or on the part of another, will be given. **REWARDS/GIFTS**

You will get some very rewarding news, as well as assistance, acknowledgment, and/or recognition in your career. And, if you are a writer, you will achieve success in publishing or literary fields. **SUCCESS**

You are going to be in the right place at the right time and before your very eyes a prayer will be answered or a wish granted. **FORTUNE**

You will be grateful for the solution to a problem, answer to a need, or opportunity to promote your business, and for the fact that things turned out better than you expected. **BLESSINGS**

Mundane: Happiness can come from many sources, whether it's one you've named or not. God works in mysterious ways. **SPECIAL GUIDANCE**
Esoteric: Just because no one sees things the way you do, or things don't appear to be working out, don't think that "this is real" and God (or the miraculous) is not. Cultivate a habit of applying your metaphysical knowledge to your everyday experiences by turning within instead of barricading the Infinite with stress, and It will become more real to you.

Relax and let ideas come and go. When the right one comes, you'll know it. **BEST COURSE OF ACTION**

Things are going to work out better than you anticipated, and an unexpected twist of fate will be a turning point for you in the attainment of your goal. **OUTCOME**

◆   THE SEVEN OF CUPS

Many 7s denote a period of introspection or solitude. They also indicate unlooked-for advantages or gain through things that come unexpectedly.

Many Cups (three or more) indicate that conditions are felt primarily in the realm of emotion or spirit, but not necessarily as an outward manifestation.

The focus is on the search for truth, gut-wrenching experiences, and life-altering events related to your family, friends, work, or love; feelings of powerlessness, inadequacy, or confusion; cosmic contact, spiritual experience.

You wish things weren't so hard and/or want to become less emotional or reactive, and to be able to throw off or cut off anyone or anything that could elicit a negative emotional response.

You will experience a lot of vacillation in matters of the heart, and will be looking for the right approach or the right mate. Or, you will have so many other things on your mind that love will be the furthest thing from it.

Someone who doesn't follow through as anticipated is going to create a sudden change of plans, or you will be surprised by an uplifting message from a corporate head or superior.

Someone is going to cause you to reevaluate a situation you had planned to go ahead with and to rearrange your plans . . . what to do?

You are going to make a resolution or compromise, and will have to give something up in favor of, or to make room for, another. This could be concerning a major purchase, or a choice between family and the one you love.

You will be trying to decide which course to take or where to go, and if you drive, drive carefully and defensively or an accident could occur.

PAPERS
You will be sorting things out effectively, getting things down in writing, and a confusing issue will be resolved. This could also indicate legal papers transferred or the commencing of a law suit.

WORK/CAREER
Your life may feel so empty that there will be nothing to do *but* your work, and at times even that will be unrewarding.

UNIONS
If you don't unite or marry at this time, a new element will make the future look more promising.

EMOTIONAL STATE
You will feel uncentered, confused and unstable, alone and introspective.

PLEASURE
Business is going to take an upward swing and you will enjoy being productive and reaping returns on investments or new enterprises.

NEWS
You are going to hear some distressing news that will make you very introspective.

FAMILY
You will want to escape from responsibilities and emotional turmoil and may seek outside counsel.

THE PHYSICAL BODY
You will suffer from anxiety attacks, or will have problems with your legs, and if you consult a doctor, tests, X-rays, more treatment, or surgery will be suggested, but a rest would do wonders.

FINANCES
There will be small gains in your finances and a bank statement, account, or error to attend to, but it will get corrected.

TIME
In time, tensions will ease off, productivity will increase, and things will become easier or more comprehensible.

FRIENDS
Your friends will boost your enthusiasm for your work or come up with new business ideas and their positive outlook will be contagious.

VISITORS/CALLERS
Your hope for one to call is a false hope and you will be disappointed when he/she doesn't.

MAIL
You will have to write a letter or make a call in order to get something you want or need . . . this could be concerning a product.

ANXIETY
You will feel that the thing you want most is light years away from being obtained (if even possible), and that you have no power whatsoever to make any changes or create miracles.

You will be disappointed in the fact that there is no love or money in your life.

DISAPPOINTMENT

Searching, seeking, questioning, or wanting will come to an end.

ENDINGS

Your faith in an idea or project will be rudely shattered, and you will feel as if you're losing all control. You won't know what to do and will want to take flight in order to escape, but won't be able to make any clear-cut decisions.

NEW BEGINNINGS

Something is going to come along that will make the way easier . . . like more information or insight into your situation.

INHERITANCE

A debt will be paid, and there will be money in the mail or news that you will soon be receiving some.

REWARDS/GIFTS

You won't feel capable of mastering the steps it takes to succeed, but someone or something will come along that will help you or make your way easier.

SUCCESS

You are going to be rescued from a life-or-death situation . . . a very traumatic experience.

FORTUNE

You will be grateful for the intervention of one who has your welfare at heart.

BLESSINGS

Mundane: Don't let conditions, appearances, or what others have to say sway you or cause you to veer from your ideal. What you want is right under your nose, just waiting to be discovered.
Esoteric: Don't alienate yourself from life-giving forces. God dwells in you *as* you and in everyone and everything else.

SPECIAL GUIDANCE

Be thankful for all that you *do* have or that which you have been given and steer clear of negative thoughts or influences. Allowing for weakness can be disastrous in that it will undermine all the work you've done.

BEST COURSE OF ACTION

You will put things together in your mind and come to a final synthesis or resolution which will bring a deep feeling of gratitude or contentment.

OUTCOME

THE EIGHT OF CUPS

Many 8s indicate a positive change of mind or status because the beneficial qualities of the number 8 are rarely diluted.

IN A READING

Many Cups (three or more) indicate that conditions are felt primarily in the realm of emotion or spirit, but not necessarily as an outward manifestation.

The focus is on recently completed projects, relationships or ideals that have gone as far as they can go, and the desire to move on or do something else.

FOCUS

You don't understand the situation you're in or why things are the way they are, and want to know if there's anyone "up there" who's listening or cares.

DESIRE

You can expect a stress-free but unfulfilling rendezvous (no fireworks). If however, your relationship already exists, pent-up pressure or negativity may create feelings of alienation or cause it to sour.

ROMANCE

You will experience an event which will change your perspective entirely . . . a change for the better caused by a friend, lover, or associate who enters your personal life or business world. This could also be due to a sudden windfall.

THE UNEXPECTED

You will enjoy the company of others and will want to make a positive impact on them, or to aid, assist, or comfort; and they will feel the same about you.

OTHERS

A trip may have to be postponed due to someone's tardiness, or an illness in the family, and you will soon travel for health reasons or to visit with a good friend.

THE HOME

You will take a drive or go on an outing with a lover or admirer, but in the process will realize that your relationship has no future, or can go no further because it doesn't "push your buttons," or it just isn't right for you.

TRAVEL

A favor involving papers will be offered.

PAPERS

WORK/CAREER — Your business will expand or your skills will be sought after or in demand, but there will also be a personal loss.

UNIONS — You will make a decision to end a personal relationship, to finish it, end cycle, and move on . . . a friend, yes, but a lover or lifetime partner, no.

EMOTIONAL STATE — You'll be dismayed at the turn of events that seems to sabotage your best intentions, but in the final analysis, things will turn around and peace will be restored.

PLEASURE — You will enjoy clothes, furnishings, new products, or outings with friends.

NEWS — News will arrive which will cause you to look at alternatives where living quarters are concerned, and/or an awaited call will finally come.

FAMILY — You will do a favor for a friend or relative who is planning to travel, or you will make tentative plans to get together.

THE PHYSICAL BODY — You will have problems with your eyes like an inflammation, irritant, blurred vision, or infection, but a soft-tissue problem or fungus infection could also be indicated.

FINANCES — You will be feeling the lack of money and will literally pray for it to come in, and every time you turn around, another expense comes up.

TIME — You are going to get the ball rolling on a new venture that could be very rewarding, but you will still be missing that significant other in your personal life.

FRIENDS — Expect to hear some good news from a friend or relative who'll be in a better frame of mind due to a sudden improvement in his/her love life or livelihood.

VISITORS/CALLERS — A short trip or jaunt will ensue because of a call or caller (could be from a lover); or an admirer will call and want to spend some time with you.

MAIL — Papers will be completed and ready to distribute or mail; and/or someone will offer to give you a mailing list.

You'll be concerned about your future, your love life, your finances, **ANXIETY**
and whether a business project will succeed or fail.

Things are not going to be as easy as you thought, or go according **DISAPPOINTMENT**
to the plans you made, but conditions will take a turn for the better
or prove to be a lucky break.

Money troubles, relating problems, or obstacles to unions will be **ENDINGS**
overcome.

You will embark on a new project, training program, or money- **NEW BEGINNINGS**
making enterprise.

You will "inherit" the opportunity to learn or implement something **INHERITANCE**
new.

You will soon give or receive a gift of gold . . . something that **REWARDS/GIFTS**
hangs.

Your success will come through a fortunate adjustment in a financial **SUCCESS**
matter or a successful litigation or lawsuit, and also through keeping
your emotions on an even keel.

Luck will be with you in the arrival of money or a long-awaited **FORTUNE**
financial settlement.

You will be thankful for a new career direction. **BLESSINGS**

Mundane: Whether you see it or not, you're being given the oppor- **SPECIAL GUIDANCE**
tunity to rise above your instinctive or habitual response patterns,
and if you make a conscious attempt to do so, they will lose their
grip on you.
Esoteric: Be still and let it be okay with you that what's happening
is beyond your present understanding. It's only in the stillness that
we hear our answers, receive direction, or commune with God.

Learn how to establish a link between yourself and God for times **BEST COURSE**
of crisis and make an effort to remember your metaphysical princi- **OF ACTION**
ple. One way to do this is to still the questions or "whys" in your
mind and just *trust*.

Things are going to end on a positive note and you will find yourself **OUTCOME**
moving in a new direction.

◆   THE NINE OF CUPS

Many 9s mean that situations or events are nearing completion or have just been completed and another plateau awaits.   **IN A READING**

Many Cups (three or more) indicate that conditions are felt primarily in the realm of emotion or spirit, but not necessarily as an outward manifestation.

The focus is on highly charged emotional events related to personal affairs and material well-being, such as love, career, food, shelter, security, or health.   **FOCUS**

You want personal fulfillment or gratification and to "keep the faith" in the ultimate workings of good, despite appearances to the contrary.   **DESIRE**

You will want the same things as before, but with a different partner or in a different way. It can't be the same as it has been . . . it must be better.   **ROMANCE**

A chance meeting or phone call is going to bring unexpected good fortune or financial gain.   **THE UNEXPECTED**

You will be disappointed in someone's actions, and will feel pressured by the problems of others.   **OTHERS**

You will be making plans to travel or considering a trip, but may postpone it till a later date because something better will come up.   **THE HOME**

You will have an unexpected diversion in your original plans and will go on a business trip as well as a shopping trip.   **TRAVEL**

You or someone in your family is going to have problems with leasing agreements, finalizing a deal, or closing an escrow; and/or you will write a resumé, work bid, or presentation.   **PAPERS**

Your work will start off bright, then turn dark, and then bright again. Don't worry, after a slight reversal you'll see material gain or a good outcome.   **WORK/CAREER**

You will be weighing the pros and cons of a relationship or partner-   **UNIONS** ship, but will be unable to reach a definitive decision (even though you want it) because of the risks involved.

EMOTIONAL STATE
You will experience a sense of emotional starvation which will get progressively worse, and you will distrust yourself, your decisions, or your future.

PLEASURE
You will enjoy the "things" that life has to offer—food, clothes, furnishings, or luxuries—and will be appeased or gratified by sensual or emotional pleasures.

NEWS
You will be wishing a particular person would call, and someone else does.

FAMILY
An emotional issue concerning the care or treatment of another will be discussed.

THE PHYSICAL BODY
You will be an emotional wreck or will have bouts with insomnia or troubled sleep.

FINANCES
Money that was promised or anticipated will be delayed, but should arrive shortly.

TIME
The future will begin to look hopeless because you can't see a way of improving your situation, selling your idea, or getting yourself established, but a new reality is just around the corner.

FRIENDS
A friend will call with exciting news about your work, finances, or a proposed endeavor; or you will call him/her.

VISITORS/CALLERS
Your wish for someone to call will be fulfilled but delayed; and, someone will call with an open-house invitation.

MAIL
If you were expecting a letter, package, or payment from someone, it will be delayed. However, a small amount of money may arrive from an unexpected source.

ANXIETY
You will be troubled by your future, your livelihood, or a complete lack of personal fulfillment or emotional gratification.

DISAPPOINTMENT
You will feel used, mistreated, or taken for granted by someone you love or care for.

You will no longer hope for personal fulfillment and will feel as if all doors are barred and you have inherited a big share of nothing. You will feel like a lost soul, fighting a lost cause. **ENDINGS**

Your energy will be transferred into areas that can provide fulfillment, and you will be surrounded by love and affection. **NEW BEGINNINGS**

You will "inherit" an advantageous meeting or conversation, happiness, satisfaction, and a feeling of accomplishment. **INHERITANCE**

You will receive gratitude, love, and support from others; or, you will prepare a gift for a friend who is away, something very generous. **REWARDS/GIFTS**

You will have success in attaining what you want, but it may take another form than that which you now envision, and/or you will be satisfied with what you've attained or accomplished. **SUCCESS**

Luck will be with you in getting your wish and making a successful barter or trade. **FORTUNE**

You'll be grateful for the material comforts that you have. **BLESSINGS**

Mundane: The past is not a barometer, so don't resign yourself to "that's the way it is, and it will never change." Anything is possible. *Esoteric:* There are no mistakes in the Universe and all things work for good. **SPECIAL GUIDANCE**

Withhold judgment for now, and don't make premature evaluations. **BEST COURSE OF ACTION**

Your wish will be realized, but only after you thought it wouldn't be, and the form or way in which it will be fulfilled will probably change. **OUTCOME**

◆ THE TEN OF CUPS

Tens are read the same as a number 1. However, they also signify a cyclical rebeginning, and a time when you must come to terms with something you may have avoided in the past.

IN A READING

Many Cups (three or more) indicate that conditions are felt primarily in the realm of emotion or spirit, but not necessarily as an outward manifestation.

The focus is on impromptu departures from home, fleeing from boring or dreary responsibilities, rest and relaxation from work or worry, and unusual or unconventional relationships.

FOCUS

You want a fulfilling and rewarding relationship and/or the support of others.

DESIRE

"Emotion will rock the ocean" in a very unusual love affair.

ROMANCE

You are going to get a surprise from a lover . . . could be an old flame who will reenter your life.

THE UNEXPECTED

Others will be friendly, sociable, or flirtatious and you will love being with them.

OTHERS

You will be contemplating a departure from home or your work, and will think that anything would be better than what you're doing or where you are now.

THE HOME

A very pleasant or relaxing trip is on the horizon.

TRAVEL

Something is going to enter the picture that will make your work a lot easier (like a new idea or program); or, if you've been hoping to get out of a contract, or binding agreement, someone or something will provide the means for you to do just that.

PAPERS

There will be correspondence connected with your work that will involve mail, phone calls, or special application.

WORK/CAREER

A budding romance or renewed love bond will evoke great feelings of love or devotion. If single, this could indicate a marriage if other cards support it.

UNIONS

EMOTIONAL STATE   At times you will be emotional or moody, but for the most part, adaptable and flexible.

PLEASURE   You will enjoy socializing with your friends or family, freeing yourself from "the cares of the world," and/or a sudden departure from home to a new environment.

NEWS   You can expect to make or receive a long-distance phone call, and many messages from your friends or relatives.

FAMILY   You will get a long-distance call from a relative, or you will make one.

THE PHYSICAL BODY   You will be subject to erratic eating or sleeping habits and/or sexual preferences. But if you've been ill, you will soon recover.

FINANCES   Money matters will be in a state of "delicate" balance, but prospects look as if they're improving, and you will enjoy spending money on others or doing for others, and may pick up someone's tab . . . or he/she will pick up yours.

TIME   In time, you will meet and talk with many people who will encourage you and help you to build more confidence in yourself or in the work you are doing.

FRIENDS   Expect a long-distance call from a friend or relative, and a good friend or loved one will soon be moving away or leaving your life . . . this could be due to a marriage.

VISITORS/CALLERS   An admirer will call or arrive, but you could be too wrapped up in your work or projects to exchange or reciprocate social amenities.

MAIL   You will get a letter or postcard from a friend or relative who's been abroad or lives in another city, or you will write a letter(s) in an attempt to encourage the support of another or to sell your work.

ANXIETY   Your troubles will stem from having too many responsibilities or irons in the fire, and feeling that there's no help or visible means of support in sight.

DISAPPOINTMENT   A frustrating attempt or aborted plan will cause a disappointment, but in no time at all, the situation will reverse itself.

A negative or disagreeable situation is going to come to an end. **ENDINGS**

Something is going to arise which will take your mind off things, or **NEW BEGINNINGS** help you to relax—something pleasurable or entertaining like an artistic project, social excursion, or trip away from home.

You will "inherit" sustenance, support, and full cooperation in all **INHERITANCE** of your affairs.

You will want to give to others and they will want to give to you. **REWARDS/GIFTS** Gifts of the heart can be the greatest gifts of all.

Your best success will come through travel, love, and pleasurable **SUCCESS** pursuits.

You will have luck in obtaining freedom from responsibilities. **FORTUNE**

You will be grateful for a helping hand in your affairs, for supply or **BLESSINGS** support from others, and/or that someone who's been ill has recovered.

Mundane: It's not going to be easy, but keep trying and you'll **SPECIAL GUIDANCE** succeed.
Esoteric: Your relationships are a direct reflection of your relationship with yourself, or the way you view your relationship with God. It follows then that if you want your relationships to improve, you must first improve your relationship with yourself. When you trust yourself, you are trusting God.

Trust a little more. **BEST COURSE OF ACTION**

You will gain the support of others and be visualizing ideas in order **OUTCOME** to mold a new future, and your wish for fulfillment or a successful outcome will be granted.

PAGE of CUPS.

THE PAGE OF CUPS

PISCES (February 19–March 20)

ASTROLOGICAL SIGN

Impressionable, reflective, sensitive, emotional, vulnerable, warm, loving, romantic, talkative, imaginative, intuitive, psychic, youthful, and sometimes flaky.

TYPE OF PERSON

Institutions, self-help organizations, occultist, poet, dancer, set decorator, make-up artist, wardrobe head, or anything that deals with illusion. Works best behind the scenes, or finishes what others start.

TYPE OF VOCATION

The focus is on unfoldment or expansion, yearning and discernment, meetings, discussions, and work-related projects for the future, and/or a person with a Piscean-type temperament.

FOCUS

You want things to come together (be it in business, health, and love or mind, body, and soul) and are anxious for the future to take shape.

DESIRE

You will be anxious about how things will turn out in the future but hope they will . . . however, involvement will be slow.

ROMANCE

You are going to receive a calm answer in an emotional storm, and get a call from an admirer.

THE UNEXPECTED

Other people will cause you to reexamine your objectives and what you want out of life, and romance could find you at your work . . . a very intriguing possibility.

OTHERS

You'll be looking for answers and trying to sort things out, and your routine will undergo a sudden and "fortunate" change. But, don't press any issues regarding money, rent, or property or you could be forced to move.

THE HOME

A journey will bring a new discovery but it may be a costly trip.

TRAVEL

You will find it to be a very slow, difficult, and unrewarding process if you try to bring matters to a head or resolve anything at this point.

PAPERS

WORK/CAREER — You will want to get on with your work but will be feeling boxed in because some basic need or element must first be fulfilled.

UNIONS — You will be driven by a need for love and companionship—the great love—because without it you'll feel like you're just going through the motions, and that is a very empty feeling.

EMOTIONAL STATE — You will feel very impressionable or sensitive, and will be struggling to assert yourself.

PLEASURE — A happier and more relaxed personal life is in store for you, as well as an increase in social activities and the entry of an ardent sweetheart or lover.

NEWS — Expect communications and messages of all kinds—business, social, and personal—and a long-distance phone call.

FAMILY — You will be fed up with one of your relatives who wants you to be his/her panacea, while another will be immensely enjoyable.

THE PHYSICAL BODY — You'll be very impressionable and may experience an emotional drain as a result. Problems with your feet, knees, or legs could also be indicated.

FINANCES — You'll be grateful for money received from your work, and that you can afford to buy whatever you want or need (within reason, of course).

TIME — Your work environment will take a distressing turn due to disturbing influences, unforeseen obstacles, or the attitudes of others, but this is only a temporary condition, and you will soon expand into even greater areas.

FRIENDS — You are going to get an invitation from a friend or admirer.

VISITORS/CALLERS — You will be taking new and decisive action with a call or caller which will solve a long-term problem.

MAIL — You are going to get a "no" answer by phone or through the mail, or you will hear that one who concerns you has decided not to pay or commit.

You will be troubled by situations that are very confusing or impossible to resolve, or by an uncomfortable personal encounter.

ANXIETY

You will be disappointed in your inability to find a solution to a business or personal problem, or in yourself for shirking your responsibilities or duties.

DISAPPOINTMENT

A long-term problem is going to be solved, but other conditions will still be up in the air.

ENDINGS

You'll offer your services to others and seek to aid those who could benefit from your experience; or you'll be on the verge of saying "yes" to a major venture or project.

NEW BEGINNINGS

You will soon "inherit" a new program or project for your future, and will also be in a position where you can express yourself and meet those of the opposite sex who are like-minded or on the same path as you.

INHERITANCE

You are going to find the perfect answer to a problem that's been plaguing you. You will also experience an "overshadowing," or sense of peace or calm, and will expand into more areas of work.

REWARDS/GIFTS

You'll succeed in work that's done behind the scenes and in any self-help or self-discovery area, and your best success will come through your ability to take decisive action, solve problems, and get positive responses or assistance from others.

SUCCESS

You will have luck in finding the right answers or making the right decisions.

FORTUNE

You're going to receive an answer to a problem or obtain that which was sought after.

BLESSINGS

Mundane: Don't bite off more than you can chew in your passion to go forward or you'll find things hard to swallow. The time is not right and you're not ready or fully prepared.
Esoteric: Don't think you're alone or that you're not being helped. It's fear and impatience that blinds you from the truth or deafens your receptivity to the spirit. When it no longer serves your growth to not know something, you will know.

SPECIAL GUIDANCE

KNIGHT of CUPS.

Clearly define what you want or hope to accomplish, and if you can't get it by yourself or do it alone, ask for assistance. **BEST COURSE OF ACTION**

The form your wish will take has yet to be materialized and so, at this point, situations will still be unresolved. **OUTCOME**

◆ THE KNIGHT OF CUPS

There is no astrological sign associated with the Knights because they indicate situations that are coming in or going out. **IN A READING**

When a Knight appears in a reading, a long-term condition will suddenly change.

The focus is on good friends, social occasions, and opportunities to travel or get away from the home environment or to advance through education or public relations, and on branching out into new worlds. **FOCUS**

You want something so badly, you think it will come to pass if you close your eyes to the possibility of defeat and hope for the best. You may also want to change your residence. **DESIRE**

A new element or flight to a different environment will ease existing tensions or loneliness. **ROMANCE**

You will be surprised by a sudden flirtation, seduction, or romantic interlude. **THE UNEXPECTED**

Others will make you think of love, or stimulate you mentally, emotionally, or physically. **OTHERS**

If you are contemplating a change of residence, you will not make a move now, and if something goes wrong around the house, you will probably try to fix it yourself. Also, watch out for small accidents around the house . . . pay attention. **THE HOME**

TRAVEL — You will have to make many short trips or jaunts, but they will be happy ones. Or, you will spend some time in the home of a relative; perhaps to take care of someone or something while he or she is gone.

PAPERS — Expect a delivery; and/or you will sign a release form.

WORK/CAREER — You are going to receive some important news and/or a decision will be made affecting your livelihood. This also indicates a happy, supportive, and nurturing atmosphere in your working environment.

UNIONS — If single, a marriage, union, or living arrangement will be proposed. A new business partnership will also be in the works.

EMOTIONAL STATE — You will have an overwhelming feeling of good, or that something good is about to happen.

PLEASURE — A new environment, project, or opportunity will offer a vacation from monotony and lift your spirits.

NEWS — A social invitation will arrive and corporate business will be discussed over the phone.

FAMILY — Your relatives will be on the move, taking up a new study or form of education or spending time away from home.

THE PHYSICAL BODY — Problems will be kept under control or cured. Don't be intimidated by doctors.

FINANCES — Expect positive changes in your financial affairs, as well as lucky breaks and cost cuts; and, if you call on those who owe you money, you will get a swift reply in the affirmative.

TIME — You will see no point in dwelling on an existing business or relationship problem, and will pull yourself out of it by directing your energies elsewhere.

FRIENDS — You will get an invitation or proposition from a friend. This also indicates happiness and camaraderie.

VISITORS/CALLERS — Expect a business proposition or social invitation soon.

You are going to receive a letter or document that will necessitate a financial decision, and/or you will be busy with forms or promotional material that can advance you in your field. **MAIL**

You will feel that you've made the wrong choice in a partnership, even though it seemed to be the right choice at the time . . . and the only option. **ANXIETY**

You will be unhappy due to unfulfilled desires. **DISAPPOINTMENT**

A business partnership or source of income through a partnership will end. **ENDINGS**

An opportunity will come to the fore in your business or personal affairs that will allow you to branch out into new and untried areas. **NEW BEGINNINGS**

You will inherit a "bridge over troubled water," or a lucky break in a financial matter. **INHERITANCE**

Someone is going to invite you to lunch or dinner. **REWARDS/GIFTS**

Your best success will come through short trips or pleasurable pursuits, and being able to tap into a sustaining power that can quell a crisis or guide you in a time of need. **SUCCESS**

You are going to receive a tip, invitation, or proposition that will prove to be lucky for you. **FORTUNE**

You will be glad that you, as well as others, are nearing your goals and things are looking up for all. **BLESSINGS**

Mundane: You will be advancing toward your goals. Expect positive changes because things are looking up.
Esoteric: Asking "why this and not that" stems from lack of faith. Pretend that you have faith and faith will be given. **SPECIAL GUIDANCE**

Leave your home environment (go alone if necessary) and accept invitations or proposals, because they will pan out later. Also, make a decision about what you want, and don't allow others to pressure you. Follow your hunches. **BEST COURSE OF ACTION**

You can expect a fresh start and a new level of experience. **OUTCOME**

◆　THE QUEEN OF CUPS

SCORPIO (October 23–November 21)

ASTROLOGICAL SIGN

Spiritual, psychic, clairvoyant, magnetic, intense, secretive, sexual, deep, complex, removed, in control, and at times overpowering or aloof.

TYPE OF PERSON

Occult work, undercover work, physician, stockbroker, acupuncturist, dentist, counselor, dramatic actor.

TYPE OF VOCATION

The focus is on books, research, study, or the occult, trying to get an idea across to others, resolution or results, the home and personal property, magnetism, attraction, romance, and/or a person with a Scorpio-type temperament.

FOCUS

You want the work you do to mean something or to have value for others and/or you want to enlist the aid of another.

DESIRE

Many social opportunities will come your way and/or someone will enter your life in whom you will be very interested (a professional-type person) and you will meet this person very close to your home, if not outside your front door.

ROMANCE

You will be unprepared for the adverse conditions and unexpected opposition, disputes, or discord that you will encounter in your home or work environment.

THE UNEXPECTED

In business, people will not respond favorably or accept what you have to offer or sell. However, they will respond very favorably in the friendship or romantic department.

OTHERS

Your home or work environment will be very discordant. This could be because of noise, children, and/or a guest who overstays his/her welcome. And if your question concerns the sale of a home or property, it will not be sold at this time.

THE HOME

If you had planned a trip or outing, something will come up that will cause you to rearrange your plans, rethink them, or postpone the trip for the time being.

TRAVEL

PAPERS   You will experience one problem after another with things involving papers, and will be unable to enlist the help of others.

WORK/CAREER   Some type of metaphysical, psychic, or clairvoyant skill will be required in the work that you do, and/or you will have the opportunity to branch out into new and different areas.

UNIONS   There will be discussions about a union, merger, or marriage and you will be very willful about what you want. You may even initiate the action toward getting it, or make the proposal yourself.

EMOTIONAL STATE   You will tend to scatter your forces (or you will feel scattered), but being around others will be good therapy.

PLEASURE   You will enjoy social or metaphysical interests, being in the company of others and being admired or sought after personally and/or professionally.

NEWS   Expect more messages and invitations than usual . . . some of which will be very uplifting.

FAMILY   You are going to experience problems on the home front. Better keep your attitude in check so you won't get sucked into an emotional storm or a situation you'd rather not be in.

THE PHYSICAL BODY   You will be upset, depressed, or under a lot of emotional strain. You may also be losing weight and/or have to go to the doctor.

FINANCES   You will attract money, favors, assistance, or leverage.

TIME   You will be looking hard for answers and in time will receive the guidance that you need. You are also going to hear a positive prediction regarding your future.

FRIENDS   A new friend will teach you, guide you, help you, train you, or enlighten you.

VISITORS/CALLERS   You are not going to see eye to eye with those who call or those you call, and will be unable to connect at a satisfactory level.

MAIL   Expect many letters, calls, or messages concerning your work . . . good fortune and progress.

You will be worried about the success of your work, because results are inconclusive or you're not aware of the whole situation or seeing the entire picture. A discordant home or business environment could also be indicated.

ANXIETY

Agents, publishers, buyers, or sellers will prove to be a disappointment.

DISAPPOINTMENT

You're going to realize that you won't be able to enlist the aid of the one you hoped would help you . . . someone you'd counted on.

ENDINGS

You will attract a lot of attention, be sought after both personally and professionally, and become all things to all people.

NEW BEGINNINGS

You will "inherit" further discussions or application, help on a project, or assistance in solving a breakdown or problem, and also the arrival of someone who thinks they can market your idea or sell your product.

INHERITANCE

Someone may give you a gift of money or clothing; you will receive the answer to a problem through a sudden inspiration; or you will be blessed with the ability to see into the future.

REWARDS/GIFTS

Your greatest success will come through your ability to make a favorable impression on others, thus attracting gifts, favors, special consideration, or advantage.

SUCCESS

You will have luck in finding answers, attracting favors, and attaining gifts or advantages.

FORTUNE

You will be grateful for a cut in expenses (maybe medical), for the speedy delivery of money or something purchased, and for a romantic introduction or opportunity.

BLESSINGS

Mundane: People might not get your concepts or see things the way you do, but you won't be left out in the cold. Someone will come to your aid or give you the opportunity to utilize some of your skills or talents.
Esoteric: There's a tremendous spiritual force present which is causing your inner hearing to increase. In time, what you couldn't see before will be clearly and explicitly revealed.

SPECIAL GUIDANCE

KING of CUPS.

Use your "charm," persuasion, and whatever resource that's available, and then let the Cosmic Forces direct your course or reveal that which is hidden. In time, you will see that your prayers have been answered.

BEST COURSE OF ACTION

You are going to have invisible help or guidance in your work or affairs but agents or go-betweens will prove to be a disappointment, and something will come up to keep your wish about, or union with, another from materializing at this time.

OUTCOME

◆ # THE KING OF CUPS

CANCER (June 21–July 22)

ASTROLOGICAL SIGN

Emotional, moody, changeable, testing, home-loving, kind, considerate, focusing, worrying, cranky, and sometimes crabby.

TYPE OF PERSON

Doctor, minister, priest, metaphysician, cook, restaurant owner, astronaut, homemaker. There's more emphasis on home life than business life, but can become well connected with big business and will get help or support if needed or requested.

TYPE OF VOCATION

The focus is on activities centering around the home or a business that you can do out of your home, financial independence; daydreaming about love and romance, and/or a person with a Cancerian type of temperament.

FOCUS

You want someone to spend time with, make love to, or share your life with; and/or to be self-sustaining or solvent in the work you've chosen to do.

DESIRE

You will be in a romantic or flirtatious mood, and life will offer several opportunities for romance, but those who try to exercise a claim will have to compete with stiff competition . . . your work and your "ideal" lover.

ROMANCE

THE UNEXPECTED   Someone is going to seek you out (and may come right to your door) who will inquire about you or your services.

OTHERS   You will suddenly find yourself in a position to promote yourself or something you do, but will run into unexpected obstacles due to the lack of consent or interest expressed by another.

THE HOME   Something new is about to be established that is going to change your outlook . . . something good. This could be news from or the arrival of a lover.

TRAVEL   Your car will be in need of maintenance or repairs (like an oil change, lube job, or tune-up), and you may soon visit someone in his/her home or travel to a new home.

PAPERS   You will put off most of your paperwork until later because it's getting too complicated or not working out the way you want and you won't want to contend with it. However, contract negotiations will go smoothly or contain a pleasant surprise.

WORK/CAREER   You will want to make it on your own, be financially independent, own your own business, or work out of your home, and a new direction or course of action is going to be proposed that will encourage that wish.

UNIONS   You may feel as if you are being mistreated, or you will be looking for a way out of a relationship.

EMOTIONAL STATE   You will have many emotional swings, and will be daydreaming about love and romance.

PLEASURE   You'll enjoy a warm emotional exchange with a loved one.

NEWS   You'll have discussions about an idea, project, or enterprise that could bring in new money and/or a talk about a business or residential move.

FAMILY   Your relatives will be experiencing emotional difficulties due to their partners or financial condition, and may discuss the possibility of moving or coming to live with you . . . or vice versa.

You will feel ill and cranky and will fear the worst, so you will indulge yourself by eating and drinking too much. A visit with or news from someone in the medical profession could also be indicated.

THE PHYSICAL BODY

Money will be acquired from a business of your own or business done out of your home. Be sure to handle financial negotiations and business transactions *before* you get started, or misunderstandings will arise.

FINANCES

Someone will seek you out or arrive unexpectedly, and things will look much brighter on all horizons. Also, new arrangements will be made that will be good for all concerned.

TIME

Expect to get a call from an old friend or lover . . . someone who cares for you a great deal and will show you or tell you so.

FRIENDS

A professional call is indicated and a family event is in store.

VISITORS/CALLERS

Letters will come in (or go out) from spiritual, metaphysical, or health-type organizations.

MAIL

You will be distraught over the lack of support you feel you are getting, or because of the emotional burden you have to carry with your family, friends, or loved ones.

ANXIETY

You will be disheartened by unfulfilled romantic desires . . . close but no cigar!

DISAPPOINTMENT

A disagreeable situation and a negative emotional condition are going to come to an end.

ENDINGS

Problems in the home or with your family will begin to ease off, but your desire for love and romance will increase.

NEW BEGINNINGS

You are going to find a new direction, line of work, or occupational outlet, something that will augment your talents or advance your position.

INHERITANCE

An admirer will call and tell you he/she has something for you.

REWARDS/GIFTS

Your success will come through exercising your personal integrity,

SUCCESS

having the courage to ask for what you want, and receiving a positive response or "go-ahead" in reply to a business query or financial matter.

FORTUNE

You are going to find something you want or need right "in your own back yard."

BLESSINGS

You will be grateful for the food on your table, the clothes on your back, and a feeling of self-worth or accomplishment for work well done.

SPECIAL GUIDANCE

Mundane: What you want or need will come to you, and you will be provided for.

Esoteric: Unfortunately, the work you're in insulates or alienates you from social involvement. However, you can rise above your emotional limitations by remembering that God is your source and works through many channels and in many ways. Open your mind to the possibility of a new beginning.

BEST COURSE OF ACTION

Don't let your desire color what is. Refuse to accept less than what is correct in people or to settle for what is "so-so." A sow's ear dressed up to look like a silk purse is still a sow's ear. Put your ideas to the test.

OUTCOME

Business will take an upward swing, new projects will be in the making, and if your "significant other" has yet to appear, you will know that there's a Divine Order sustaining your fundamental needs, and the time is drawing near.

THE
SUIT
OF
SWORDS

ACE of SWORDS.

◆ THE ACE OF SWORDS

An Ace marks a fresh start. The Ace of Swords foretells the dawning of a period of action, movement, or struggle.

IN A READING

WINTER (December–January–February)

SEASON

Many 1s indicate that a situation is about to begin or is in the beginning stages.

NUMBER 1

The focus is on a period of pressure, tension, anxiety, and explosive situations related to correspondence, communications, and responses from others.

FOCUS

You want career satisfaction, recognition, or personal gratification.

DESIRE

You will get an unexpected message, call, or response from someone who has a crush on you or loves you. This could also indicate a new love that will take you by storm.

ROMANCE

A declaration of love or affection is coming your way. This could also indicate an unsolicited kiss!

THE UNEXPECTED

All of your friends or loved ones will be tense or under some kind of strain, and their behavior will intensify the pressures you already feel.

OTHERS

Someone will call on you or come to see you. This could be an admirer, or it could be an emissary from a company that will change your ideas or plans about the future.

THE HOME

You will be contemplating a move to a new area or state and/or may have to change or rearrange your plans because of a "must-go" or "must-do" trip.

TRAVEL

Expect good news regarding papers or concerning a new enterprise that involves papers.

PAPERS

Someone is going to express an interest in the work that you do or have done . . . they could also express an interest in you.

WORK/CAREER

Strong emotions will be brought out by a business or romantic involvement; and, a marriage or partnership could be on the rocks.

UNIONS

EMOTIONAL STATE   You'll experience frustration and tense conditions, but you will be determined not to let it fluster you, so it won't last for long.

PLEASURE   You will enjoy working with new ideas and creative projects and developing new concepts. Also reading or writing.

NEWS   Expect to hear a voice from out of your past, and good news about your work or career.

FAMILY   Conditions around the home front will be very tense and communication taut because everyone will be under some kind of pressure . . . so much so that you will want to pack your bags and never return.

THE PHYSICAL BODY   You'll be extremely tense but determined to correct deficiencies, and some new action will be taken in an effort to better your condition or diagnose the problem.

FINANCES   Expect tension related to financial affairs or money matters; your income will be nominal and/or you will be sick and tired of hearing "The check is in the mail."

TIME   You will be strangely detached from the problems of yesterday and balance will be restored in every area of your life.

FRIENDS   You will talk with or meet with friends, and one of them will help you with a very important project.

VISITORS/CALLERS   You are going to get an unexpected phone call from an unexpected source—someone you had forgotten about or given up hope on. This could be a lover and/or a business emissary who will speak or act in your behalf.

MAIL   There will be a slight setback concerning a letter because of an unforeseen difficulty or misunderstanding on the part of another.

ANXIETY   You will be extremely touchy or edgy about an idea, venture, or product and will fly off the handle at the slightest provocation.

DISAPPOINTMENT   You will be distressed by a problematical home life and bad news concerning your finances or career. This could be as a result of unfair competition, or because someone can't afford to pay you or wrote you a bad check.

You're going to say good-bye to pressure, tension, and anxiety and hello to satisfaction, emotional fulfillment, and increased popularity!

ENDINGS

You will make the decision to act on, or move into, a less problematical environment or situation, and to let a business problem ride rather than forcing the issue.

NEW BEGINNINGS

You will "inherit" the opportunity to expand your business and improve your finances.

INHERITANCE

You will purchase a gift for a friend or relative.

REWARDS/GIFTS

You are going to be acknowledged for your work, skills, and ability; and if you need someone to help you get a project rolling, help will come.

SUCCESS

A new career direction will arrive and good fortune will come through a friend or admirer.

FORTUNE

You are going to be grateful for the support and confirmation you get from others . . . a significant vote of approval for your efforts.

BLESSINGS

Mundane: You are going to get what you want.
Esoteric: Despite apparent odds, you're on a course that's so strong, it's destined to succeed. Nothing can halt or divert you.

SPECIAL GUIDANCE

Have faith in yourself and know that your work is good and stands on its own. Persevere, be determined, and let nothing divert you from having what you want.

BEST COURSE OF ACTION

Tensions will ease off and you will have a renewed sense of clarity about yourself and the world around you. You will also experience career satisfaction, recognition, and improved financial conditions.

OUTCOME

THE TWO OF SWORDS

Many 2s indicate a waiting period where there will be partial success but more to be revealed later. They can also indicate a reconciliation, a reunion, and/or an element of surprise. **IN A READING**

Many Swords (three or more) predict tremendous activity, agitation, or acceleration, because Swords show the last stages of effort before the final result.

The focus is on moving ahead with anticipation in spite of fear, doubt, or confusion; making decisions; and aligning yourself with supportive or responsive friends. **FOCUS**

You want to move ahead without restriction, and want a lover or romance. **DESIRE**

The unexpected is going to happen . . . a new romance or potential love affair with one who is extremely charming, comforting, or well-to-do. **ROMANCE**

You are going to find something you thought was lost or impossible to acquire. This could be an actual object, or it could be a person who enters your life, likes you or your work, and wants to assist you. **THE UNEXPECTED**

You will help others with their problems, but will feel that you are being drained, are in need of a "transfusion," and could use a little help and support yourself! **OTHERS**

A decision will be made soon and/or surprising news could lead to an unexpected trip. Be ready to move quickly. You may also be considering a major purchase. **THE HOME**

Expect some contradictions or an unexpected event or occurrence to arise over travel plans. **TRAVEL**

Mediocrity will be replaced by perfection, and an unexpected problem will prove to be a blessing, because the solution will supersede the original concept. **PAPERS**

WORK/CAREER   Expect a surprise or an unusual event, and a new idea will be acted on that will go exceptionally well.

UNIONS   A proposal will be made and accepted.

EMOTIONAL STATE   Your emotions will be a mixture of confusion, excitement, worry, and hope.

PLEASURE   You will be pleasantly surprised when your work brings an opportunity to mix business with pleasure, or a dinner invitation from an admirer arrives.

NEWS   A surprising letter or message will spread a "magic carpet" over difficulties.

FAMILY   You will make an agreement with a relative and/or if you have been at odds, will reconcile your differences or declare a truce.

THE PHYSICAL BODY   At times you will have great surges of energy, but at other times have to fight to keep your energy level up, and if you don't watch your health during the low-energy periods, you will contract a flu virus.

FINANCES   You will be concerned about an investment or business partnership and will wonder if you should force the issue, or if the problem will get resolved on its own.

TIME   There is going to be a temporary delay in your plans because of unforeseen obstacles, and you will be forced to make some changes in your game plan before you can go on.

FRIENDS   Expect a surprise meeting or encounter that will benefit you personally or financially. This could happen where you work or even when you're out with another.

VISITORS/CALLERS   A caller will arrive bearing gifts.

MAIL   Don't expect to receive much mail, and what you do get will be mostly bills.

ANXIETY   You'll have mixed emotions regarding a personal relationship or business associate and the "kinks" that need to be ironed out before you can move ahead in good conscience or progress can be resumed.

You will think that you will never have that someone special, or that love will pass you by, or that if you sever a relationship in favor of another, you could wind up losing them both. **DISAPPOINTMENT**

Troubles or disputes are going to end and an ironic twist is in store . . . you will find that you want what you didn't want before. **ENDINGS**

You will find that most of your worries were completely unfounded. **NEW BEGINNINGS**

Someone will come into your life who is willing to help you with what you want to get across or sell, and your business or profits will take an upward swing. **INHERITANCE**

Someone is going to help you get something you wanted or facilitate the success of a project or endeavor. **REWARDS/GIFTS**

You will be successful in implementing new ideas, motivating or helping those in need, and attracting the romantic advances or an admirer or two. **SUCCESS**

You will be lucky in romance or will benefit through chance meetings or encounters. **FORTUNE**

You will be thankful for help, assistance, and/or backing on a (new) project or venture. **BLESSINGS**

Mundane: Expect a surprise in your business and personal affairs . . . the past is on its way out and a new element is about to emerge that will make the old way obsolete.
Esoteric: Everything in the universe follows a natural rhythm and order just as day follows night and harvest follows fallow. Your time for harvest is drawing near and when that time comes, a new spirit of enthusiasm will reign. **SPECIAL GUIDANCE**

Allow others to help you and don't be afraid to take a chance. **BEST COURSE OF ACTION**

Some success will be attained but some obstacles will still remain. **OUTCOME**

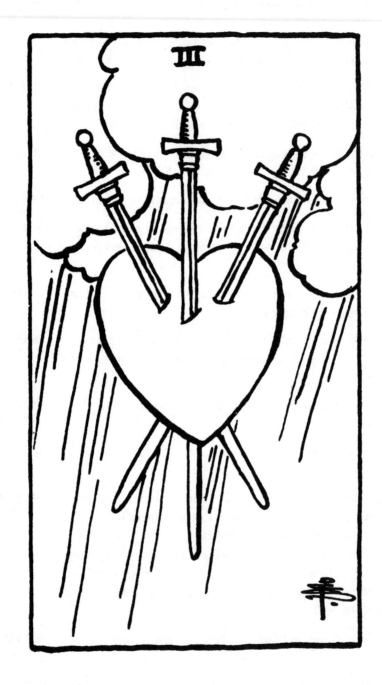

THE THREE OF SWORDS

Many 3s indicate group activities or situations involving more than one person. They can also indicate delay, but with the promise of future success.

IN A READING

Many Swords (three or more) predict tremendous activity, agitation, or acceleration, because Swords show the last stages of effort before the final result.

The focus is on personal relationships, business delays, and exterior influences; and on strife, adversity, separations and disappointment, followed by restructuring, rebuilding, and renewing.

FOCUS

You want your lover to come back; or you have run out of hope or stamina and need to see results before you can get out of the doldrums or start something new.

DESIRE

Because you have experienced suffering and heartache in the past, you may not be willing to extend yourself now.

ROMANCE

You are going to be very surprised by the appearance of someone you didn't expect to see or hear from. This will be a very positive development.

THE UNEXPECTED

You will be hurt, impatient, or angry with your friends and distraught about your love life, but that is going to change.

OTHERS

You will be "fixing up," improving, or reconstructing your home or things around the home.

THE HOME

A trip is going to establish something better. However, if traveling with a companion, ill health may befall one of you.

TRAVEL

You will have many problems with papers because you won't see the results you'd hoped to see or be able to enlist the aid of buyers, sellers, or agents, but in time that will change and setbacks will turn out in your favor.

PAPERS

A business proposal or the possibility of a new avenue to pursue or follow up on will soon be presented, but you won't leap at the idea.

WORK/CAREER

UNIONS

You may *think* that all is lost or that your relationship is over, but you are going to have a change of heart.

EMOTIONAL STATE

You will be unhappy or in a state of turmoil over your relationships, love life, or problems in the home, but that condition will not last much longer.

PLEASURE

No matter what you have felt or are presently feeling, you will soon establish something much better . . . you can also expect a surprising twist in your business or love life.

NEWS

You will have to confront an unpleasant issue with a friend (could be over travel plans), or lie to get out of an invitation or engagement.

FAMILY

Someone in your family may be in pain, and/or will *be* a pain because they ask too much of you or are continually asking for something.

THE PHYSICAL BODY

You need a vacation from tension, work, and worries and will soon take one. Tears, sadness, sickness, or physical pain are also indicated.

FINANCES

You will soon receive money that was held up or delayed, and/or financial gain will come through time investments, speculations, or a well-thought-out plan of action.

TIME

Expect a complete change. Negative conditions or delays will clear up and a new order will be established . . . something much better.

FRIENDS

You will feel the need to break out of a restricting problem (or attitude) and to overcome the fear of confrontation in order to establish a better or easier relationship.

VISITORS/CALLERS

You will not connect with the one you love or want to be with at this time, but you will later on.

MAIL

A letter, package, or card you've been waiting for, or a letter containing money, will arrive.

ANXIETY

You will be upset about faulty household equipment, lost checks or payments, and not being able to connect with the one you want to see or get the thing you want the most . . . like personal fulfillment or assistance in your work.

You will feel that what you cherished most is gone forever and that it will never return or be recovered. **DISAPPOINTMENT**

The hope that someday things will get better will end and you will feel that everything you want is completely out of reach or that what you want the most is never going to happen. **ENDINGS**

Whether you like it or not, changes will have to be made, but you will get what you need and what looked like a defeat or lost cause will be the dawning of something better. **NEW BEGINNINGS**

You will "inherit" a gift of love or affection . . . this could be something home-made. **INHERITANCE**

You will be "awarded" a fresh start in business or romantic affairs. **REWARDS/GIFTS**

Your best success will come through venturing away from your original goals, plans, or ideas and developing new ones. **SUCCESS**

You will be lucky in repairing or rebuilding something that had been damaged, or unexpectedly connecting with someone you thought was a "lost cause" or gone for good. **FORTUNE**

You will thank God for the establishment of something better in your life or affairs after you thought that all was lost. **BLESSINGS**

Mundane: Abortive attempts or delays are in your favor. New ideas or actions will replace old ones, and something better will be established that could not have happened otherwise. **SPECIAL GUIDANCE**
Esoteric: Surrender that which is painful or obsolete and let God make changes or resurrect the situation.

Don't panic, fly off the handle, or do something rash . . . this experience is only temporary. **BEST COURSE OF ACTION**

You will salvage what you can, but things will not yet be completed or resolved. **OUTCOME**

THE FOUR OF SWORDS

Many 4s indicate fruition or the manifestation of an idea, along with the foundation or "space" where things can grow.

IN A READING

Many Swords (three or more) predict tremendous activity, agitation, or acceleration, because Swords show the last stages of effort before the final result.

The focus is on *activity,* with special emphasis on printed materials such as letters, papers, and graphs, as well as money matters, social affairs, self-promotion, and starting or renewing a business of your own.

FOCUS

You want desires to be fulfilled and/or want spiritual support or transformation.

DESIRE

You will experience a feeling of being "cut off" or "out of touch," but your determination to overcome negative conditions will win out.

ROMANCE

You will be surprised by someone who calls, asks you out, or strikes your fancy. An encounter with someone who is in the news media, police department, or legal field could also be indicated.

THE UNEXPECTED

You will be looking for a way to handle a situation that seems unjust, unfair, or not right, but people you conduct business with will be encouraging or eager to extend themselves.

OTHERS

You'll be immersed in your work, and someone you didn't expect to hear from is going to call, like an admirer who's a voice from out of the past. This could also indicate a call from the law or someone in a legal profession.

THE HOME

You will be discussing travel plans. Better to put them off, as they will cause unhappiness.

TRAVEL

After a brief respite, a past project will be renewed and there will be important documents to attend to. Work involving printing, drafting, graphics, or books is also indicated.

PAPERS

WORK/CAREER   Your work environment will be very unpleasant due to tension you can cut with a knife.

UNIONS   You will feel that your partner's not holding up his or her end, participating enough, or willing to sustain the relationship by applying effort toward maintaining it.

EMOTIONAL STATE   No matter what you have suffered in the past, you'll be on purpose again, and your hope and determination will be renewed.

PLEASURE   You will be very happy because something you wanted will be given, or someone you wanted to see will arrive.

NEWS   You can expect lots of calls, messages, and communications, but this could also indicate discussions of sickness, death, or misfortune.

FAMILY   You will want to help or make amends with your family, but are at the end of your rope. A death could also be indicated if other cards or categories support it.

THE PHYSICAL BODY   Your health will be in need of repair, and medical attention or treatment will be needed.

FINANCES   You are going to have an upset or dispute over finances and/or money will be very slow in coming, but in time your worries will be over.

TIME   Whatever has been (or is) troubling you is not going to last. You will soon have a change of heart . . . a happy change.

FRIENDS   You are going to experience some form of displeasure due to a remark or comment made by a friend or relative.

VISITORS/CALLERS   Someone will call and want to see you . . . someone from out of your past. This could be a lover, someone who is married, or someone who is involved with the law or legal profession.

MAIL   You will be involved with business papers, letters, or mail; and if you mail a letter to a company, it will respond in kind.

ANXIETY   Your involvement with the law, an official-type person, or someone who's married will cause much anxiety.

You will feel mistreated, let down, or cheated by life, circumstances, or a lover and fear that you will never get "your share of the pie." **DISAPPOINTMENT**

Something you imagined would be the case is not going to transpire . . . something regarding a planned activity connected with your work, travel, or romance. **ENDINGS**

You will experience frustration, anger, or tears resulting from un-fulfilled desires or insurmountable difficulties, but that condition will not last long. **NEW BEGINNINGS**

You will "inherit" renewed or increased activity in business and social affairs. **INHERITANCE**

A small gift will be given and the person who receives it will be very glad. **REWARDS/GIFTS**

You are going to "have your way" and/or gain the help or support of others. You will also be successful in attracting love or romance. **SUCCESS**

You will have luck in obtaining the thing you worried about or asked for. **FORTUNE**

You are going to receive an answer to a prayer. **BLESSINGS**

Mundane: You will get what you want.
Esoteric: Your affairs are in accord with Heaven. **SPECIAL GUIDANCE**

Pray or ask for what is rightfully yours and continue to apply your-self to the work at hand. **BEST COURSE OF ACTION**

You will need a rest before any further activity can be resumed. **OUTCOME**

◆ THE FIVE OF SWORDS

Many 5s indicate change, challenge and fluctuations (lucky or un- **IN A READING**
lucky). They also indicate material prosperity but spiritual poverty
if not properly balanced or understood.

Many Swords (three or more) predict tremendous activity, agitation,
or acceleration, because Swords show the last stages of effort before
the final result.

The focus is on unforeseen problems, conflicts, and defeats which **FOCUS**
cause a depressed or distressed turn of mind. You won't feel like
expending energy on superficialities and will be frustrated in work,
love, and health.

You will feel that there are more obstacles ahead, and won't want **DESIRE**
to face the ordeal you know you must if you are to have what you
want.

You will be longing for love, but will not be willing to "sell your **ROMANCE**
soul" to get it.

You won't be prepared for the inner (or outer) struggle you'll have **THE UNEXPECTED**
with yourself after a decided course of action is taken.

You'll want to be gregarious, but you won't be able to fulfill that **OTHERS**
wish because you'll be so stifled by all the things you don't want in
your life that you'll withdraw or just want to be left alone.

If you intend to revamp something in your home or purchase some- **THE HOME**
thing for your home, you'll run into problems. Either it won't be
right, delivery will be delayed, or it will cost more than expected.
Some dismal weather is also indicated.

You will be irritated in your travels, or will have problems with cars **TRAVEL**
or transportation.

Papers, letters, or printed material will only provide partial answers. **PAPERS**
More work will have to be done before they're completed to your
satisfaction, results can be seen, or conclusions drawn.

WORK/CAREER — Things will not go as well as they should, and you will have conflicts or clashes of will with others or people in business will infuriate you.

UNIONS — You will experience regret, nostalgia, and remorse over unfulfilled dreams or promises.

EMOTIONAL STATE — Other people who promise and then fail to deliver will cause great unhappiness or bitter disappointment.

PLEASURE — You will be pleased about your success in a new venture and a surprise call from a lover or admirer.

NEWS — You will hear of some misfortune befalling a friend or loved one, and some rather depressing news for you.

FAMILY — A relative will do a favor for you or give you something you want. Or, if there is a question concerning a medical test, the outcome will be favorable.

THE PHYSICAL BODY — You will be troubled by a recurring illness or physical problem, and taking medication or vitamins, but more treatment or rest will be necessary and, unfortunately, the problem may never go away completely.

FINANCES — You will be self-sufficient, financially solvent, and able to sustain yourself on your earnings or income, but you will still be fearful about your finances and your future security.

TIME — In time, things will let up and you will be more relaxed about your situation.

FRIENDS — You will be frustrated over the constant effort it takes to deal with your friends or romantic relationships.

VISITORS/CALLERS — Expect the unexpected where callers are concerned.

MAIL — You will have work to get out or letters to mail, but a health problem will cause a delay.

ANXIETY — You will be troubled by doctors or a health condition that needs attention, and by machinery or electrical appliances.

You will get little or no help, understanding, or compassion from others, just added pressure, frustration, or responsibilities, and you will have to wait much longer than you should have or were promised.

DISAPPOINTMENT

A negative condition or attitude is going to end.

ENDINGS

In spite of everything, you will confront issues head on and tackle every "crisis" one by one.

NEW BEGINNINGS

You will have to be utterly self-reliant.

INHERITANCE

You will have to return, exchange, or add something to a product because it won't be right or the way you want it.

REWARDS/GIFTS

You will be successful in getting something you've wanted for a long time and rather than your having to go after it, it will come to you. You will also find that your predictions about a situation concerning another were accurate.

SUCCESS

You will feel unlucky or thwarted.

FORTUNE

You'll be grateful for proof that your efforts have been effective and your faith in the Universe has been restored.

BLESSINGS

Mundane: You're in for a struggle and there will be more work or problems ahead than you're aware of now.
Esoteric: If God wants you to do something, He will give you the desire for it and the power to do it.

SPECIAL GUIDANCE

Consider the source and avoid dwelling on the negative side of things. Don't allow an inconsistent or indecisive attitude to get the upper hand. Use positive affirmations and count your "wins," no matter how small.

BEST COURSE OF ACTION

The outcome will be one of conquest and defeat; you will succeed in some areas but not in others, and while you may get what you want, it may not be the way you want it.

OUTCOME

◆ THE SIX OF SWORDS

Many 6s indicate adjustments in thoughts, attitudes, or conditions. **IN A READING**
They also represent the ability to transcend difficulties.

Many Swords (three or more) predict tremendous activity, agitation, or acceleration, because Swords show the last stages of effort before the final result.

The focus is on evaluations or opinions and obstacles or problems **FOCUS**
related to public or professional people, career goals, and working relationships.

You are having problems with relationships, partnerships, or per- **DESIRE**
sonal property and want them to be resolved.

A promising situation will turn out to be a disappointment. Expect **ROMANCE**
a delay, or more of what you don't want.

A debilitating illness, a business disagreement, or an emotional issue **THE UNEXPECTED**
will cause a loss of employment or earnings.

You will encounter many disturbing events which you will be unable **OTHERS**
to exert any influence over, and because of this, you will be left to your own devices and will have to master the situation internally.

Expect problems, setbacks, and some rethinking. Also, something **THE HOME**
broken, disconnected, or not functioning correctly will need to be repaired. If you are considering a move or a new home, you will have second thoughts.

A short trip will change things for the better, and you will soon **TRAVEL**
travel for health reasons.

You may need to revise a document, and/or a conflict over papers **PAPERS**
could sever a working relationship if you don't keep your cool.

You will have an upsetting confrontation or argument at work or **WORK/CAREER**
related to your work with an employer, competitor, or someone you conduct business with. It will be adjusted or resolved, however.

UNIONS

You will not go ahead with an intended partnership or consummate a merger because you're going to go with a different partner.

EMOTIONAL STATE

You will be sick and tired of problems, complications, and things not going the way you want them to, and will make a concerted effort to focus your attention on the now and to forget about the future *and* the past.

PLEASURE

You will restructure your thinking and find a sense of solitary satisfaction, self-worth, or well-being.

NEWS

You're going to have a conversation concerning a loss of some kind (this could be financial) . . . something important.

FAMILY

Problems with your family will remain but the tension will resolve.

THE PHYSICAL BODY

Ill health will befall you, and you will suffer from stomach problems, headaches, or a more serious illness; or, problems with medical or insurance papers will arise.

FINANCES

You'll make a pittance as far as money goes, and will have a tough time making or collecting money that is owed or due, but through a fortunate turn of events, you'll have enough to pay your immediate bills and will make more money sooner than you think.

TIME

In time you will reap many rewards (especially material), and your work environment will vastly improve.

FRIENDS

You are going to establish new and better relationships with your friends even if you've had a falling-out in the past.

VISITORS/CALLERS

Expect a disappointment, a postponement, or a cancelation of plans; also, someone you'd rather not hear from is going to call.

MAIL

You'll have to make a call or write a letter in order to get what you want or need, and/or you will be angry because someone has failed to deliver what was promised.

ANXIETY

You will be troubled by business problems and unfulfilling, unrewarding, or disappointing relationships.

DISAPPOINTMENT

You'll be dismayed or disappointed in your personal relationships because the road to success was not as smooth as you hoped it would be.

A major problem or obstacle related to your work or personal affairs is about to be resolved. You can't see it coming, but it's very near.

ENDINGS

A negative period will end, a new partnership will be established, and you will be involved in a new project or enterprise where both parties are in accord.

NEW BEGINNINGS

A situation will look very promising and your goal almost in sight, but there will be more problems to deal with before the results you want will be realized.

INHERITANCE

A gift will have to be returned or exchanged, and/or you will do a service for another or receive a compliment or display of affection.

REWARDS/GIFTS

You will find it very hard to succeed or virtually impossible to pursue your goals at this point in time, and co-workers or others could make your environment rather unpleasant.

SUCCESS

Your timing will be excellent and you will acquire something that will relieve your tensions or correct for losses.

FORTUNE

You will be grateful for the arrival or realization of a new platform for future endeavors.

BLESSINGS

Mundane: The first step in correcting a problem is to acknowledge the fact that you have veered off your course or are moving in the wrong direction. That recognition is enough to stop the momentum from continuing.
Esoteric: Your pain could be an indication that you are healing. On the physical plane, when one has surgery the next step is recovery, which can be just as painful. When the spiritual or emotional body undergoes "surgery," the healing process is much the same.

SPECIAL GUIDANCE

The problem is not going to go away of its own accord. You must alter your stance or take action to resolve it.

BEST COURSE OF ACTION

You will do some rethinking but in the end, will decide to pass on, withdraw from, or sever a partnership.

OUTCOME

THE SEVEN OF SWORDS

Many 7s denote a period of introspection or solitude. They also indicate unlooked-for advantages or gain through things that come unexpectedly. **IN A READING**

Many Swords (three or more) predict tremendous activity, agitation, or acceleration, because Swords show the last stages of effort before the final result.

The focus is on attempts, efforts, uncertain or unstable conditions, introspection, analysis, perfection, priorities, self-protection, family members, partners, and health. **FOCUS**

You want someone to call or come by, to correct a problem area, and/or to get away from work or responsibilities. **DESIRE**

An admirer will want to see you and will phone or come to call. **ROMANCE**

You will be surprised by an unexpected reunion or the sudden appearance of an old friend, lover, or business associate. **THE UNEXPECTED**

You will enjoy the company of others and will be happy to be spending time with them. **OTHERS**

You will be trying to put things in perspective or perfect an idea but will have problems trying to establish priorities, meet scheduled plans, or follow through with a course of action. **THE HOME**

There will be tension related to travel plans, cars, or schedules, and you may have to travel alone. **TRAVEL**

There will be much paperwork to do, but don't rush or you'll make a mistake or miss significant information. Also, changes can be costly, so make sure they're worth it. **PAPERS**

You will want to get away from your work but it will keep pulling you back. **WORK/CAREER**

No matter how much you want someone or something, you will do without it before you will put yourself in a compromising position. **UNIONS**

EMOTIONAL STATE   Your plans will not go smoothly and you'll be under a lot of pressure trying to perfect things, correct them, or put them in order because you're taking on more than you're capable of, or prepared for.

PLEASURE   A surreptitious advantage is coming your way (in your finances or love life) that will put a smile on your face and a song in your heart.

NEWS   You will attempt to reach someone but he/she will be out of touch or his/her phone will be disconnected.

FAMILY   You may struggle, argue, or sometimes be at odds with your family, but deep down, you love them very much and will have their welfare at heart.

THE PHYSICAL BODY   You could be experiencing problems with your breasts, and trying to accomplish too much will result in tension aches and pains. Stop, or head problems could result. A rest and/or a muscle relaxer would greatly help.

FINANCES   You will experience anxiety over the receipt of money or a check thought lost, but it will shortly be recovered. An unexpected financial gain could also be indicated.

TIME   In time you will conclude matters successfully, and take time off to rest and relax.

FRIENDS   A friend will help you to overcome whatever problem is plaguing you by steering you in the right direction; or, a friend from out of state will call.

VISITORS/CALLERS   A message or caller is going to elicit an antsy or giddy feeling and conflicts will arise over time slots, schedules, appointments, or meetings.

MAIL   A health letter, legal notice, or bureaucratic "reminder" will irritate you.

ANXIETY   Striving for perfection and trying to establish priorities, meet deadlines, or keep appointments will be a constant source of aggravation for you.

You will be upset with or disappointed in a business associate, partner, or friend who will let you down.

DISAPPOINTMENT

A business partnership, labor dispute, or conflict with employees, partners, or associates will be resolved amicably.

ENDINGS

You'll begin to see things as they really are in terms of objectives and establish a precedent; and, if you have been working too hard, you will take some time off for R and R.

NEW BEGINNINGS

You will "inherit" an invitation to an event. This could be a spiritual event.

INHERITANCE

An unexpected advantage or gain is coming your way (this may be acquired surreptitiously, however), and someone will present you with a gift of wine or food.

REWARDS/GIFTS

You're going to have unexpected financial gains, and your good judgment and ability to establish correct priorities will prove to be successful.

SUCCESS

You'll be lucky in establishing better conditions. Finding bargains and getting gifts and good fortune will come through business affairs, social activities, and unexpected events.

FORTUNE

You are going to be grateful for an unexpected financial gain or surreptitious advantage.

BLESSINGS

Mundane: Things are going to clear up and work out.
Esoteric: Perfection is a concept that was derived from something you decided was "good" or "right," and what you're doing now is being compared to that decision. But in reality, perfection is nothing but an idea.

SPECIAL GUIDANCE

Maintain mental or emotional balance, keep things in their proper perspective, and take things slow and easy. If you're having a problem, don't struggle with it; take time off, or just drop it for now.

BEST COURSE OF ACTION

A friend, lover, or new alliance will be very beneficial to your life, your work, or your career.

OUTCOME

◆   THE EIGHT OF SWORDS

Many 8s indicate a positive change of mind or status because the beneficial qualities of the number 8 are rarely diluted.

IN A READING

Many Swords (three or more) predict tremendous activity, agitation, or acceleration, because Swords show the last stages of effort before the final result.

The focus is on withdrawal, imprisonment, "endarkenment," restriction or oppression, handicaps, accidents, health problems, danger, hardship, deadlock, or limbo.

FOCUS

You want to get out of an oppressive situation or change your present line of work.

DESIRE

You will be feeling restricted or boxed in but are actually in a protective (spiritual) box so you won't be diverted from your higher purposes.

ROMANCE

You will be caught off guard by many unexpected problems and sudden handicaps; but, on the positive side, if you want to sell your home or property, you will.

THE UNEXPECTED

You will feel limited, restricted, or immobilized by others and as a result, will experience many hardships.

OTHERS

You will entertain a lover or admirer or both.

THE HOME

Transportation activities will include an unexpected financial break; or, a beneficial trip is in the offing.

TRAVEL

Circumstances will warrant the abandonment of a project involving papers for the time being because you won't feel like pursuing it, or you won't be able to.

PAPERS

You may take some sick leave, or "blow out" of an unpleasant job or work situation; or, you could change your mind about taking a job you really didn't want anyway but felt you had to because of financial considerations.

WORK/CAREER

You will be afforded the opportunity to regenerate in a different environment (or with a different partner) and because of this, will

UNIONS

experience a positive change of mind or status, and will no longer feel restricted, bound, or imprisoned.

EMOTIONAL STATE   You'll feel trapped in a negative cycle of events and will worry that the future holds more of the same.

PLEASURE   There will be many surprising developments in your social affairs; and romance will inspire several exciting (if elusive) moments.

NEWS   A situation will arise creating conflict or uncertainty about an issue you thought you had handled, or hoped was resolved; but don't worry, it will work out.

FAMILY   Some of your relatives will be oppressive, but you will enjoy the company or conversation of other family members.

THE PHYSICAL BODY   Watch your health, be very careful of accidents around the home or in your car, and be especially cautious of electrical gadgets, sharp objects, and other drivers.

FINANCES   You'll be feeling stuck or strapped and will want to make more money, because even though you've got it to spend, the supply is decreasing. Don't worry; it will be made up, even if you've had problems getting it in the past.

TIME   In time you will overcome oppression, or prisons of the heart or mind, and a new area of relaxation or emotional fulfillment will come to the fore.

FRIENDS   You will want to escape from an oppressive or abusive personality and probably will. Choose your friends wisely, and use more discrimination.

VISITORS/CALLERS   You will be upset over a call or caller and will wish he/she had never called.

MAIL   A letter (or news) you've been waiting for is going to arrive.

ANXIETY   You will worry that you're in a negative or "bad luck" cycle that may never end and you will be hesitant to embark on anything new for fear that it too will be tainted.

Handicaps, deficiencies, or misfortune caused by others and being forced to accept conditions that are not of your choosing are going to cause a great deal of mental, physical, or emotional distress.

DISAPPOINTMENT

Trouble in personal relationships will end, followed by a change of heart. Someone will find that when given the freedom he or she wanted, he or she won't want it after all.

ENDINGS

New freedom will be found through the resolving of restrictive conditions, or getting out of an oppressive commitment.

NEW BEGINNINGS

You will get a business referral or a lucky break in a legal matter; or, financial gain will come through an investment or profit sharing.

INHERITANCE

You will be "given" the power to overcome unfortunate circumstances . . . don't worry.

REWARDS/GIFTS

You will escape from oppressive situations and have unexpected gains in business or finance.

SUCCESS

A new venture, purchase order, or business opportunity will come right to your door.

FORTUNE

You will be thankful for a release from pressure and/or a new partnership or business contract.

BLESSINGS

Mundane: The problem's not with you but with others. They're the ones who aren't coming through, living up to their end, or causing misfortune. But even though the problems are great, they can still be overcome.
Esoteric: It's not "what is" that stands in your way but your fear of it or resistance to it. Try to remember that *every* experience has a positive end in view no matter what it looks like now.

SPECIAL GUIDANCE

Don't blame yourself for the faults of others . . . walk away, or say "no."

BEST COURSE OF ACTION

You will escape from oppressive situations or prisons of the mind or body, and will acquire whatever "means" or resources you need, as well as finding a new outlet for your talents or abilities.

OUTCOME

◆ THE NINE OF SWORDS

Many 9s mean that situations or events are nearing completion or have just been completed and another plateau awaits.

IN A READING

Many Swords (three or more) predict tremendous activity, agitation, or acceleration, because Swords show the last stages of effort before the final result.

The focus is on deprivation, discord, and suffering through an ideal or cause; progress that appears to be blocked, stymied, or aborted just at the moment of conception; and worry or anxiety about your future or about someone else.

FOCUS

You have been subject to prolonged periods of depression and are not happy with your present situation and want things to come together and work out.

DESIRE

You will be separated from one you love, but a lot of what you fear is not true and will not be the case at all, and in a very short time you will be reunited.

ROMANCE

What you feared would happen in a romantic situation will not. The unexpected arrival of a sweetheart could also be indicated.

THE UNEXPECTED

Someone will cause you to question your values, needs, and responses and you'll worry that if you follow your heart and hold out for what you really want, you will end up with nothing. Or, you will have to confront some unpredictable changes and temporary losses but will soon see that everything has worked out after all.

OTHERS

You will experience anxiety over another who is away on business; and/or, an offer made will be rescinded or declined.

THE HOME

If you travel, you will find it difficult to attain that which was sought after; and/or, someone you love or care for is gone or will leave you behind and you will miss them very much.

TRAVEL

You will be involved with calculations, contracts, journals, books, data banks, or business documents, and money will be received for something that involves papers.

PAPERS

WORK/CAREER New ideas or avenues will come to the fore . . . expect substantial gain and supreme success.

UNIONS There will be an uncontrollable and irreconcilable separation or broken marriage caused by a work situation or love affair with another.

EMOTIONAL STATE You will have bouts with inconsolable depression or nostalgia over a lover who is gone . . . so much so that you will feel like a zombie or become so wrapped up in your work you won't feel anything.

PLEASURE You'll be pleased about a compliment, social invitation, or receipt of money.

NEWS A date or plan will be canceled and the person left out will not be pleased.

FAMILY Relatives will be experiencing difficulties, losses, or sorrows; or a relative will take your side against another.

THE PHYSICAL BODY You will have stomach problems, be subject to nausea, or have trouble with your prostate gland.

FINANCES Your financial situation will be especially good because you will acquire money through a new project, business deal, or settlement, and through another source as well.

TIME You will persevere and exercise great self-discipline in your work and affairs, but your heart will beat for only one . . . and he/she is gone.

FRIENDS You will be parted from a friend or loved one and will be very sad or lonely without him/her.

VISITORS/CALLERS A surprise is in store. Also, a visitor will arrive . . . someone you are very happy to see.

MAIL A new source of income will come in through things involving papers, letters, books, or mail.

ANXIETY You will wonder why things have to be the way they are instead of the way you wish they were or if you're missing a point that's causing your karma to be repeated over and over again.

Not being able to be with the one you love, and things that didn't work out when you tried so hard and put so much of your heart or effort into them, will break your heart.

DISAPPOINTMENT

You may think that everything is over, but it's not. You will soon have a change of heart.

ENDINGS

You're going to have a new reality or awareness about your future and your relationship with another and feel that maybe things *are* going to get better or work out after all.

NEW BEGINNINGS

You will "inherit" new inspiration or spiritual guidance.

INHERITANCE

A gift will be given for "good karma."

REWARDS/GIFTS

New avenues will spring from old, in both your business and your personal affairs.

SUCCESS

You will have luck in returning, repairing or replacing something damaged or useless, and will be surprised by a "stroke of luck" that will happen to you in the very near future.

FORTUNE

You will be grateful for a new venture involving papers (a very workable or lucrative idea) and positive developments in your personal affairs or love life.

BLESSINGS

Mundane: You will have good fortune later on. Time will prove to be advantageous and you'll get what you want after all.
Esoteric: What looks like failure or loss is instead an opportunity to grow internally, in that it provides the space for a new quality or awareness to emerge. One of the qualities could be (spiritual) maturity and/or the elimination of fear.

SPECIAL GUIDANCE

Wait for things to resolve themselves.

BEST COURSE OF ACTION

You will have a new state of consciousness and a revised experience caused by a new venture, partner, or lover.

OUTCOME

◆ THE TEN OF SWORDS

Tens are read the same as the number 1. However, they also signify a cyclical rebeginning, and a time when you must come to terms with something you may have avoided in the past.

Many Swords (three or more) predict tremendous activity, agitation, or acceleration, because Swords show the last stages of effort before the final result.

The focus is on unfinished business or conditions that have become stagnant and must be cleaned up, cleared away, or corrected before any further progress can be made, be it in yourself, your family, your home, your business, or your community.

FOCUS

You fear poverty or ruin and want to find a way out of an impossible dilemma.

DESIRE

Though the worst is over, anguish will continue because you won't be able to bury the past or start anew. You will vacillate between "Do I want it or don't I?" and the moment you try to pin anything down or make a firm decision, it changes.

ROMANCE

You are going to have to face some hard, cold, and rather unpleasant facts about yourself, your situation, or another.

THE UNEXPECTED

People will make you take action to correct situations, change the way you respond to them, or move in a different direction.

OTHERS

You will be making corrections or repairs in your home, health, appearance, wardrobe, communications, and relationships.

THE HOME

You will have unexpected good luck in your journeys which will bring positive changes or a happier outlook; but, if you go on a shopping spree and buy impulsively, you may regret it or have to return what you bought.

TRAVEL

You are going to have problems sorting things out, correcting errors, or filling out documents, and anger or frustration will arise over inconclusive answers.

PAPERS

WORK/CAREER — Things will not go smoothly in your dealings with others because of obstacles or adverse conditions, hardships, or disputes, and you may quit, be demoted, or dismissed.

UNIONS — Things are not going to go as you hoped or planned, and although you will be disappointed, you will put it behind you and move on.

EMOTIONAL STATE — You will be questioning the motives or behavior of another and feeling a bit left out or abandoned, and will also feel that your life, occupation, and the people you have to deal with have become a tedious and encumbering chore.

PLEASURE — You will be displeased with the quality of your life and will find it difficult to derive much pleasure or satisfaction from it.

NEWS — Someone will call with an inquiry or invitation and you will be uncertain how to answer; or, you will be hurt or insulted by a rude response (or lack of response) from another.

FAMILY — Your family will be more in focus than usual, and conditions all around won't be at their best.

THE PHYSICAL BODY — Expect increased activity (could be outdoors), exercise to improve circulation, and/or recovery from an accident or injury. Tears can be an excellent catharsis.

FINANCES — Financial problems will soon be relieved or resolved, and a flurry of business or an adjusted financial statement will give you an unexpected bonus.

TIME — You are going to feel absolutely devastated or defeated, betrayed by your friends, your lover, or life itself; but hold tight . . . it's not the end but a new beginning, and from now on things can only get better.

FRIENDS — You will have the realization that you have outgrown a friendship and/or will be very upset over the actions of a friend.

VISITORS/CALLERS — Someone will call and want to see you, and you will meet with him/her.

MAIL — You will get a letter or message that you find insulting or that dashes your hopes concerning a hoped-for venture or merger.

You will be troubled by other people's "predicaments" or lack of commitment and your inability to do anything about it.

ANXIETY

Though you will try not to let it bother you or get under your skin, you will be distressed by the thought that things are not going to go the way you want them to or that you're not going to have what you want the most.

DISAPPOINTMENT

Your affection for or infatuation with a person, place, or thing will come to an end. A decision not to go back to work at your current place of employment could also be indicated.

ENDINGS

A new job assignment or complicated work project is going to begin.

NEW BEGINNINGS

You will have to take an objective look at yourself, your situation, or others.

INHERITANCE

Someone will give you a very nice or unexpected gift, something personal; or, you will get a pleasant financial surprise.

REWARDS/GIFTS

Your greatest success will come through progressive financial gains in your business or trade and finding a new method of operation which can increase your potential or allow you to do your work without interference.

SUCCESS

You will consider yourself lucky because you have the ability to solve a problem by removing yourself from it or by remaining neutral and accepting it; or, luck will be with you in a financial matter, bringing an unexpected bonus.

FORTUNE

You will be grateful for help or comfort in times of crisis and/or for a favor someone will do for you.

BLESSINGS

Mundane: Don't give up on yourself or another or consider the situation (or the person) hopeless.
Esoteric: Your lack of faith in yourself (or God) is hindering your ability to see what *you* really want. Remember, God dwells in you *as* you.

SPECIAL GUIDANCE

Come to terms with what is, but turn away from negative thinking patterns or habits and look for alternatives. Learn to have more faith in that which can't be seen but nevertheless exists.

BEST COURSE OF ACTION

PAGE of SWORDS.

Things are going to go in a different direction than you anticipate and though the future looks rather grim, there are positive vibrations on the way and other recourses will become apparent. **OUTCOME**

◆ THE PAGE OF SWORDS

TAURUS (April 20–May 20) **ASTROLOGICAL SIGN**

Practical, thoughtful, persevering, possessive, realistic, down-to-earth, security-minded, patient, sensual, and sometimes reserved. Needs concrete results and knows how to get them. **TYPE OF PERSON**

Serving, singing, sales, finances, negotiations, consulting, leasing, working with buildings or homes. **TYPE OF VOCATION**

The focus is on unexpected developments and occurrences in love affairs or personal relationships; motion, messages, and controlled reactions; workable ideas and concepts to further growth; and/or a person with a Taurean-type temperament. **FOCUS**

You want success or cooperation in business and/or matters of the heart. **DESIRE**

You will want to walk away from or forget a painful relationship, but won't be able to. **ROMANCE**

You are going to be very surprised by the return of a lover, and an unexpected turnabout in matters of the heart . . . a positive development. **THE UNEXPECTED**

You will be put in a position you won't want to be in and will feel incapable of finding a solution; but a significant adjustment will be made, and pressure will ease off. **OTHERS**

You will be preparing to travel and an unexpected and distressing event will occur upon your arrival or return home. At some point, you will be considering a roommate. **THE HOME**

TRAVEL

You may be disappointed in connection with a trip or journey, or a plan will fall through. Expect the unexpected and use caution if driving.

PAPERS

You won't be sure you want to finish a project now that it's begun because there's no guarantee of success once it's completed.

WORK/CAREER

Emotional problems will interfere with your work and as a result, you may leave your job or business partner and start developing or researching projects designed to further you in another direction.

UNIONS

An unexpected occurrence will cause grave concern over the activities of another; or, a very unexpected development will occur.

EMOTIONAL STATE

You will be trying to maintain a "cool" or detached attitude when confronted with upsetting circumstances or people who oppose you, and you will succeed. You may lose your temper first, however.

PLEASURE

You will enjoy working on a creative or expressive project and/or flirting with others.

NEWS

A call from, or the arrival of, an admirer will change many things. This will be a very unexpected and much-welcomed turn of events in the feelings department.

FAMILY

A relative will call or arrive (or you will call on him/her), and you or someone in your family will be planning to travel or go abroad.

THE PHYSICAL BODY

You will be more sexually active or stimulated than usual and could also experience problems with your teeth, gums, or muscles.

FINANCES

You will be concerned about your financial condition and will make an effort to straighten out your affairs in that area, but they still won't get resolved.

TIME

In time, an unpleasant or unworkable business situation or personal relationship will end and a new start in a new direction will begin.

FRIENDS

Unseen elements will begin to surface which will be like a second wind in your relationship.

VISITORS/CALLERS

A friend from the past will come or call and so will a lover.

You will be concerned about a letter which could be the deciding factor in a future event or business-related venture; or, a letter containing money could balance out a business that only made a small profit.

MAIL

You won't want to be in the position you're in and will be very upset and confused about how to deal with it.

ANXIETY

You will be disappointed because your ventures are not going to go the way you expected them to and more problems must be dealt with.

DISAPPOINTMENT

You will want to end a relationship and will almost break up, but it won't end, it will continue in spite of everything.

ENDINGS

Previous obstructions will begin to break down and you will be given a fresh start . . . a "token" of what is to come that will herald the beginning of a better and brighter tomorrow.

NEW BEGINNINGS

You will "inherit" a new direction or method of operation in your career, finances, and love life.

INHERITANCE

You will receive money, gifts, and/or emotional support, and you will do a generous and considerate favor for another. You could also buy yourself a gift or two.

REWARDS/GIFTS

Your success will come through deliberate effort, gradual development, and unexpected business and social opportunities that turn precarious events into new possibilities and future potential.

SUCCESS

You're going to hear something in a very important business or personal matter that will assuage your fears or keep you from going off the deep end.

FORTUNE

You will be greatly relieved when the truth in a situation is revealed, and previous ambiguities or misunderstandings in a romantic relationship get resolved in a *very* satisfactory way.

BLESSINGS

Mundane: The situation in which you feel trapped is only temporary. Your pessimism will soon be replaced by great joy, and someone will be very instrumental in changing things for the better.
Esoteric: If what you think or hear is negative, don't believe it.

SPECIAL GUIDANCE

KNIGHT OF SWORDS.

Don't give up . . . a new beginning is at hand.

BEST COURSE OF ACTION

You will find what was sought after, successful conclusions or agreements will be reached, and all will end well.

OUTCOME

◆ THE KNIGHT OF SWORDS

There is no astrological sign associated with the Knights because they indicate situations that are coming in or going out.

IN A READING

When a Knight appears in a reading, a long-term condition will suddenly change.

The focus is on renewed business activity, financial security, or potential enterprises; rising from obscure status to a more prominent or fruitful position; and decisions concerning investments, partnerships, and love affairs.

FOCUS

You have established a link with someone (or something) and want the chain of events to continue.

DESIRE

Though you don't see it coming, you will soon be swept up in a powerful love affair that is going to change your life dramatically.

ROMANCE

You'll be pleasantly surprised by some unexpected good news about your career and positive changes in your home or work environment. A new romantic interest could also be indicated.

THE UNEXPECTED

You can expect many social calls, business calls, and inquiries, as well as a commission or call for work.

OTHERS

You will be doing a lot of socializing, entertaining, and coming and going, and that's good because you won't want to hang around the house; you'll want to be out having fun.

THE HOME

There will be several short trips or jaunts (one could be with a sweetheart); or, a lover who's been away will soon call or be at your door.

TRAVEL

PAPERS   Something you planned to do involving papers will not be completed at this time and you could take a tentative step toward a legal action.

WORK/CAREER   A very prosperous and influential period is at hand, and someone could enter your life who could manage your career, subsidize you, or move you into a much more prominent position.

UNIONS   You will trust, then distrust, but progress will continue and your relationship will go on.

EMOTIONAL STATE   Your emotional state will greatly improve through the intervention of another.

PLEASURE   You'll be pleased about the possibility of a new enterprise to embark on, and the appearance of those who suddenly change your life both personally and professionally.

NEWS   A message from an admirer (someone you like and feel comfortable with) will brighten your day, and new information in a personal relationship will arrive that will change your perspective about that person . . . a positive change.

FAMILY   There will be emotional discussions between you and a family member and you will be trying to sort things out.

THE PHYSICAL BODY You will hear news of severe illness or death befalling another.

FINANCES   Someone will be the unexpected catalyst to a brand-new business venture or bring an opportunity that could increase your earnings substantially.

TIME   You will trust, then distrust, your future, but progress will continue and you will be favorably aided in some way.

FRIENDS   A new friend will change the course of your experience or eliminate a problem of concern.

VISITORS/CALLERS   You will discuss a trip or journey with a caller, and a suitor or potential lover will arrive.

You will be hoping a letter will arrive, and you will soon receive a license or legal certificate.

MAIL

You'll be worried that others are not keeping their agreements or commitments or that they're unreliable, irresponsible, or inept.

ANXIETY

Unresolved problems and disappointing or depressing elements will dishearten you.

DISAPPOINTMENT

Your allegiance to an "era," establishment, or untrustworthy partnership will end.

ENDINGS

A new reality is going to dawn for you, one of simplicity, acceptance, and grace; you will come to the full realization that there is no need to contrive solutions or assert any fixed ideas and will be willing to let the Universe direct your course.

NEW BEGINNINGS

You will "inherit" an increase in finances and activity.

INHERITANCE

Someone is going to enter your life who'll be willing to promote you or move on your idea.

REWARDS/GIFTS

You're going to be very successful in your career, favorably aided by others, compensated for your work or efforts, and increasing your assets or finances.

SUCCESS

Luck will be with you in love, in money matters, or in gaining influence, support, or prominence.

FORTUNE

Someone is going to assist you or bring about changes in your present condition or status, and you will be very grateful.

BLESSINGS

Mundane: This is a very good time for embarking on new projects. Problems will be solved (whether they're mental, physical, emotional, or spiritual) and you'll attract whatever you need in the way of help or assistance.
Esoteric: Your ability to visualize what you want and your deep desire to make it happen brings about not only material rewards but inner transformations as well.

SPECIAL GUIDANCE

Don't give up, you will receive an answer or clear-cut direction that will solve your problem(s) and get you back on the right track.

BEST COURSE OF ACTION

QUEEN of SWORDS.

Someone or something is going to enter your life that will resolve past difficulties or cause your concerns to vanish, and you'll be swept up in that life-altering event or powerful force.

OUTCOME

◆ # THE QUEEN OF SWORDS

VIRGO (August 23–September 22)

ASTROLOGICAL SIGN

Mental, analytical, scientifically minded, objective, factual, "Vulcan" in nature, ingenious, perfectionist, discriminating, independent, cold.

TYPE OF PERSON

Scientist, secretary, analyst, researcher, editor, computer programmer, astrologer, numerologist.

TYPE OF VOCATION

The focus is on development, research or investigation, science or electronic devices, instruction, training, or the desire to break into a new area; deep thinking, change, or new thinking; and/or a person with a Virgo-type temperament.

FOCUS

The past is gone and the future looks uncertain, but you don't want to be faithless or fearful. You want to be at peace with yourself or your predicament and for your incentive to be restored.

DESIRE

You'll be separated from the one you love and feel that the most important thing about your life is gone and can never be replaced.

ROMANCE

A friend or relative will call unexpectedly or drop by unannounced.

THE UNEXPECTED

You'll hear of a death (or of someone about to die) and also of a couple who have separated, and will take it very much to heart; or, you will feel alone even when you're not.

OTHERS

You'll be alone and separated from a loved one; and/or, if your home or something in your home is in need of repairs or maintenance, someone will do the work at the price you want or at no extra cost to you.

THE HOME

TRAVEL

You'll take a short or sudden trip, but expect some changes or altercations along the way.

PAPERS

There will be a delay or setback with things involving papers.

WORK/CAREER

Some areas will be at a standstill while you wait for things to develop, and you will cut someone or something off cold in your working environment. You may also be considering a new line of work or money-making venture.

UNIONS

You will be alone or separated from a partner or loved one and will feel an emptiness that nothing can fill (this could be due to a death, if other cards support it).

EMOTIONAL STATE

You will work with "what's so" in an effort to go with the flow and because of this will find the way easier, but you will be troubled by the feeling that your success was at the cost of personal fulfillment.

PLEASURE

You'll be happy that conditions are changing and that what you want in the way of confirmation, recognition, or profit is coming your way.

NEWS

You will hear some news or information that will elicit a tearful response. Loss is indicated for a relative.

FAMILY

Expect to hear some unhappy or upsetting news.

THE PHYSICAL BODY

A health problem will make it difficult to work or follow through with plans, but you'll press through it.

FINANCES

Someone isn't honoring agreements or making payments on time, and you will call on him/her or take action on it.

TIME

A new plan will erase any previous grievances and change your outlook completely.

FRIENDS

A call from a friend (or relative) will cause sadness . . . this could be concerning the loss of a loved one or the end of a relationship.

VISITORS/CALLERS

An opportunity will arise to move out of your isolation and into "the dating game."

MAIL

You'll get a document in the mail, perhaps of a legal nature.

You will be annoyed by misleading information or cursory facts that postpone your progress or delay your launching date.

ANXIETY

An unexpected event, like being left at the altar or a business deal gone sour, will leave you feeling alone and abandoned.

DISAPPOINTMENT

A proposed business plan will fall through and new projects will be difficult to launch.

ENDINGS

You'll make a decision to resolve a conflict by cutting off the person who caused it or by withdrawing emotionally.

NEW BEGINNINGS

You will "inherit" faith and fearlessness in the face of the unknown.

INHERITANCE

You will prepare a gift or do a favor for a friend or loved one.

REWARDS/GIFTS

Your accomplishments will not be great because you'll be hampered by conditions beyond your control and your sphere of activity will be limited, but because of your faith and perseverance, success will eventually come.

SUCCESS

A fortunate adjustment will be made and a proverbial "path through the wilderness" will be found.

FORTUNE

You'll be grateful for a new avenue to pursue and a change in your outlook.

BLESSINGS

Mundane: A feeling of emptiness is sometimes necessary. A cup that's already full has no room for more.
Esoteric: Relinquish self-guidance (ego) and allow the Higher to lead. There are times when earthly desires must be sacrificed in order to make room for a Divine plan.

SPECIAL GUIDANCE

Wait for new ideas or products to develop and in the meantime, do something pleasurable. Learn to find satisfaction in that which you can do on your own.

BEST COURSE OF ACTION

Though you won't know how, what, or why, you'll stay emotionally detached, trying to do the right thing until what you need to know is revealed.

OUTCOME

KING of SWORDS.

◆ THE KING OF SWORDS

LIBRA (September 23–October 22)

ASTROLOGICAL SIGN

Fair, just, balanced, perceptive, humanistic, poised, sensitive, compassionate, selfless. Can appear wish-washy because weighs all sides before making decisions.

TYPE OF PERSON

Lawyer, law enforcer, armed forces, internal affairs, public relations, psychologist, relationship counselor, interior decorator.

TYPE OF VOCATION

The focus is on trying to get ahead or make it in the world; inner and outer conflicts; behavior modifications; clarity or discernment; legal matters, police, or professional assistance; and/or a person with a Libran-type temperament.

FOCUS

You will be fearful about your future and will want to see things more clearly, obtain a new perspective, or enlist the aid of a professional-type person.

DESIRE

Dwelling on the past only causes pain, so you'll release it and let it go. This could concern someone who's in a legal or law-enforcement profession.

ROMANCE

You will make new friends, mend relationships with old friends, and set things straight in your mind or affairs. A call from someone in a uniform could also be indicated.

THE UNEXPECTED

Challenging situations will arise that will cause you to close off or guard yourself, and you'll be so caught up in defending your position, you'll fail to see the feelings of others. When you realize it, you'll feel ashamed.

OTHERS

You will think about moving or living with someone in order to save money or cut down expenses, and/or will wish something would come along and "save your ass."

THE HOME

You should use caution when traveling; slow down around curves and watch your rear in an upcoming trip or journey; and be prepared for unforeseen obstacles like a roadblock or rerouting of traffic.

TRAVEL

PAPERS — You'll be concerned about a delay in a financial matter or legal deal, or will worry about the status or credibility of another. This could also indicate legal papers signed.

WORK/CAREER — You will be very apprehensive about your work and your future (could be because you've lost your faith or sense of purpose), but you will keep trudging on in the hope that somehow, some way, things will change.

UNIONS — You'll come to the realization that you've been living in a dream world.

EMOTIONAL STATE — You will experience tension, frustration, and anxiety with regard to your work or your future and will feel as if it's a constant uphill battle to succeed.

PLEASURE — You will take pleasure in completing a task or project successfully in spite of the difficulties you encounter.

NEWS — An upsetting message or communication breakdown will make you feel challenged, blocked, or thwarted.

FAMILY — You're going to have discussions about travel plans, relationships, and finances with your relatives. Friction is also indicated, so don't expect much help.

THE PHYSICAL BODY — You, or someone you know may need to consult a doctor or specialist and you could be suffering from a low-grade infection or virus. An herbal treatment or anti-inflammatory medication could be the best medicine.

FINANCES — There will be tension related to money matters, and even if you're making money, the atmosphere will be taut and unpleasant.

TIME — In time, your perspective will change, pressure will be relieved, and your future will look more promising. You will also gain great insight into how you interact with others and how your attitude comes across.

FRIENDS — Challenging situations or conflicts are going to arise, or you will have friends in the police department, the legal field, or government.

Expect a letdown; the one you want to see won't call or come by. **VISITORS/CALLERS**

An "inconvenience" will necessitate a letter or phone call; an untimely bill will arrive; or a letter will provide the evidence you need to file a lawsuit or get out of a contract. **MAIL**

You will be troubled by an uncertain future because you won't be able to see your way clear on any level, and you will worry about your interactions with others. **ANXIETY**

You will think that the Universe is against you and all of your plans, because you have lost faith in yourself or God and will feel that to continue on will be a fight every step of the way. **DISAPPOINTMENT**

Separateness and being alone are going to come to an end. **ENDINGS**

You'll cut through adversity, see things the way they really are, and set things straight in your personal affairs. Also, someone you've been putting off or "stringing along" is going to call. **NEW BEGINNINGS**

You will "inherit" a questioning and introspective mind about the "whys and wherefores" or motives of others and an alternative course of action or "Plan B." **INHERITANCE**

A gift that was given may take its toll in blood. **REWARDS/GIFTS**

Your best success will come through the discovery of a new way of relating that will allow you to see things through the eyes of others and to embrace a new dimension of experience. Success in legal matters is also indicated. **SUCCESS**

You'll be fortunate because you'll recognize the truth in a situation *before* you say or do something you'd regret. **FORTUNE**

You will be grateful for the ability to ward off conflicts, negative behavior patterns and physical, or emotional assaults. **BLESSINGS**

Mundane: Stay detached and you will be able to perceive the truth in situations, and your impressions or perceptions will later be confirmed.
Esoteric: Don't be afraid to be defenseless or "lay your cards on the **SPECIAL GUIDANCE**

table." It *can* make a difference, because what's consciously or unconsciously being expressed is coming from genuine concern.

BEST COURSE OF ACTION   Still your unruly thoughts and don't respond in a preconditioned way. Be impartial, unprejudiced, and nonjudgmental.

OUTCOME   You will be determined to carry on despite the obstacles or trials you have to endure, and you will find an alternative course of action.

THE
SUIT
OF
PENTACLES

ACE of PENTACLES.

◆   THE ACE OF PENTACLES

An Ace marks a fresh start. The Ace of Pentacles foretells the dawning of a period of manifestation, realization, proof, and prosperity.

IN A READING

SPRING (March–April–May)

SEASON

Many 1s indicate that a situation is about to begin or is in the beginning stages.

NUMBER 1

The focus is on continuation and/or things that come together later on; new things replacing old; investments of time or money; potential partners or partnerships; and pleasure, satisfaction, and prosperity.

FOCUS

Everything you were once immersed in (be it in your love life or your business) has either been cut off, cut back, or completely severed and you want it to spring back or be replaced by something else.

DESIRE

You'll be thinking about romance and will want to have a significant love affair. If already involved, you will wish your partner would be more loving or responsive.

ROMANCE

You will be very surprised at the unsolicited attention you're going to get from one who really piques your romantic interest.

THE UNEXPECTED

You will not be willing to compromise or associate with those who don't support you, your growth, or the way you want to feel about yourself, and you won't let your heart rule your head.

OTHERS

If in business for yourself or working out of your home, you will have a sudden surge in activity and you may soon buy something that you couldn't afford or put off buying before ... perhaps a house.

THE HOME

You will be considering a trip abroad, or a letter will arrive from a distance containing money you should have received before.

TRAVEL

You will be engaged in a project involving paper(s) which could be very successful, and if you were experiencing problems in the past, they will be amended or resolved.

PAPERS

WORK/CAREER — Activity may have been slow in the past but your business interests will soon begin to thrive.

UNIONS — You will be unfulfilled with your present partner and will want to come together with someone else.

EMOTIONAL STATE — You'll be in a fun-loving frame of mind and material rewards or sensual pleasures will take center stage.

PLEASURE — Pleasure pursuits, financial agreements, and spiritual matters are going to bring you a lot of personal satisfaction, and something that was cut off (or you thought was dead) in the past is going to spring back again.

NEWS — Expect good news concerning your business or finances.

FAMILY — Your family will be experiencing better times, better health, or improved conditions.

THE PHYSICAL BODY — If you've been ailing, you'll be on the road to recovery, or good news concerning a medical issue will come. This could also indicate a "new age" or herbal-type treatment.

FINANCES — You will soon be receiving money from something that was held up or that you should have gotten in the past (and you will be notified of this) . . . something that has to do with time or a time investment.

TIME — In time, a romance you thought was over will be revived, bringing great happiness and a renewal of joy and pleasure.

FRIENDS — You and a friend (or loved one) you haven't seen in a while will soon be talking.

VISITORS/CALLERS — You will make a call on a friend, and a gift will be given, purchased, or discussed.

MAIL — You will get good news about money, or money you didn't expect to get will arrive (something stemming from the past) and it will be more than you anticipated.

ANXIETY — You'll be troubled by your inability to make a definite decision in a romantic situation, and/or by constantly having to redo or revise work that should have been done right the first time.

You will not be able to have your heart's desire or find an outlet for your talents and as a result, will feel very lonely and unfulfilled. **DISAPPOINTMENT**

A new opportunity or relationship is about to spring from something cut off or thought dead, and your loneliness is going to end. **ENDINGS**

You will take action to repair, correct, or reinstate yourself or your affairs, and will also embark on a pleasure pursuit, shopping spree, or new business venture. **NEW BEGINNINGS**

You're going to receive money you should have gotten before and/or an invitation to a social event, dinner party, or fund-raising benefit. **INHERITANCE**

If you buy a gift, you will get a good deal at a good price; or, you will do a very charitable act for another, or give to the poor or needy. **REWARDS/GIFTS**

Your success will come through pleasurable pursuits and profitable investments of time, money, or energy. **SUCCESS**

Luck will be with you in financial matters, in bringing things together later on, and in resolving a romantic dilemma. **FORTUNE**

You will be very grateful for the generosity bestowed upon you by another. **BLESSINGS**

Mundane: It may take a while, but what was cut back or pruned *will* spring up again. "All things come in time." **SPECIAL GUIDANCE**
Esoteric: If you've come to a dead end, it's because you lack the kind of knowledge that only time and experience can acquire.

Keep an optimistic attitude and let time be the deciding factor. Also, take time out to play, and don't be afraid to spend money on pleasurable pursuits or enjoyable commodities. **BEST COURSE OF ACTION**

Your world will be transformed and you will prosper. **OUTCOME**

◆ THE TWO OF PENTACLES

Many 2s indicate a waiting period where there will be a partial success but more to be revealed later. They can also indicate a reconciliation, a reunion, and/or an element of surprise.

IN A READING

Many Pentacles (three or more) indicate that conditions are taking form, or are in the process of being demonstrated.

The focus is on emotional tribulation due to difficult schedules; endeavors that seem to be in vain; ineffective verbal or written efforts; and business losses or discouragements.

FOCUS

You want endeavors to go well, but feel as if you're between a rock and a hard place.

DESIRE

You will be trying to maintain emotional control when faced with upsetting news or circumstances; yet, unbeknown to you, your lover feels the same.

ROMANCE

You're going to have a romantic change of heart and find a solution to a problem through a different source, another person, or in a different way than you expected.

THE UNEXPECTED

The effect of others will be felt primarily in the work environment, and though you will handle whatever comes up, you will feel star-crossed in matters of the heart.

OTHERS

You will be trying to maintain emotional equilibrium but will find it very difficult because all of your endeavors or plans will be going awry.

THE HOME

You'll be considering a trip or rendezvous to meet with a friend or loved one, but the conditions surrounding this venture will be very unstable.

TRAVEL

You will be very discouraged because printed matter is not producing the desired result or moving as fast as you would like; and/or, legal action for breach of contract could be taken against someone.

PAPERS

You will be upset or discouraged about an idea or project, but it will get straightened out or dealt with through a new approach.

WORK/CAREER

UNIONS

You will have a release or overcome an emotional crisis through the entry of several new factors (both personal and professional).

EMOTIONAL STATE

You won't like being in the predicament you're in and things will be getting even harder. Schedules will be too full, business will be a strain, and the little time you'll have to spend with the one you love won't be enough.

PLEASURE

You'll enjoy getting or giving gifts, doing favors for others, and resolving a personal and very emotional dilemma.

NEWS

You will feel misrepresented or deceived by a very upsetting message, phone call, or conversation.

FAMILY

You won't be able to really relate to or connect with your relatives due to outside influences that will be pulling or possessing your attention.

THE PHYSICAL BODY

You will have tension-related problems, stiffness, aches and pains.

FINANCES

You will have discussions about work or finances which will be agreed upon by everyone, and if in business for yourself, you'll make money but will have to make some concessions. If traveling for work, you will have an expense account.

TIME

You will be looking for a way out of a dilemma and wondering what you should do, but someone will solve the problem for you in a very propitious way by providing an alternative or letting you out of your commitment.

FRIENDS

A social event will provide a buffer between you and a romantic problem and could very well mark the end of your troubles.

VISITORS/CALLERS

You will not connect with, or talk to, the one you want to see (like a loved one), due to scheduling problems or a lack of effort on your part or on the part of the other.

MAIL

A letter you've been waiting for will not arrive, or an advance or subsidy will be delayed, or a package containing a cassette will come.

You will be troubled by ineffective or misrepresented efforts and by not being able to see, talk to, or express your feeling with a loved one, but that is going to change.

ANXIETY

Disappointing elements in your love life, discouraging news, or endeavors that seem to be in vain will cause you to lose your incentive in your work or career goals.

DISAPPOINTMENT

Internal conflicts and emotional tribulation will come to an end.

ENDINGS

Someone is going to enter your life who will instigate change and a new direction or course of action.

NEW BEGINNINGS

You are going to get a positive response from another in answer to your efforts, query, or demands.

INHERITANCE

A small gift or token of love will be purchased, and if it's for a lover, it will in some way be the catalyst to winning him/her over or to getting him/her to reveal more of his or her feelings.

REWARDS/GIFTS

Your success will come through a new career direction or a romantic change of heart . . . a happy change.

SUCCESS

New solutions will come through someone who enters into your situation and puts a new slant on things, and you will have the good fortune to know what is true and what to do.

FORTUNE

You are going to be grateful for a small gift or sum of money.

BLESSINGS

Mundane: Good *will* prevail . . . a positive change is in store.
Esoteric: Trying to take on too many things at once is taking its toll. You're spreading yourself too thin. All is going out and nothing is coming in.

SPECIAL GUIDANCE

Narrow your choices down to one, and maintain a sanguine attitude and balanced disposition.

BEST COURSE OF ACTION

The balance will be restored, pressure will ease off, and hope and cheer will be regained.

OUTCOME

THE THREE OF PENTACLES

Many 3s indicate group activities or situations involving more than one person. They can also indicate delay, but with the promise of future success.

Many Pentacles (three or more) indicate that conditions are taking form, or are in the process of being demonstrated.

FOCUS

The focus is on activities pertaining to work or career goals, papers, mail, literature, words, meetings, plans, construction, and practical application.

DESIRE

You want to get things accomplished and to improve the quality of your life or your work.

ROMANCE

Memories of the past will begin to fade away, freeing you to accept new opportunities.

THE UNEXPECTED

You're going to be surprised by a sudden and unexpected business opportunity, a valuable product, and a long-distance phone call.

OTHERS

Someone will come along that will change your outlook or "liven up the party" and you'll enjoy the company of good friends, new friends, and new acquaintances.

THE HOME

You will be actively involved in your work or hobbies and an unexpected caller will arrive bearing gifts or opportunities.

TRAVEL

You are going to take a short trip or jaunt but may want to leave sooner than you thought.

PAPERS

You will be making corrections and adding new ideas to a project involving papers in order to improve the quality or ensure the best result, and may enlist the aid of another in order to speed things up.

WORK/CAREER

You will come together with someone to discuss a business idea or venture and to toss around ideas that could improve or market your work, and all will be in accord.

UNIONS

In business-related affairs, you will be making preparations to begin a new undertaking. If you are involved in a personal relationship, you will be discussing living arrangements and making plans for your future.

EMOTIONAL STATE   You will feel uplifted, renewed, and in a sociable mood.

PLEASURE   You'll derive pleasure from your talents, work methods, and social exchanges.

NEWS   An awaited message will arrive with very positive results . . . could be from an admirer.

FAMILY   Your relatives will be concerned about the outcome of a proposed venture and may seek outside assistance or legal aid to determine the verdict.

THE PHYSICAL BODY   You will overindulge in food or drink for emotional gratification or compensation; and, if you thought you would have a chance to rest and recuperate, you've got another think coming, because you'll be inundated with work or chores.

FINANCES   Someone will help you collect money that is owed to you, or you'll soon begin a new enterprise (or retrieve a past one) that will bring in more money or supplement your income.

TIME   You'll be discussing the future and future projects with someone and it will be a very positive encounter.

FRIENDS   A friend will help you in your work or give you something at cost, and/or you will go on an outing with a friend.

VISITORS/CALLERS   You're going to have more calls than usual and will be discussing or arranging a future event, project, or get-together.

MAIL   Something concerning a letter, contract, or document will cause you to change your plans or take new action.

ANXIETY   You will be troubled by communications, mergers, or meetings, and trying to effect solutions or plan ahead.

DISAPPOINTMENT   You'll be disappointed that you can't communicate with someone you want to talk to or externalize your ideas, but this will pass.

Communication problems, withholds, and hard feelings will come to an end. **ENDINGS**

You'll get together with someone on an idea or partnership and will also be making revisions in your work or presentation in order to increase your earnings or make your returns more lucrative. **NEW BEGINNINGS**

You will be inspired by a new vision, project, or product that you can do in your home and sell, or that you can adorn yourself with. **INHERITANCE**

You will give a gift and get a gift. **REWARDS/GIFTS**

You'll succeed in getting your ideas across to others and will have profitable discussions, transactions, and/or returns. **SUCCESS**

You're going to meet a new associate who will clear up a problem area, help you in a business endeavor you're trying to promote, or get you back on target with a previous business attempt. **FORTUNE**

You'll be grateful for a meeting you will have with another that will inspire your confidence and shine a bright light on your future. **BLESSINGS**

Mundane: You'll have to revamp, redirect, or make some alterations in your current work or plans.
Esoteric: The goal is worth the suffering. **SPECIAL GUIDANCE**

Don't be reticent when it comes to accepting new opportunities or pushing yourself, your ideas, or your product. **BEST COURSE OF ACTION**

You'll be in the process of embarking on a new business venture and considering activities with an eye toward the future. You will also make arrangements to talk with someone or meet with him/her again. **OUTCOME**

◆ THE FOUR OF PENTACLES

Many 4s indicate fruition or the manifestation of an idea, along with the foundation or "space" where things can grow. **IN A READING**

Many Pentacles (three or more) indicate that conditions are taking form, or are in the process of being demonstrated.

The focus is on work, success, and financial security; a "safe" space or environment, making every effort count, and not wanting anything to go to waste. **FOCUS**

You want success in your business, finances, or material affairs and are contemplating the impact of a new relationship or partnership. **DESIRE**

There will be obstacles to getting together (such as logistics, business priorities, or geography), but if both parties are in accord and want to be together, the obstacles can be overcome. **ROMANCE**

You will be pleasantly surprised by an unexpected business transaction and/or a new business that will begin to show a profit. **THE UNEXPECTED**

Confronted with personal loss or unfulfillment, you will turn your attention toward business and material rewards. **OTHERS**

A financial opportunity, business transaction, or sale is going to come right to your door. **THE HOME**

A plan to meet with someone is going to be canceled or postponed, but you will go out anyway. Or, you will buy a car. **TRAVEL**

A significant sale or large purchase will be decided upon but won't be completed until a later date. **PAPERS**

Your heart won't be in your work, but you'll know you must forge ahead in spite of it or you won't accomplish what you need to get done. **WORK/CAREER**

You won't unite with someone on any real level because your heart belongs to, or is committed to, another. **UNIONS**

Your thoughts will be on your work and it will be a blessing because if they were on your love life, you would be unhappy. **EMOTIONAL STATE**

PLEASURE   You will be pleased about your professional advancements, co-workers, and/or a financial transaction.

NEWS   Expect a very positive financial message.

FAMILY   You will be discussing relationships or the pros and cons of a financial move with someone in your family or a close friend.

THE PHYSICAL BODY A health condition that needs medical attention will trouble you and you won't be able to get the help you need; and, if you go to the doctor, it will be a very painful ordeal.

FINANCES   You will have enough money to cover your bills and take care of your needs, and any outstanding debts will be paid. A bill of sale could also be signed and important papers transferred.

TIME   Most of your energies will be directed toward your work and you will examine or evaluate what's been done so far and make necessary changes or improvements.

FRIENDS   You can expect honest communications and a surprising disclosure.

VISITORS/CALLERS You will make a call on another and/or a caller will arrive.

MAIL   You will be tired of hearing "the check is in the mail," but a check *is* in the mail.

ANXIETY   You will be troubled by financial setbacks and delays or unknowns regarding another.

DISAPPOINTMENT   You will be discouraged about your unfulfilling or unrewarding personal unions, wasted efforts, or loss of money through your own carelessness.

ENDINGS   A debilitating health condition will come to an end, and/or someone you love may die . . . if an animal, it may have to be put to sleep.

NEW BEGINNINGS   You're going to be directing your energies toward material gain or profit and will soon begin a new venture with someone you like very much.

INHERITANCE   You are going to get some unexpected money, a new possession (like a car), or a new job.

You will buy a gift for yourself and another. **REWARDS/GIFTS**

You'll be successful in business transactions that involve bartering, **SUCCESS**
calculating, and analysis, and in forming new partnerships.

Luck will be with you in getting what you want. **FORTUNE**

You will be thankful for someone's help in an undertaking or the **BLESSINGS**
kind words, intervention, or concern expressed by another.

Mundane: What is success really worth? Are you willing to pay the **SPECIAL GUIDANCE**
price?
Esoteric: If obstacles are confronting you, it's because you're moving in the wrong direction or proceeding in error. More facts need
to be uncovered.

Be honest with yourself. **BEST COURSE OF ACTION**

You will establish a new approach or foundation, but in romantic **OUTCOME**
affairs you will remain detached, guarded, or noncommitted until
you see which way the ball is going to bounce.

◆ THE FIVE OF PENTACLES

Many 5s indicate change, challenge, and fluctuations (lucky or un-lucky). They also indicate material prosperity but spiritual poverty if not properly balanced or understood.

IN A READING

Many Pentacles (three or more) indicate that conditions are taking form, or are in the process of being demonstrated.

The focus is on self-doubt or confusion; difficult dealings with oth-ers; unfortunate circumstances in love, business, or marriage; mis-fortune, suffering and loss; and upsets or pressures caused by someone or something.

FOCUS

You don't want to deal with a situation or confront an issue insti-gated by it.

DESIRE

You will long to be with the one your heart yearns for . . . no other can take his/her place or fill the void, and try as they might, others will not succeed. An illicit love affair could also be indicated.

ROMANCE

You will hear of or talk of a health problem, accident, or injury which may need medical attention or hospitalization and/or of mis-fortune befalling another.

THE UNEXPECTED

You will feel alone or unwanted and will lack confidence in yourself or your work; and even if love is offered, you will be unable to find refuge or solace in it because your heart, dream, or path is some-where else.

OTHERS

You will be feeling discouraged or melancholy and in need of a rest from mental or emotional stress.

THE HOME

Prepare for the worst if traveling, and you may be confronted with some bad news on your arrival. You will also be contemplating a major move or journey.

TRAVEL

You will think your paper work in ineffective, substandard, or shal-low in quality, or that it needs a lot more work or detail than you've got so far, or that it will *never* get done or be completed to your satisfaction.

PAPERS

WORK/CAREER   You will experience troubles, dissension, and possible loss in your work or career, as well as difficult dealings with others; and/or you will have a heated debate over papers or contractual agreements.

UNIONS   If single and hoping to unite, there will be no marriage or union. If married, it will be an unhappy marriage that has failed through the lack of communication, misunderstandings, or sexual problems.

EMOTIONAL STATE   You will be anxious, depressed, or filled with doubt and will feel inadequate, unconfident, or insecure; but a lot of what you're feeling is a direct result of being overtaxed (mentally or physically) and pushing yourself beyond your limits.

PLEASURE   Your finances are going to improve, but your pleasure will be dimmed by hardships and suffering.

NEWS   An unhappy message will cause a letdown or failure to unite as planned. Discussions about the breakup of a relationship or business partnership could also be indicated.

FAMILY   Someone in your family will be unhappy about his/her finances, partner, or an infidelity. The trouble is that you will be too emotionally exhausted to help or lend any comfort.

THE PHYSICAL BODY   A health problem will need attention (but it's not as bad as you think). This could, also indicate a visit to a doctor as a result of a fall, accident, or injury . . . be careful.

FINANCES   You can expect financial success regardless of obstacles or problems. Money spent or received for spiritual or metaphysical work could also be indicated.

TIME   Lovers or friends will be unable to come together as planned or hoped for (this could be due to a legal complication).

FRIENDS   You will feel very deeply for your friends or loved ones but won't see your way clear to unite or come together, so you won't.

VISITORS/CALLERS   You will hear of a tragedy or discuss a serious illness or accident.

MAIL   You are going to get a health notice or reminder.

ANXIETY   You will have trouble fulfilling an act or duty and will begin to realize the futility of want or desire (and the frustration and pain that ensues), and so will be very reluctant to pursue any course that could elicit more.

You will be very sad that your love for someone is unrequited, or that you can't be together, and will wonder if it's because of a karmic debt or predetermined course. A mechanical breakdown or car accident could also be indicated.

DISAPPOINTMENT

That which was imperfect, not right, or ideal will be sacrificed no matter how much you hoped it could be otherwise, and you will not put up with people whose ethics are ruthless or who have an "I'm aboard, pull up the ladder" attitude.

ENDINGS

You will attract people with whom you have more in common or who mirror your experience.

NEW BEGINNINGS

You will come to the realization that the only thing worth seeking is wisdom and understanding.

INHERITANCE

You're going to get an unexpected financial surprise, or someone will shower you with gifts or money.

REWARDS/GIFTS

You will get an unexpected bonus or promotion in your work, but your greatest achievement will be in attaining spiritual insight or assistance, and in your ability to unravel life's mysteries and channel that wisdom.

SUCCESS

Luck will be with you in money matters and in attaining a sought-after position, but it may come through what appeared to be an unfortunate experience that caused unnecessary suffering.

FORTUNE

You will be grateful for spiritual assistance, guidance, or inspiration in a time of stress.

BLESSINGS

Mundane: You're going to develop a new method of operation which will be an asset to your work or assist you in utilizing more of your potential. And you'll have to straighten out your relationship(s), even if it means ending one.

SPECIAL GUIDANCE

Esoteric: You're in need of a spiritual transfusion. Platitudes and handout philosophies from your fellow man will not alleviate your

despair. But this kind of suffering develops compassion, and spiritual deliverance must have an empty vessel to pour itself into (one in which all hope or promise has been stripped away) before it can descend.

Drop any preconceived notions or expectations in romantic matters because your hopes will not be realized. Concentrate on business, trade, or commerce, because those areas will prosper.

BEST COURSE OF ACTION

You will have to deal with uncomfortable issues whether you want to or not, but in times to come will realize that it was for the best or the only way you could have grown.

OUTCOME

◆ THE SIX OF PENTACLES

Many 6s indicate adjustments in thoughts, attitudes, or conditions. They also represent the ability to transcend difficulties.

IN A READING

Many Pentacles (three or more) indicate that conditions are taking form, or are in the process of being demonstrated.

The focus is on token starts, promising enterprises or career opportunities, investment potentials, health decisions, solvency, and gratification.

FOCUS

You want what's rightfully or legally yours to be given back or to be reinstated in your profession or status.

DESIRE

You will be wishing or hoping a lover will call or come by.

ROMANCE

A new program, plan, or promised venture will fall through or fail.

THE UNEXPECTED

You will enlist the assistance of another (one who's been an uncooperative or elusive associate) and if you approach him/her in person, diplomacy will win out where threats and ultimatums have failed.

OTHERS

You're too socked into your work; you need to get away from it to relax and unwind. If you keep pushing yourself, you'll have an uphill battle the whole way.

THE HOME

TRAVEL

You will travel for work, social events, or group activities.

PAPERS

New information will make something impossible suddenly possible.

WORK/CAREER

New elements will come to the fore in your work environment, but you will still be unsettled because you have not yet established yourself or landed in the position in which you want to be.

UNIONS

Even if you come together, you will experience a sense of separateness and will feel as if the distance is increasing.

EMOTIONAL STATE

You will be in a positive mood and looking forward to something new.

PLEASURE

You will be pleased that you are doing better work than you thought you were capable of.

NEWS

You will hear from someone you love very much, and/or you will get or make many calls about your work.

FAMILY

A family member will be very unhappy with his/her lot in life and will soon travel or move.

THE PHYSICAL BODY

Guard against accidents on the home front and be careful of what you eat . . . you could harm yourself or experience a life-threatening situation.

FINANCES

You will have money troubles or problems trying to collect what is owed to you, and the situation will still be unresolved.

TIME

Several prospects will be in the making, all of which look promising, and someone will surprise you with a charitable act or deed.

FRIENDS

You will experience an undercurrent of tension or discomfort with your friends or business partners because something will be unsettled in your mind that will need to be discussed and resolved.

VISITORS/CALLERS

You are going to get a call from one you were thinking about or concerned about, as well as a business call or a call for work.

MAIL

Debts will be paid or a small sum of money will be enclosed in a letter.

You will be anxious about an uncomfortable undertone of unfinished business because your affairs will not be clear, resolved, or settled in your mind.

ANXIETY

You will be disappointed in something that wasn't all that it was cracked up to be (like a proverbial wooden nickel) or because of the loss of an important document.

DISAPPOINTMENT

Your preoccupation with money or security will cease to be a problem because money will begin to flow in from many sources.

ENDINGS

You will feel insecure about the success of a current venture and uncertain about how to proceed in the future.

NEW BEGINNINGS

You will "inherit" money through your work or career, an offer of financial assistance, or a debt paid in full.

INHERITANCE

Someone will relay their appreciation for that which you've given them, or you will receive an offer of sponsorship or a gift of money.

REWARDS/GIFTS

Your best success will come from educational resources or a new kind of work that will surpass or supersede the old.

SUCCESS

Luck will be with you in bringing things out into the open and discussing them and in initiating a new venture or method of work that could be very beneficial in time to come. You will also be given a small gift or token of love.

FORTUNE

You will be thankful for the opportunity to make more money and the development of a new kind of work or business enterprise.

BLESSINGS

Mundane: There *are* answers available, and the key to solving problems is to stop thinking about them.
Esoteric: Problems exist only as long as you think about them. Keep your attention on the now and act as if it were the first and last moment you will ever have on earth. As Don Juan once said, "There is no guarantee that you are going to live a single moment longer."

SPECIAL GUIDANCE

Follow through with your original decision and be willing to defer instant gratification.

BEST COURSE OF ACTION

Your affairs will still be unsettled, but you'll move into a happier atmosphere.

OUTCOME

THE SEVEN OF PENTACLES

Many 7s denote a period of introspection or solitude. They also indicate unlooked-for advantages or gain through things that come unexpectedly. **IN A READING**

Many Pentacles (three or more) indicate that conditions are taking form, or are in the process of being demonstrated.

The focus is on a situation or a pause in progress which causes great dissatisfaction, anxiety, or depression, and on a reevaluation of goals, aspirations, or life itself. **FOCUS**

You want to be productive, make more money, or move on to something else entirely. **DESIRE**

You will be disappointed in love and will unhappily resign yourself to the prospect of continuing on alone. **ROMANCE**

You will be pleasantly surprised by someone who inadvertently provides the key ingredient or missing link needed to reinforce your determination and ensure the success of an idea, project, or enterprise . . . something you wanted or were looking for but didn't know existed. **THE UNEXPECTED**

Someone or something will inadvertently provide the means for you to turn a frustrating or negative situation into an extremely positive one. **OTHERS**

You will experience fear and anxiety over money that should have been paid but hasn't arrived and may not. But, money will arrive through another avenue that will more than make up the difference. **THE HOME**

You will travel or be away from home, and though you will enjoy yourself, the weather will be hot and sticky. **TRAVEL**

You will be bogged down with paperwork and progress will be very slow. Watch out for plagiarism or theft of ideas. **PAPERS**

You'll be dissatisfied with your progress and experience anxiety about your business or financial state, and will want to be much more successful or solvent. **WORK/CAREER**

UNIONS

A marriage, union, or partnership will be reviewed, proposed, or discussed . . . is it what you really want?

EMOTIONAL STATE

Your attitude will be unresponsive, "apart," or indifferent toward people and events because of a deep-seated depression stemming from wanting to succeed but feeling that every effort has come to naught and there's nothing you can do to change it.

PLEASURE

You are going to be pleased with a new possession that you purchase for yourself or your home, and a new discovery will bring unexpected joy.

NEWS

Expect a pleasant surprise, and/or someone from a doctor's office will call.

FAMILY

You may be spending some somber times at home.

THE PHYSICAL BODY

You will suffer from extreme anxiety or nervous exhaustion and will be unable to take on anything that would be mentally, emotionally, or physically taxing; and, you or someone you know will have to go to the doctor soon.

FINANCES

Your financial situation will look very precarious, with very few options available, but good news will arrive concerning a financial gain that will shed new light on the way you view your future security.

TIME

Things will look as if they are going from bad to worse, but you're on the threshold of a new discovery.

FRIENDS

Your friends will be beneficial and a friend from a long distance could call.

VISITORS/CALLERS

Someone is going to call as anticipated. Something unusual will transpire, but they will call.

MAIL

A letter that was promised, hoped for, or planned on is not going to arrive at this time.

ANXIETY

You will be anxious to move in a new direction but nothing is being presented.

You are going to be disappointed in the time it may take for your goals to materialize and will wonder if they will ever be attained. **DISAPPOINTMENT**

Patience and complicity will end. **ENDINGS**

You are going to reevaluate your position to see if it's worth pursuing (especially if it relates to business), but will carry on in spite of everything. **NEW BEGINNINGS**

You are going to "inherit" a new possession and/or a complete understanding of something you sensed but hitherto had not been able to consciously formulate or put together in your mind. **INHERITANCE**

You are going to receive some news containing a financial opportunity or "win." The purchase of a rather expensive gift could also be indicated. **REWARDS/GIFTS**

Unfortunately, you won't see the results you'd hoped to see and will find it very hard to get yourself established. **SUCCESS**

You will be fortunate in romantic affairs that take a sudden turn for the better. **FORTUNE**

You will be grateful for a new possession or gift. **BLESSINGS**

Mundane: You have what it takes; you just need someone who can help you get where you want to go or put it all together. Hang on, help's coming. **SPECIAL GUIDANCE**
Esoteric: If you plant a seed, it doesn't blossom overnight—it takes time. No amount of wishing it to be otherwise will make it grow any faster.

Don't attempt to take on more than is as yet safe or sound. New ideas will come to the fore that will help you carry on or ensure a successful outcome. **BEST COURSE OF ACTION**

Because you are determined to succeed, you will apply the type of constructive energy it takes to ensure success. **OUTCOME**

◆ THE EIGHT OF PENTACLES

Many 8s indicate a positive change of mind or status because the beneficial qualities of the number 8 are rarely diluted.

IN A READING

Many Pentacles (three or more) indicate that conditions are taking form, or are in the process of being demonstrated.

The focus is on assistance or backing on an idea or project, and on risks, finances and assets, enlargement, accomplishment, employment or commission, kinship, friendship, romance, and betterment.

FOCUS

You want enterprises to be successful and for things to go well.

DESIRE

Love may be difficult to ground, but someone will light up your life (or be the best thing about life) and, if there's no one special now, you'll attract romance like a bee to honey.

ROMANCE

You'll be surprised by the entry of a possible romantic interest and/ or the reconciliation of two people you thought would never come together again. News of an unjust or untimely death could also be indicated.

THE UNEXPECTED

You will be greatly affected or impacted by an encounter with another. You will also be acknowledged for being bright and/or making a positive impact on others.

OTHERS

You will be looking for the solution to a problem (be it external or internal) or the best action to take in order to effectively get a handle on it or clear it up.

THE HOME

You will be considering a trip or outing (if you go it will be beneficial), and if you hoped to travel with someone special or meet someone special, you will get your wish.

TRAVEL

You will be involved with release forms or legal, medical or corporate papers, and if you've made a mistake that has halted your progress, someone will correct it for you or show you the procedure so that you can continue.

PAPERS

If you've been depressed or bored with your work, it will soon lift and you will have a change in attitude brought about by a compen-

WORK/CAREER

sation for a previous effort, new orders, or new projects to embark upon.

UNIONS

You will wonder if your relationship is really practical or if you're living in a dream world that can never be reconciled with the life-style you're accustomed to or have chosen to live.

EMOTIONAL STATE

You will be uncomfortable or off balance because you will feel the advent of change or the necessity to implement changes and you won't want to leave the safety or security of your home or what's been previously established.

PLEASURE

You will enjoy the fact that you are making a positive impact on others, or making a difference in their lives, and will be pleasantly surprised by an unexpected romantic possibility that will intrigue you or pique your interest.

NEWS

You will speak with one who will assist you in a project you've been contemplating or send some business your way. Also, news from a lover will arrive when you least expect it.

FAMILY

You will have a difficult time with family members or in trying to make travel arrangements or schedule outings together . . . try to avoid contention.

THE PHYSICAL BODY

There will be cost considerations, a loss of appetite, and possible weight loss. Sexual arousal, or a warning that too much sun or heat could make you ill could also be indicated.

FINANCES

Expect material gain and increase, but in small sums only.

TIME

You will soon sever a relationship with one who's been difficult or disappointing, and you will form a new alliance.

FRIENDS

Public or social activities will be highlighted, bringing opportunities to diversify your skills or advance your position. Business and friendship could mix nicely now.

VISITORS/CALLERS

Expect to get a late-night call from an admirer.

MAIL

You will receive a letter or package you've been waiting for.

ANXIETY

Feeling as if you're being pushed into making a commitment you're not prepared to make because it doesn't feel right, will cause much anxiety.

You will be disheartened by unsuccessful ventures or love affairs and difficulties in achieving your goals.

DISAPPOINTMENT

Most of your problems or conflicts are going to end and your business efforts will no longer be in vain. Expect a change for the better.

ENDINGS

You will begin a new project or venture and some of your ideas will be backed by someone who will provide tangible assistance or an offer of sponsorship.

NEW BEGINNINGS

You will "inherit" an offer of financial assistance or backing for a new enterprise and recognition for your talents and abilities.

INHERITANCE

You are going to get an offer of financial assistance or a gift of money.

REWARDS/GIFTS

You will be praised or recognized for your skills and your ability to make a difference in the lives of others. You will also attain backing or financial assistance on a project or enterprise if you concur.

SUCCESS

You are going to regain a sense of peace, clarity, or assurance about yourself or your position in life, and a phone call to a loved one or a call from a suitor will reinstate your relationship.

FORTUNE

You will be grateful for the help or assistance of others as well as a financial bonus, employment opportunity, or offer of backing on a project.

BLESSINGS

Mundane: Circumstances are going to change for the better. *Esoteric:* You're not equipped to change conditions or better your situation on your own. The answers or assistance you require must come from others whose experience, understanding, or knowledge is greater than yours.

SPECIAL GUIDANCE

Don't try to force issues, but wait for things to change. This is not a time to assert yourself. If you try, you won't get what you're after or will lock horns with your peers. If you just sit tight, you will gain considerable help or means.

BEST COURSE OF ACTION

You will have small successes but not big ones.

OUTCOME

◆   THE NINE OF PENTACLES

Many 9s mean that situations or events are nearing completion or have just been completed and another plateau awaits.

IN A READING

Many Pentacles (three or more) indicate that conditions are taking form, or are in the process of being demonstrated.

The focus is on business, business partnerships, corporate enterprises, and promotion or advancement, and/or mediation to change or revitalize existing conditions.

FOCUS

You want to promote yourself and/or form a (new) partnership or alliance.

DESIRE

Friendship or love will be offered through work, service, health, or restaurant environments.

ROMANCE

You'll be pleasantly surprised by a gift of money, an offer of financial assistance, or an employment opportunity.

THE UNEXPECTED

Your interactions with others will be primarily business-oriented and you'll be in a position to promote yourself or your business ideas in a conducive environment. An unexpected offer of money or employment will also come your way.

OTHERS

You will be busy with work projects that are done out of your home or that you can do over the phone or through the mail.

THE HOME

You will soon travel for business or social reasons and/or will have to put out money for car maintenance or repairs.

TRAVEL

You'll be busy with papers geared to self-promotion or new business ideas such as presentations, business cards, or biographies. News that a payment is about to be received could also be indicated.

PAPERS

You will be concentrating on making money or bettering your financial condition so you'll busy yourself with activities geared to promoting or advancing that endeavor.

WORK/CAREER

There will be time spent away from your partner or mate but this is

UNIONS

only temporary, and a decision to hold out for what you really want
will prove to be the right choice.

EMOTIONAL STATE   Being productive in your work will compensate for the lack of fulfillment in your personal life and give you vicarious satisfaction.

PLEASURE   You'll be pleased that you are making money at your craft or profession, and will derive a great deal of satisfaction in being praised for
your work or efforts . . . a just reward.

NEWS   You will discuss finances and business-related ventures over the
phone. Also, a plan that looked "iffy" will go through after all if
you still want it to.

FAMILY   Your family or friends will be helpful and supportive and if you ask
for something, it will be given.

**THE PHYSICAL
BODY**   Beware the demon rum, which will give you the courage to act
impulsively; or, someone you know may have a drinking problem.
This also indicates that one who's been ill or had surgery is on the
road to recovery.

FINANCES   You will soon experience better financial conditions and a pleasant
surprise.

TIME   You will be preoccupied with business affairs and making money.

FRIENDS   You're going to have discussions about your work or work projects
designed to bring people closer together. Also, a new friend or alliance will be found and a friend will pay you for your services.

VISITORS/CALLERS   You will have many business calls bringing opportunities to make
money or concerning the receipt of money, but plans to combine
business and social activities will go awry.

MAIL   You are going to receive a surprise letter or expression of gratitude.

ANXIETY   You'll be afraid to trust yourself or your decisions because you've
been wrong in the past or couldn't make what you wanted to hap-
pen, happen.

DISAPPOINTMENT   You're going to hear an unkind disclosure or negative prediction
about your future . . . consider the source.

Your sense of connectedness with another is going to end, a partnership will look as if it's over, and/or a business is about to fold.   **ENDINGS**

You will have a change in consciousness.   **NEW BEGINNINGS**

You're going to receive an offer of love, friendship, or support from another . . . someone who will try to diagnose your needs and fulfill them.   **INHERITANCE**

You will give of yourself or your talents and provide substance to others; and someone will give you a very nice (or expensive) gift.   **REWARDS/GIFTS**

You'll be successful in business or financial agreements and in attaining results through the cooperation of others.   **SUCCESS**

Luck will be with you in anything connected with your work.   **FORTUNE**

You'll be grateful for the opportunity to make money, advance yourself, or better your position.   **BLESSINGS**

Mundane: A situation will arrive that will lure, entice, or beckon you on . . . a very tempting offer. And, your wish for a union will soon be fulfilled.
Esoteric: Think the situation out before you approach it. If you're sincere, you'll get whatever help you need. If not, you will run into obstacles.   **SPECIAL GUIDANCE**

Eliminate weak points and promote yourself, your own business, and social activities. Go for it!   **BEST COURSE OF ACTION**

You will serve others, increase your earnings, and promote yourself or your business, but unless you make a move (or amends), your desire for a partnership or union will be unfulfilled.   **OUTCOME**

◆ THE TEN OF PENTACLES

Tens are read the same as a number 1. However, they also signify a cyclical rebeginning, and a time when you must come to terms with something you may have avoided in the past.

IN A READING

Many Pentacles (three or more) indicate that conditions are taking form, or are in the process of being demonstrated.

The focus is on the home, family, or dwelling; daily living costs and expenses; domestic matters; friends, community, and working environment.

FOCUS

You want to establish better relations with others and hope that a proposed plan or business project will be successful.

DESIRE

There will be no love life at this time (your only bond will be a psychic bond) because all of your activities will be geared to daily living, family ties, or your home.

ROMANCE

You'll be caught off guard by an unexpected event, confrontation, or petty argument elicited by another (someone very important) which will mark a major change of direction. This could be the result of a financial matter, personality clash, or misunderstanding.

THE UNEXPECTED

Your family and friends will be your primary concern.

OTHERS

You will make plans to go on a social outing and to visit with family or friends.

THE HOME

You will make plans to visit the home of a relative or travel with a relative.

TRAVEL

You'll have a hard time with papers or presentations, and new projects will be difficult to launch.

PAPERS

There will be discussions concerning travel, schedules, or marketing; new groups or unions; and philanthropic endeavors.

WORK/CAREER

You will be communicating or uniting with friends or relatives, but not with a loved one or business partner.

UNIONS

EMOTIONAL STATE   You could be in the doldrums, but new elements will enter your life that will make your outlook on the future more hopeful.

PLEASURE   You'll enjoy getting away from your work or responsibilities for a bit, socializing with friends, family, and admirers; and/or will be pleased by a clean bill of health.

NEWS   You'll be angry about a lack of clientele or a business associate who isn't sticking to his/her agreements, and will soon take action and do something about it.

FAMILY   You will talk about future events, projects, or trips; and if someone in your family has been planning to travel, unexpected changes will cause him/her to rearrange plans or return sooner than expected.

THE PHYSICAL BODY   You, a family member, or a pet will need attention, shots, grooming, or looking after.

FINANCES   Money will be fair or alternating from good to bad, and will be spent on household items, living expenses, and various sundries. And, if a financial transaction has been bothering you, you'll soon have a pleasant surprise. Also, money will come in through clients, dividends, or legacies.

TIME   You'll be involved with activities centering around your family or domestic environment such as home repairs or maintenance, and much of your time will be spent alone.

FRIENDS   You'll soon be forming a new union with a small group of business associates or friends.

VISITORS/CALLERS   You will be gathering together with a group, and someone from your job (or in your job) will call and cause you to make different arrangements.

MAIL   An unexpected financial notice, statement, or large bill that you were not prepared for will come.

ANXIETY   You'll be troubled by your inability to establish or cement the type of relationship you want to have with another. A misunderstanding, falling out, or argument with a friend or employer could also be indicated.

You'll feel invalidated or unappreciated for who you are, what you're trying to do, or what you want to represent. **DISAPPOINTMENT**

You will not accept things as they are, and will take action to correct problem areas by canceling arrangements that don't suit you or by severing a relationship (be it business or personal) altogether. **ENDINGS**

You will call someone in an attempt to resolve a problem, locate a new job, or handle something connected with your work. **NEW BEGINNINGS**

You'll receive a dividend, legacy, or inheritance and positive reinforcement in your profession or a new method of operation. **INHERITANCE**

A caller will arrive with a small gift. **REWARDS/GIFTS**

Your best success will come through areas related to friends, family, household, and/or personal appearance. **SUCCESS**

You'll consider yourself lucky that you're able to meet the costs of living, or for the resurrection and redirecting of energies into constructive channels. **FORTUNE**

You'll be grateful for the resolving of arguments. **BLESSINGS**

Mundane: You'll be frustrated in your attempts to unite with others or gain the support of your superiors in your working environment, and will have little or no assistance from the spiritual realm in the form of guidance or direction.
Esoteric: Look and see if somewhere along the line you created a role model that no longer serves you. **SPECIAL GUIDANCE**

Attend to day-to-day living or household affairs that need maintenance or attention and stick close to those who support you or the way you want to feel about yourself. **BEST COURSE OF ACTION**

An era or chain of events is going to culminate and be completed, which will detach you from your problems and eliminate apprehension. A new group or union will also be in the making. **OUTCOME**

PAGE of PENTACLES.

◆ THE PAGE OF PENTACLES

CAPRICORN (December 22–January 19) **ASTROLOGICAL SIGN**

Studious, persevering, productive, professionally inclined, ambitious, patient, responsible, practical, conservative, and sometimes moody, morbid or subject to depression but never gives up. **TYPE OF PERSON**

Producer, regional manager, chief executive, boss, headwaiter, photographer, student, laborer. **TYPE OF VOCATION**

The focus is on employment, profession and status, scholastic or romantic endeavors, mental labor, practical idealism and dynamic efforts, and/or a person with a Capricorn type of temperament. **FOCUS**

You want to be successful or make more money in your work but feel thwarted in all of your attempts. **DESIRE**

"How do I handle this?" will be the issue concerning a romantic interest, and because you will meet it with a sense of responsibility for your actions, you will feel very good about yourself, whether your relationship has a future or not. **ROMANCE**

You are going to get some good news from someone who cares . . . something very unexpected and very much appreciated. An unexpected social invitation could also be indicated. **THE UNEXPECTED**

A friend will want to play matchmaker or bring you and another together in a business endeavor; or, a friend will help you in a business matter. Whatever the case, it will be a pleasurable experience. **OTHERS**

You will be feeling pensive, moody, or depressed, and may leave to go shopping or out for breakfast, lunch, or dinner. You will also have a lot of work or chores to do. **THE HOME**

You will soon leave your home to go on a shopping spree, social excursion, or scholastic endeavor. **TRAVEL**

You will be disappointed in the results you'd hoped you'd see in an **PAPERS** enterprise that involves a great deal of time and/or detail, and will contemplate abandoning the project altogether.

WORK/CAREER

At this moment, you may feel that there is nothing you can do that will lift you out of the slump you're in, but someone or something is going to come to your aid and brighten your spirits.

UNIONS

Because of basic incompatabilities and irreconcilable differences, you will not be able to unite, and if you are already committed, you will feel the only recourse left is to sever the relationship or get a divorce.

EMOTIONAL STATE

You will be up and down (mostly down) and rather gloomy, trying to sort out your feelings and the feelings of others.

PLEASURE

You will be happy with the results of a social outing or scholastic or academic project, lecture, or tour.

NEWS

You will make a call that will clear up a snag or error in a commercial venture or program and will be pleased that it gets resolved.

FAMILY

You will want to cancel your plans with your family, or will have to postpone.

THE PHYSICAL BODY

You may experience choking sensations, backaches, or problems with your stomach, ears, or throat. If it's your throat or ears, it could be that you are not saying something you know you should, or willing to hear something being said.

FINANCES

Money will be slow in coming, and not as much as you hoped for, and you will have conflicts with others or worry about what you should do. However, there will be unexpected financial gains soon.

TIME

You will experience many fluctuations and ups and downs (mostly downs), related to your profession, finances, or status.

FRIENDS

A new direction or promising lead or venture will not pan out or come to fruition, and you will be disappointed.

VISITORS/CALLERS

Someone will unexpectedly phone who will propose a new avenue to pursue.

You will get a legal notice or letter from a lawyer, and/or you will be informed that an account has been or will be closed. | **MAIL**

Efforts to complete your work quickly and easily will be harder than appeared at first glance. | **ANXIETY**

Unfavorable news concerning your business or finances or a promising lead that doesn't pan out will be a disappointment. | **DISAPPOINTMENT**

You are going to stop trying. | **ENDINGS**

Someone will help you make a change for the better by revealing a new approach or alternative to a matter of great concern. | **NEW BEGINNINGS**

You will "inherit" a business referral and a personal introduction or blind date. | **INHERITANCE**

You will be rewarded with friends who will offer their assistance and positive input about your future, your career, or your financial affairs. | **REWARDS/GIFTS**

Your success will come through an impromptu business proposal or social invitation that will change things for the better. | **SUCCESS**

Luck will come through a social invitation that will offer a new business lead. | **FORTUNE**

You will be grateful for unsolicited praise for your work or literary efforts and a fortunate business/social call. | **BLESSINGS**

Mundane: Realize the futility of effort. If something is meant to be, it will come of its own accord. When you stop seeking, searching, or expecting, it will begin to happen.
Esoteric: Since you're not the cause and are powerless to change what is happening, it's futile to be upset. | **SPECIAL GUIDANCE**

Be willing to listen to, or act upon, new ideas. | **BEST COURSE OF ACTION**

You won't want something that isn't right, no matter *how* much you want it, and you won't give up until you get what you want. | **OUTCOME**

KNIGHT of PENTACLES.

◆ THE KNIGHT OF PENTACLES

There is no astrological sign associated with the Knights because they indicate situations that are coming in or going out.

IN A READING

When a Knight appears in a reading, a long-term condition will suddenly change.

The focus is on travel, promotion or advertising, and real estate or property investments; but your heart and mind will be on life, love, and the pursuit of happiness and that will take precedence over all else.

FOCUS

You want the kind of peace or personal fulfillment that only love or the grace of God can bring and to enjoy the simple things in life and all they have to offer.

DESIRE

You will experience apprehension or disquiet over a schedule because you'll feel it will wipe out your chances for a relationship; and/or, you will intuitively sense that which is to come.

ROMANCE

You'll be surprised by a promotional opportunity that will give you the chance to sell yourself or advertise your product through the media, trade, or radio.

THE UNEXPECTED

People will run hot and cold (mostly cold) in your business world, creating a lot of stress or uncertainty, and an unexpected assault or confrontation will occur in your working environment or travels. Accidents happen close to home.

OTHERS

You will go on a pleasure trip or shopping spree, and/or will soon go house hunting.

THE HOME

A short trip with someone you like or love is in store.

TRAVEL

You will get caught up with paperwork that has been piling up, and an idea for a new project will be in the making which will require an outline or presentation.

PAPERS

Business may have been slow in the past, but things are going to take an upward swing and improve greatly.

WORK/CAREER

UNIONS

You will be seriously considering a marriage or union and all of its ramifications.

EMOTIONAL STATE

Love will be the most important and all-encompassing thing in life. It's all you want, and all you think about. You won't want to work or do anything else, because it will be such an all-consuming emotion.

PLEASURE

You will enjoy the loving rapport you'll share with another and also a temporary escape from your work or busy schedule.

NEWS

An inspirational message will bring a new slant on an old reality . . . this could be something a lover says or does.

FAMILY

You won't see eye to eye with your family or want to talk to or share your feelings with one of your relations; also, someone in your family will be discussing real estate or looking for a new home.

THE PHYSICAL BODY

You'll be surprised at what a little honesty can do. Withholds are a terrible energy-zapper . . . and boredom is worse.

FINANCES

You'll have financial problems or experience difficulty in attaining or collecting money or payments, but in the final analysis, you will come out ahead.

TIME

You could butt heads with someone close or experience a sense of alienation.

FRIENDS

If there were problems in the past, they will be eliminated and the fences will come down, and/or deeper bonds are about to be established.

VISITORS/CALLERS

Analysis or circumspection will be demanded as a result of a call or caller.

MAIL

You will get a card, letter, or message from an old admirer.

ANXIETY

You will be troubled by insecurity and the fear of failure, or be upset because of a business partner or associate who doesn't support you, or who is cold or indifferent toward you or your goals.

DISAPPOINTMENT

The lack of resolution in matters of the heart or (emotional) distance that can't be bridged, along with financial problems and family difficulties, will dishearten and depress you.

ENDINGS

You will not be able to progress any further on a business course you wanted to complete by a certain time, but a new avenue will present itself that can't be refused.

NEW BEGINNINGS

You will be spending time with an easy-going, intelligent, and likable person and will enjoy his/her company very much. This could also prove to be a significant connection in times to come.

INHERITANCE

You will "inherit" inner peace and calm.

REWARDS/GIFTS

If you've been trying to figure what to get or buy, the perfect idea will come to you.

SUCCESS

You are going to get a positive response or "go-ahead" on a new business idea, and in your personal affairs, an open, honest, and direct communication with another will turn an ordinary event into an extraordinary experience.

FORTUNE

You will be fortunate in attaining increasing nourishment in matters of the heart and a spontaneous outpouring of love or affection from another.

BLESSINGS

You will be grateful that some of your desires were realized and that you have the ability to sustain yourself.

SPECIAL GUIDANCE

Mundane: Your efforts will be rewarded in more ways than one. *Esoteric:* Set aside a time to be still, a moment away from the hustle and bustle and all the thoughts that occupy your mind. . . . "In the stillness you shall know Me."

BEST COURSE OF ACTION

Follow your heart, your "hunches," or your "gut reaction" . . . do what feels right and don't do what doesn't.

OUTCOME

In time you will get your wish, and your desires will be realized.

QUEEN ofPENTACLES

◆ THE QUEEN OF PENTACLES

AQUARIUS (January 20 - February 19)

ASTROLOGICAL SIGN

Idealistic, public-minded, charitable, magnanimous, determined, opinionated, pragmatic, hopeful, influential, dedicated, aspiring, compassionate, friendly but sometimes impersonal. Is strongly affected by outside events which are usually unexpected or out of his/her hands.

TYPE OF PERSON

Serving the planet, New Age teacher, minister, healer, psychologist, painter, writer, inventor.

TYPE OF VOCATION

The focus is on hopes, wishes, and aspirations; verification and tangible results; compassion for or service to mankind (or the ministry); finance and profit; and/or a person with an Aquarian-type temperament.

FOCUS

You want to establish yourself *to* yourself . . . to find your "center" or place where you belong, and for words (prophecies) or ideas to come to light.

DESIRE

You are going to meet or be attracted to a very unusual or "striking" person who will be just as interested in you.

ROMANCE

Someone is going to call that wants your services or is in need of your assistance. You will also get a job offer or employment opportunity.

THE UNEXPECTED

You'll be confused as to which way to turn in a personal dilemma.

OTHERS

You will be preparing for a future event concerning a work project, making social plans, and responding or reacting to events concerning your family or close friends.

THE HOME

A very happy trip is in store for you and you will soon see the one you've been meaning to visit or hoping to see.

TRAVEL

Expect the receipt of money or a letter containing money for something that involves papers.

PAPERS

WORK/CAREER Some new information concerning your work or a "working product" will change your perspective and cause you to look at things in a much brighter light.

UNIONS You will want a supportive relationship based on love, commitment, honesty, and integrity, and will be weighing a relationship to see if it measures up. If it does, you will unite or marry . . . if it does not, you will drop it.

EMOTIONAL STATE Though you will be somewhat moody, you will soon break into a smile.

PLEASURE You will enjoy helping, serving, or giving to others and/or handling a problem with conviction and integrity, resulting in a great deal of personal satisfaction.

NEWS Expect a social invitation from a relative, friend, or admirer.

FAMILY A friend or relative will need some consoling and you will aid or assist him/her.

THE PHYSICAL BODY A spiritual cleansing would be very good for you and if you have been ailing, you will soon experience better health. If contemplating a health profession, it should be very rewarding.

FINANCES You'll begin to feel more secure as money starts to come in or free up.

TIME In time, a fondest wish will be fulfilled and you will feel very fortunate.

FRIENDS Ideas will come to light through your friends, and what you thought about regarding another will be verified.

VISITORS/CALLERS You are going to get a business call or an offer of employment different from your usual work.

MAIL If you were expecting a letter to arrive, you will have to wait another day. A financial transaction done by mail could also be indicated.

ANXIETY You will feel as if you're compelled to follow a dream that will never come to pass or materialize.

You will be disheartened by a quest that looks impossible to attain . . . can't have and can't let go.

DISAPPOINTMENT

You won't be able to reconcile the (spiritual) ideal with the (earthly) reality, so there will be no possibility of a union at this time.

ENDINGS

An admirer could come to visit, and stay!

NEW BEGINNINGS

You will "inherit" answers, verification, or tangible results; words that come to light; rewards for your efforts; as well as profit, gain, or financial increase.

INHERITANCE

You are going to receive answers or tools for living. You will also be discussing an appropriate gift to give someone.

REWARDS/GIFTS

You will have success in financial affairs and obtaining results in your field of endeavor, and/or you will do very well in healing professions.

SUCCESS

You are going to receive a positive sign or omen of what is to come.

FORTUNE

You will be grateful for verification or confirmation on an idea, and for gifts and/or special favors.

BLESSINGS

Mundane: Keep following your star and you will get your wish. You may have to wait, but what you want *will* come.
Esoteric: Things are working out better and faster than you think, and problems that looked like mountains will prove to be molehills.

SPECIAL GUIDANCE

Clarify your objectives and when faced with a circumstance you previously would have bent under, recognize it as an opportunity to be at cause (instead of effect) and press through it.

BEST COURSE OF ACTION

You will attain some results for your long-sustained efforts, but you'll have more to go before major results can be realized or you're firmly established in the "place" you want to be.

OUTCOME

KING of PENTACLES.

◆ THE KING OF PENTACLES

GEMINI (May 21 - June 20)

ASTROLOGICAL SIGN

Mental, versatile, adaptable, diversified, capable, alert, confident, studious, curious, enterprising, skillful, energetic, communicative, changeable.

TYPE OF PERSON

Writing, directing, lecturing, fashion, arts, motion pictures, radio, dealing with the public at large. Capable of doing two or more jobs at a time.

TYPE OF VOCATION

The focus is on communication, expansion and mental absorption, arts or media arts; contacts with those in positions of power, authority, or influence; completing old projects and beginning new ones; and/or a person with a Gemini-type temperament.

FOCUS

You want to make money, to be more successful, and/or to unite or reunite with someone.

DESIRE

Expect an impasse. A lover is not going to act or call as expected and it's going to annoy you because you will feel that it was thoughtless, inconsiderate, or irresponsible.

ROMANCE

You are going to get some very unexpected validation from important or influential people or department heads and/or public acclaim.

THE UNEXPECTED

You will associate with gifted, influential, or powerful people who will be instrumental in your life or in that which concerns you.

OTHERS

You will be immersed in paperwork and/or many assorted projects.

THE HOME

If you were planning a trip to the beach or seashore, you will cancel your plans as weather won't permit, but if your trip concerns a business venture, it will be successful.

TRAVEL

You'll be completely absorbed in and involved with paperwork of all kinds, be it writing, drawing, journal-keeping, screen plays, art, fashion, or books.

PAPERS

WORK/CAREER

You will be very popular and in demand, and will make a very good impression on your superiors or peer group.

UNIONS

The give and take will be lacking in your relationship and your efforts to communicate or pull together will fall on deaf ears. You will have problems related to children, community, work, or time investments.

EMOTIONAL STATE

Your emotions will be buried under mental activity and you will be preoccupied and completely absorbed.

PLEASURE

A new project or potential enterprise is going to spring from your past (or work that was done in the past) that is going to give you a great deal of unexpected satisfaction.

NEWS

Expect a very positive message or response from an influential person who will admire the work you do, and will tell you so.

FAMILY

You will want to escape from responsibilities toward your family, but won't.

THE PHYSICAL BODY

If you've been under the weather, you will definitely be making improvements—mentally, physically, emotionally, and spiritually—and if you consult a physician, he/she will tell you so.

FINANCES

Financial transactions in the home or field will be very prosperous.

TIME

You will be involved with the public and with professional people and your affairs will come to a head very quickly. What was wrong will be set right, what was missing will be found, and what was needed will be provided.

FRIENDS

You will have many helpful and influential friends, professional friends.

VISITORS/CALLERS

If you are hoping to hear from someone, you will get your wish.

MAIL

A mistake in your financial records will be found and will have to be straightened out (an error on your part); or a forgotten bill will arrive.

ANXIETY

You will feel as if you're just spinning your wheels and going nowhere, where your love life or career aspirations are concerned.

You will be disappointed in things connected with papers, books, or personal relationships, and will feel that no real progress is being made or that there are no new avenues to pursue or doors to open.   **DISAPPOINTMENT**

Regrets, pain, anguish, or sorrow will come to an end. You will review the past and all that has gone before, and then release it and let it go . . . what's done is done.   **ENDINGS**

You will be completely absorbed in new projects and activities, and if you have been estranged from a friend or loved one, you will be reunited or reconcile your differences.   **NEW BEGINNINGS**

You will "inherit" a reunion or reconciliation with an old friend or loved one.   **INHERITANCE**

You will get an artistic commission or business assignment, and money or some kind of special attention, advantage, or honor.   **REWARDS/GIFTS**

Your success will come through admirers of the opposite sex, business and social activities, and any project that deals with the public or professions.   **SUCCESS**

You will be fortunate in meeting influential people who could benefit you or your career and in resolving personal arguments, reconciling differences, and reuniting with a sweetheart or loved one.   **FORTUNE**

You will be grateful for help, praise, or assistance from a professional.   **BLESSINGS**

Mundane: The standstill will be overcome, and/or a reunion is at hand.
Esoteric: You are never alone; all you have to do is reach out.   **SPECIAL GUIDANCE**

Be patient, persistent, and diligent in your efforts.   **BEST COURSE OF ACTION**

You will be completing an era and closing the door to the past to begin anew, in a new direction.   **OUTCOME**